Determinations

Essays on Theory, Narrative and Nation in the Americas

NEIL LARSEN

VERSO

London • New York

For Emma Luna

. . . and in memory of Michael Sprinker
(1949–1999)

First published by Verso 2001
© Neil Larsen 2001
All rights reserved

Verso
UK: 6 Meard Street, London W1F 0EG
USA: 180 Varick Street, New York, NY 10014–4606

Verso is the imprint of New Left Books

ISBN 1–85984–619–X
ISBN 1–85984–329–8 (pbk)

British Library Cataloguing in Publication Data
A catalogue record for this book is available from the British Library

Library of Congress Cataloging-in-Publication Data
A catalog record for this book is avilable from the Library of Congress

Typeset by Exe Valley Dataset Ltd, Exeter, Devon, England
Printed by Biddles Ltd, Guildford and King's Lynn

Contents

Acknowledgments

All intellectual shortcomings and poverties in the essays that follow are the author's alone. Any worth to be found in them is, on the contrary, the ultimate result of an immense wealth of intellectual associations and friendships stretching back years and involving many more people than I can name in this space. But a few must be openly acknowledged here, among them my editor at Verso, the late Michael Sprinker, whose support for this project, never without the bracing criticisms that Michael was known for, was a precondition for its realization. Many of my colleagues in Spanish and Critical Theory at the University of California, Davis have been unfailingly generous and encouraging as well. But I especially want to acknowledge my students in two graduate seminars, taught in 1998 and 1999 at UC Davis, for whom the material and arguments contained in the final two chapters in *Determinations* were initially conceived and developed. I am particularly grateful to three of them: Sebastiaan Faber, awareness of whose ready, critical and sympathetic intelligence encouraged me to re-think my own ideas with the utmost care and concentration; Julia M. Pigg, whose assistance in the research for the final section of this work was essential to its completion; and Jennifer M. Valko whose help in the final preparation of the manuscript was invaluable.

Parts of *Determinations* have appeared earlier in the following publications: chapter 1 as "Imperialism, Colonialism, Postcolonialism" in the *Companion to Postcolonial Studies*, eds Sangeeta Ray and Henry Schwarz, Oxford: Blackwell Publishers, 2000; chapter 2 in *The Preoccupations of Postcolonial Theory*, eds Kalpana Seshadri-Crooks and Fawzia Afzal-Khan, Durham: Duke University Press, 2000 (an earlier version appeared in *Dispositio/n*, vol. XX, no. 47, 1995, pp. 1–16.); chapter 3 in *Cultural Logic: an Electronic Journal of Marxist Theory and Practice* vol. 1 number 1 Fall 1997; chapter seven in *Julio Cortázar:New Readings*, ed. Carlos J. Alonso, Cambridge: Cambridge University Press, 1998; chapter 8, under the title "*El siglo de las luces*: Modernism and Epic," in *Modernism at its Margins*, eds José B.

Monleón and Tony Geist, New York: Garland Press, 1999; chapter 9 in an earlier version as "Surrealismus und Marxismus in Lateinamerika," in *Weg und Ziel* (Vienna), no. 2, May 1997; and chapter 10, in an earlier version, as "Más allá de lo 'transcultural': Rulfo y la conciencia histórica," in *Revista canadiense de estudios hispánicos*, vol. XXI, no. 2, November 1997.

Preface

Not the least of my difficulties in writing and assembling the work that follows has been the selection of its title. The only word that seemed a given from the first was "essays," since that, unambiguously, is what *Determinations* is made up of. These, enumerated as twelve "chapters," fall into two broad and reasonably distinct sections: "Theory in the 'Post'-Colony," a sustained polemical engagement with what has come to be known as "postcolonial" theory; and a second body of more traditionally literary critical essays on writers and texts of the modern Latin American canon. (The final, twelfth chapter of *Determinations* returns in a speculative and abbreviated mode to more abstractly theoretical questions regarding the nation and narrative form.) I have subtitled this second section, awkwardly and perhaps too ambitiously, "Nation and Narration on a North/South Axis: Case Studies for a Regionally and Historically Grounded 'Postcolonial' Studies." The "ground" I refer to here—modern Latin America—makes, in fact, a theoretical virtue out of one my own personal-intellectual necessities. Though at times it seems to me that I have done nothing for the last five or six years but dispute the meaning and pertinence of "postcolonialism," I am—to paraphrase Marx—not a "post-colonialist" but a former student of Comparative Literature trained as a Latin-Americanist. I read books written in European languages (English, Spanish, Portuguese, French and German) and have access to the literatures of Asia and Africa not written in these languages only through translation.

By this empirical standard, of course, there may be no such thing as a "postcolonialist" anyway—an argument Aijaz Ahmad, a significant influence on some of the work that follows, has been making to many, probably reluctant ears for some time now.[1] As Terry Eagleton noted in a 1999 review[2] of Gayatri Spivak's *Critique of Postcolonial Reason*, the first requirement for admission to the ranks of "postcolonialists" may be to deny being one. Still, the fact is that it has become impossible, at least in the United States, to write and speak as a Latin-Americanist with any connections to literary and cultural theory without engaging the question of the "post-colonial," even if only to question its value or legitimacy. This is one of the immediate circumstances that led to the writing of chapters 1 through 6.

In *Notes to Literature* Adorno characterizes the essay-form as "determined" by "the unity of its object along with that of the theory and experience that have migrated into the object."[3] Thus, if I am justified in claiming the form of "essay" in this sense for the critical texts that follow, a deeper, less circumstantial unity of focus and concern should become evident to readers of *Determinations*. Into what possible unitary object have "theory" (postcolonialism, Marxism, etc.) and "experience" (Latin–Americanism) "migrated" here?

The most immediate answer is, of course, the nation or "national question" itself as (to anticipate here the first, introductory chapter of *Determinations*) that which both grounds and mediates among the diverse intellectual—and at times pseudo-intellectual—nuclei that drift about in the "postcolonial" ether.

But then *Determinations* is as much a book about narrative as it is (if it is) a contribution to debates about the nation, making necessary still further determinations and delimitations of its "object." I will hazard the one most essential of these: not nation *as* narration—or not *only* this—but nation and narration *both* as, simultaneously and inseparably, a problem of history *and* a problem of *form*. Here I anticipate the final essay of this collection (itself, in essence, an anticipation of a more elaborate and systematic critical study) in which a case is made for a rigorously and genuinely dialectical method of "political narratology," starting from the elemental historical forms of social relation that in fact underlie and precondition the immediate affinity of nation and narration.

But to delimit still further: into such historical *forms*, finally, there must enter a conceptual space for historical *variation* itself. If nation and narration lead back genealogically to a third mediating term, *the specific form of this mediation* itself will obey historical specificities and determinacies of its own. To suggest that the concept (or mere term?) "postcolonial" names such a specific determination seems, to me, too dubious to declare outright, even hypothetically. A better case might be made, however, for locating in the regional/historical unity of Latin America such a determination. And that— again, as much out of personal necessity and fortuitousness, in my case, as out of any intellectual virtue—accounts for the third, "American" delimitation of the immanent, essayistic object of the present work.

Finally, an acknowledgment of intellectual influences. If I am not a "postcolonialist" I am a Marxist. The point in saying so is not to belabor the obvious, nor is it to deny, *a priori*, the legitimacy of such a claim when it is made by more than one "postcolonial" theorist. (This is a question addressed at length in chapter 4.) The careful reader will note that the range and meaning of "Marxism" itself varies significantly throughout the essays making up *Determinations*. My point here rather is to recognize one of several parallel and 'virtual' objects of this work, theoretical and political foregrounds that, in the final analysis, are perhaps what these essays really ought to have been about in the first place.

Still this is, *almost* a book about two other, closely related 'virtual' objects. The first is the work of the Brazilian Marxist critic Roberto Schwarz, cited, consulted and reflected upon repeatedly throughout the pages of *Determinations*, and the subject of a separate essay (chapter 5). The reader could do no better than defer the reading of these pages and proceed directly to a work such as *Misplaced Ideas*[4] for a "regionally and historically grounded case study" in what, within Schwarz's Brazilian intellectual element, could be called "postcolonialism" only in a generously ironic spirit, if at all. Here and there—mainly 'there'—concepts and ideas still take intellectual precedence over jargons.

This might also have been a book about the critical theory and Marxist philosophy of Georg Lukács. From "Narrate or Describe?" to *The Historical Novel* to *History and Class Consciousness*, the Lukacsian stamp is ubiquitous in these pages. This is, nowadays, an unusual influence among Marxists, not to mention among Latin-Americanists and "postcolonialists." In a certain way every idea contained in *Determinations* has been generated within the peculiar intellectual space defined by these two seemingly disparate poles. Why on earth consult Lukács on questions of postcoloniality or Latin-Americanism? My answer, briefly and unapologetically, is that one *must* do so if one is to pose questions of narrative form, no matter what their 'location,' in relation to the thinking of Marx. Revisions of Lukácsian theory, some of them quite significant perhaps, may as a result be in store. (See, for example, chapter 8.) But my conviction is that, though Latin America and the third world as a whole seem not to have been on Lukács' conceptual map, the full range of Lukacsian narrative theory nevertheless 'travels' quite well.

My own 'travels' in Lukacsian Marxism, as it happens, chart a definite and unorthodox course. They begin in places like *The Historical Novel* and *Studies in European Realism*, pass back through *History and Class Consciousness*, and come to a strange kind of conclusion in *The Theory of the Novel*. Perhaps the book about Lukács that this Lukacsian book is not could have discovered a reason for this. In the meantime, readers are offered the following, rather centrifugal reflections on matters that in the end may orbit around what is also a kind of 'postcolonial' condition: that of the North American Marxist and Latin-Americanist saving the meaning of his own, profoundly aporetic 'national' experience, post-1968, for last.

Part I
Theory in the "Post"-Colony

Imperialism, Colonialism, Postcolonialism: An Introduction

I. Coming to terms: from slogans to jargons

Any general introduction to the subject(s) of "imperialism, colonialism and postcolonialism" ought to be a fairly straightforward matter of marshalling the best, or most influential definitions and theoretical illuminations of these terms according to the vaguely historical sequence already implied in this triad. ("Colonialism, imperialism, postcolonialism" would, from this point of view, be the more appropriate sequence.) But this is already a problematic undertaking. However current or fashionable in academic circles, "postcolonialism" is, by anyone's reckoning, a term whose use is also virtually restricted to the metropolitan academy and its satellites. Indeed, its circulation within this academy itself is still far from universal, being further limited mainly to the discourse of literature departments and "cultural studies." The superficial circumstance of its origins as a term in a 1970s debate between political scientists and the fact that historians, sociologists and even journalists may have now begun to adopt it is largely irrelevant here.[1] The generic use of the term to refer to any formerly colonized political or social entity brings into play none of the polemical and often refractory questions—especially those, as we shall see, regarding the nation—that the term or concept evokes within left and "theoretical" circles in the humanities and cultural studies.[2] Yet another "post-al" jargon to its detractors, a challenge to metropolitan, Eurocentrist doxa according to its defenders, the term (in whichever of its variations: postcolonialism, postcoloniality, postcolonial studies, postcolonial theory, etc.) signifies little more than its own (waning) novelty or exoticism *outside* the walls of the academy.

It's possible and sometimes even routine to speak of "colonialism" and "imperialism" *inside* these walls too, but these terms—and the rather more discreet realities they denote—had to force their way in from the outside. I doubt whether the history or social studies textbooks that I read as a 1960s high school student in the midwestern United States made any reference to "colonialism." "Colony" or "colonization," perhaps, as in "the thirteen colonies." "Empire" I do seem to remember (as in "Roman" or "Spanish") but "imperialism", I am certain, never. "Imperialism" (as in "US") was a term that those of my peers with sufficient temerity had begun to utter after 1967 or so, about a reality entirely outside the textbooks. Its utterance usually meant trouble. With reference to the war in Vietnam, it implied sympathy for the "enemy." "Colonialism" was safer for us, since, so we had been taught, the United States had no "colonies"—only the "commonwealth" or "free associated territory" of Puerto Rico. But one can assume a similarly fraught politics of diction for those speaking of "colonialism" in the Paris of the 1950s, not to mention the Algiers of that same period, or the India or China of decades earlier. These words, whatever else they were, had come to signify injustices, causes, social movements and revolutions, massive historical upheavals and changes. They had their accompanying, opposing slogans: national liberation, revolution, socialism. Perhaps, within its much more modest sphere of common usage, "postcolonialism" has become a slogan as well—powerful enough to secure the publication of an article in a journal, or, on the other hand, troublesome enough to result occasionally in denial of an academic appointment or of tenure. But no genuinely mass social or political movement I am aware of paints the word "postcolonialism" on its banners. How, after all, would one know whether to be for it or against it?

"Imperialism, colonialism, postcolonialism" risks conveying an illusion of conceptual parity or symmetry—a species of category mistake—as a result of which a crucial *historical* perspective is eclipsed. To guard against this false, ahistorical symmetry, however, does not require that we drop the last of its terms. That would incur the opposing, anti-intellectual fallacy, much in vogue on the neo-conservative right in the United States, according to which academics and intellectuals generally communicate only in esoteric jargons with no bearing on the general form of existence. (Consider whether such could be said of terms such as "relativity," "mode of production," or "the return of the repressed.") But, despite its intramural genealogy, the "postcolonial" may in fact point at a concept, or at least at a conceptual place-holder, made necessary by the continuation of the same history that turned "imperialism" and "colonialism" into fighting words. For jargons, too, have their histories, and perhaps just enough negativity to point beyond themselves. The gesture of exasperated dismissal on the grounds of "trendiness," unless it can account for the origin of the trend itself, is reduced to the intellectual level of that which it thinks it dismisses.

Think, for instance, of how, before the coinage of "postcolonial," one was accustomed to speak of what the novels of Gabriel García Márquez and Chinua Achebe had in common over and against, say, those of Margaret Drabble and Alain Robbe-Grillet. The reference, unless my memory deceives me, was to the "third world." By way of tarring its utterer as a "sixties" relic, "third world" conjures up an entire historical conjuncture, and accompanying political culture, in which one naturally went on to utter the above-cited slogans of "national liberation," etc. For reasons that the discussion to follow will, if successful, help to clarify, we who once un-self-consciously said "third world" now hesitate, if only for a second, to utter it in the same contexts. This hesitation I think reflects the decline of the national liberation movements of the "Bandung era" (see below, sections III and IV) leaving us with the question of why and with what effect this decline has occurred, but helping to explain in the meantime the currency of "postcolonial" as, if nothing else, a *euphemism* for "third world." Whether the term "postcolonial" or the "theory" and/or the "condition" that are designated this way point us beyond the crisis of third worldism, or merely serve to mystify it yet again, is a matter for genuine debate. But it seems no less certain that a terminology—and thus perhaps a conceptual spectrum—limited to "imperialism" and "colonialism" will incur the risk of historical mystification as well unless it can account for suspicions (often its own) that it has grown somehow anachronistic. There may, in the end, be no particularly good reason for saying "postcolonial"—as distinct from the earlier practice of referring to the "neo-colonial"—and yet be quite good ones for not saying "third world."

The danger of confusing slogans with jargons, once avoided, still leaves us, however, with certain nagging questions of conceptual protocol. "Postcolonial," within its narrow domain, now routinely qualifies a certain class of "theory" and even of literature and culture. A Gayatri Spivak or Edward Said may now prefer to issue disclaimers or "critiques" but no one blinks before referring to them (along with the third member of the celebrated triumvirate, Homi K. Bhabha) as "postcolonial theorists." Salman Rushdie and Derek Walcott are, at least in the world of academic conferences and publications, "postcolonial" authors, and the films of an Ousmane Sembene, a Wang Zhimou and even, perhaps, a Jane Campion may be said to belong to a "postcolonial" cinema. Whether these all, in turn, partake of a common condition or reflect a common ideological standpoint called "postcolonialism" is a more difficult and very likely futile kind of question. (Here already the mechanical utility of the generic gives way to the conceptual counterfeit and nullity of the jargonistic.) But is there, on the other hand, a "colonialist literature", or a "literature of imperialism"? Although it would make obvious sense to designate, say, James Anthony Froude's *The English in the W. Indies, or the Bow of Ulysses* as "colonialist," or the John Wayne movie *The Green Berets* "imperialist," in view of the now transparently apologetic content of such narratives in relation to the ideologies of colonialism and imperialism, what say, of Gertrudis Gómez de Avellaneda's *Sab* or Joseph Conrad's *Heart of Darkness*? Both of these literary works—the former a Cuban abolitionist novel written in the first half of the nineteenth century, the latter one of the most celebrated fictional narratives of Britain's late imperial heyday—are also the products of historical periods that gave rise to colonialist and imperialist ideologies, and might even be said to be their cultural products. But the abolitionism of *Sab*, while scarcely dreaming of independence from Spain, lends it an incipiently anti-colonial flavor nevertheless, and Conrad's novel, however staunch its belief in British (as opposed to Belgian) civilizational probity, is in no *overt* way a defense of imperialism.

Shifting the ideological axis over to the oppostion—the "anti-"—might be the best next move here. Aimé Césaire's *Notebook of a Return to my Native Land* is unambiguously anti-colonialist and yet not reducible to a propagandistic core the way Froude's travel narrative is. Bolivian director Jorge Sanjinés's 1960s film *Blood of the Condor* is "anti-imperialist" cinema in an analogous sense. "Postcolonialists" of all stripes ought to find some common ground here in the acknowledgment that conscious opposition to imperialism and colonialism is, while no guarantee of artistic integrity, one of the latter's likelier symptoms.

But *anti*-imperialism/colonialism, in the end, remain no less problematic as indices for literary or cultural research or critique. Most of what furnishes the reader, student or scholar within the humanistic disciplines with his or her intellectual objects simply stands in too ambiguous, unmediated a relationship to the conceptual domain of imperialism or colonialism. "Postcolonialism" seems better suited to the task, but only insofar as it has been emptied of most ideological referentiality. Although the two are worlds apart ideologically, V.S. Naipaul is as readily classified a "postcolonial" writer as is Ngugi wa Thiong'o. No less ideologically divergent, Hans Magnus Enzensberger and, say, Tom Wolfe are taxonomically if not generically joined in negative correlation with the "postcolonial." There are, no doubt, possible reasons for such pairings, but "postcolonialism" in its currently vernacular usage doesn't get at them.

It is evident, then, that between the intellectual entry point of a terminology—"imperialism, colonialism, postcolonialism"—and the endpoint of these terms' real conceptual purchase for the general-purpose humanist, there are some missing links to be supplied. The most crucial of these, I propose, is the concept that prompts the terminological question itself, and that, at the same time, mediates between it and the protocols and methodologies of literary or cultural research. This is the concept of *nation*. Imperialism, (neo)colonialism and postcolonialism are, in variant but broadly overlapping ways, things done to, said of, opposed or embraced by nations. In relation to both imperialism and colonialism, the nation becomes an object or a projected space of emancipation—although, as I shall discuss below, as part of ultimately divergent emancipatory projects. And it is in relation to this nation as a "liberated territory," real or imagined, that the mimetic, narrative, obliquely ideological operations of literature and culture can now be fairly rigorously analyzed and classified.

In its outright claim that all third world literature was on some level a "national allegory," Fredric Jameson's celebrated and still controversial essay, "Third World Literature and the Era of Multinational Capitalism," may indeed have over generalized this relation to the point of distortion. But its fundamental methodological proposition (not *its* discovery alone, of course) remains a crucial one for postcolonial studies: that "third world" literature[3] is not about imperialism or colonialism *per se* but about the *nation* as that concrete, lived immediacy that itself, on another historical plane rarely so immediately or concretely experienced, is, or resists being colonized, etc. (See section III of this chapter for further discussion of "national allegory.") And only in relation to the question of the nation does postcolonialism shed *its* jargonized and euphemistic properties and begin to assume true, although still perhaps conceptually negative form: albeit here with the difference that the nation has become that lived space in relation to which the liberatory or utopian desire of culture seems, perversely, to have become misplaced.

Keeping the category of the nation in the foreground, what I propose to elaborate in what follows is a general correlation between three terms—"imperialism, colonialism and postcolonialism—and

(A) a concrete, world-historical conjuncture in relation to which a definite emancipatory politics of the nation (or of nationalism) becomes dominant;

(B) a key theoretical formulation of (A);

(C) an aesthetic or meta-literary idea—in this sense perhaps a "poetics" — of the nation corresponding to (A) and conceptually inter-linked with (B).

I should clarify first, however, that the history we are concerned with in what might now be thought of as a material-intellectual genealogy of "postcolonialism" begins with the first great global crisis of capitalism in the late nineteenth century (1873–95)[4] and is therefore an interval of the *modern*. (Thus the genealogical sequence in which "colonialism" follows on "imperialism"—if not the superficial chronology—is the more accurate one after all.) Neither the imperialisms of the ancient world nor the colonialism of the early modern epoch (1492, etc.) bear on the precise genealogy under scrutiny, except as a source of images and roles in which to play out a modern drama. This is because the national problematic or "question" at the core of postcolonialism presupposes as historically defunct the "classical" national movements of bourgeois Europe, the "great", more or less democratic revolutions and attempted revolutions in England, France, Italy, Germany, etc. However contested or simply nebulous their positions on what the emancipatory powers and spaces of the national are now, postcolonialists are tacitly unanimous in seeking these anywhere but in the metropolitan West of today. The nationalisms of a Jean-Marie Le Pen, the Northern Italian "Ligas," or, for that matter, of Michigan or Idaho "militias" are aspects or symptoms of the global conjuncture to which postcolonialism is critically directed, but their neo-fascist, Euro-chauvinist politics place them on the side of a global divide opposite to even the most Euro-centered of postcolonialists. The history that occupies us here dates from that moment, unevenly registered, after which it has become irrevocably clear that the destiny of all modern nations is no longer to become—or to simulate the condition of being—Western . . . if only because the West itself now forbids such an entelechy. Whatever this destiny may be (and perhaps its very thought is already a kind of trap) it cannot avoid the thought of itself as *centered elsewhere*.[5]

II. Imperialism

A. *"Oppressed nations"*

Contemporary references to "imperialism", though less and less frequent, it seems, in the discourse of postcolonialism, point to what is fundamentally still an unlapsed, if much modified historical reality universally heralded in two events: the outbreak of World War I in 1914, and, in its midst, the Russian Revolution of October, 1917. In a more philological sense, such references tend to be conscious or unconscious re-inscriptions of a single text, Lenin's *Imperialism, the Highest Stage of Capitalism*, first published in 1916.[6] We shall have more to say in a moment about the general theory of imperialism advanced by Lenin. But it was the events of 1914/1917 themselves that put paid to what had still been, up until then, the widely held belief that the unity of the European working classes, under the political direction of Social Democracy, would prevail over the predatory interests of monopoly capitalist powers bent on a violent re-division of saturated world markets. As Lenin himself put it in 1915, "the times when the cause of democracy and socialism was associated . . . with Europe alone have gone forever."[7] Only the most reactionary ideologues, shortly to coalesce in European fascism, could any longer affirm that the national destinies of England, France or Germany were the historical roadsigns pointing to universal emancipation. The European proletariat had defaulted at the decisive moment, and, after the revolutionary shocks brought about by world "imperialist" war left a beach-head against monopoly capital only in peripheral, semi-colonial, quasi-"Asiatic" Russia, the nation as an "arena of struggle," as a determinate space for a dialectic of emancipation, had suffered a radical transformation. It was now a space in which the centrality and world-historical ascendancy of bourgeois Europe might still be redeemed, but only if the latter looked beyond itself to the margins of its global hegemony for political, not to say spiritual leadership. The multinational, archeo-imperial territory over which Soviet political organs had assumed a tenuous control was, from a "classical," nineteenth-century European perspective, still a kind of pre-national polity, tending towards, but now, it appeared, poised to surpass its bourgeois-revolutionary phase. The nation as emancipatory space had thus seemingly entered into a new historico-philosophical dialectic, unsuspected by Romantic, Hegelian and even, perhaps, classical-Marxist notions alike: still European in form, if only because Europe still seemed the almost exclusive site of "material civilization," the same nation had become quasi- or even non-European in content. The nation, as one might summarize it here, had become *trans-europeanized*. The highly organized and "cultured" European working class that was to have donned the mantle of eighteenth- and nineteenth-century bourgeois democracy had to look to a fledgling, "under-developed" Soviet counterpart for its historical lessons in self-liberation. But this meant in turn looking for such a lesson to an even more "backward" Russian and Central Asian peasantry—only tenuously "Soviet" and just a half-century freed of serfdom—since it was only, in the end, due to the mutinous peasant army of the Czars, in volatile but epoch-making alliance with Soviet power, that the predations of "imperialism" had been dealt a (temporary) historical defeat. The cause of social revolution was, already in the language of the *Communist Manifesto*, pronounced to be international in "substance," but still national in "form."[8] But 1914/1917 disclosed this form as "national" only if the following corollary were added: there were *oppressor* and *oppressed* nations as well as classes,[9] and the agency of social revolution now appeared to flow from a conjuncture of oppressed class and oppressed nation in relation to which Europe had become "de-centered."

B. Lenin

The writings of Lenin on such questions, especially nowadays, are unlikely entries on any academic reading list or bibliography, "postcolonial" or otherwise. And it is important to note that despite what was, for decades, the orthodox left's canonization of Lenin's *Imperialism* as the supreme authority when it came to this subject, Lenin himself had neither coined the term nor cornered the market on theories of imperialism when he wrote his "pamphlet" in Zurich in 1916. His principal empirical source was the work of the English liberal J.A. Hobson and he wrote his own work, as usual for him, in an intensely polemical mode, framed by earlier works on the subject by Kautsky, Hilferding, Luxemburg and Bukharin.[10] In the "postcolonial" mind-set that now dominates much radical academic thinking, moreover, references to "imperialism" as the "highest" or "last" stage of capitalism[11] have come to seem painfully anachronistic: does not capitalism's ability to survive two World Wars, outlast the "actually existing" socialism of the USSR and its allies, and, thanks in part to technologies of production and exchange undreamt of by Lenin, to penetrate any and all local, political barriers erected against it, render Lenin's 1916 text finally obsolete?

One might answer here that, electronic capital transfers and the like notwithstanding, to those it most damages "globalization" (see section IV) still resembles in most ways what pre-"postcolonial" theory termed "imperialism,"[12] and that "highest" stages can go on much longer than such phrases encourage us to believe. But whether or not a general, humanistic interest in "imperialism" requires one to read Lenin, the genealogical centrality of his thought in relation to postcolonial studies must be recognized. In *Imperialism* and throughout his writings on the national question, Lenin assumes the social standpoint of those whom modern capitalism as a world system most exploits and oppresses, even when they are not "proletarians" in a conventional sense. As a Marxist, and thus as an inheritor of European "civilization" at what is arguably its intellectual zenith, he nevertheless breaks uncompromisingly with the "oppressor" nations of imperialist Europe and North America while still refusing to indulge in the counter-myth of an "inverted Eurocentrism."[13] Without discounting in the least the *political* importance of nationalism and national movements in relation to the new imperialist order, Lenin divests the nation both of its Eurocentrist mystique *and*—as we would now say—of its generally "essentialist," fetishized form in oppositional consciousness. Think, for example, of what is implied in the theoretical metaphor most popularly associated with Lenin's theory of imperialism, that of the "weakest link." If the entire globe has now become part of one vast, interlocking system of capitalist production, reproduction and accumulation—riven, of course, by ever deeper global crises—then the theoretical question of how to rupture or undermine such a system can no longer confine itself to a *national* framework. Given, moreover, the unevenness of this global system in terms of wealth and degrees of exploitation, breaks in the chain are more likely to occur where capitalist development is relatively lacking but where its social impact is, for this reason, most devastating. Czarist Russia, Lenin argued, was such a place, which explained why the relatively small and new Russian proletariat was able to seize and hold power (from a relatively *weak* bourgeoisie, it is true) where its larger, longer-organized European (especially German) counterpart had been unsuccessful in this during the post-war period of crisis. Lenin, indeed, went further and argued that the European labor movement that had failed to stop World War I had been effectively *corrupted* by its higher degree of development. Its leaders, if not its rank and file, had become a "labor aristocracy" with a material interest in keeping the imperialist system—or at least the historical pact with their "own" imperialist bourgeoise—intact.[14] The "weakest link," that is, revealed the existence of a chain that was not only economic but political, and even, in a sense, ideological and cultural in nature. The new reality of imperialism marked the crisis not only of older, nineteenth-century models of national economy but of national culture and civilization as well. It exposed the Western European and North American metropolis as captive to its own global economic and political "reach" —and hence compelled to launch world wars—but also to be a place of moral and spiritual *decadence*. The destiny of the modern, "Western" metropolis was not to become a New Athens but rather a New Babylon.

Historical developments subsequent to 1917 undermine, of course, the erstwhile faith in either the "socialist" citadel of Stalin's USSR or Maoist China's "East Wind" as the new, de-linked centers of a post-European, post-bourgeois civilization. But the fact that even the most arcane, historically and sociologically oblivious postcolonial theory can regard "Western civilization" as a myth long since shattered rests, genealogically, on the historical and social transformation climaxing in 1914/1917 and on its uncompromising theorization and de-mythification at the hands of Lenin.

"Imperialism," then, understood both as a world-historical conjuncture and as the index of a theoretical and critical discourse denotes an approach to the "national question" that is both "trans-europeanizing" and radically secularizing. By placing the nation in its newly global, economic context, critiques of imperialism such as Lenin's make possible the following step, which is to regard the nation from a consciously historico-political, even strategic perspective. Imperialism's "other" in this sense is not a nationalist "anti-imperialism" but a (proletarian) "internationalism," grasped here, also, as primarily a political and strategic question. The modern nation— the supreme creation of bourgeois Europe—is not something to be re-invented but to be superseded. To do so, however, requires that the nation be confronted theoretically and practically as a form or limit imposed on an internationalist politics.

C. An International of form

Can one, then, go on to identify a "poetics" of the nation—or the "inter-nation" —in this sense? As discussed earlier, the links between the literary and imperialism are plentiful but invariably contingent, thematic or merely propagandistic in nature. But if we re-consider such links in relation to the new, paradoxically "national" experience of the *inter*-nationality brought into being by imperialism—from world wars to mass migrations—we find ourselves in more familiar literary, or, at least, literary-historical-territory: is not this "poetics" of internationalism equivalent to that of the twentieth-century avant-garde now (for a "postmodern" culture) canonized in movements such as Cubism, Futurism and Dada and in figures such as Apollinaire, Grosz, Mayakovsky, etc.? All students of modern "Western" literature and art have learned by heart the art-historical meta-narrative that traces the birth of the first, truly cosmopolitan, international aesthetics to the trenches of Word War I. In a four-year interval, as the story goes, the Romantic idols of national culture (European, at any rate) were smashed to pieces. A modern—much less a modern*ist*—aesthetic could no longer be confined within a national tradition, or even experience. Non-Europeans and "postcolonialists" are not long in detecting the Eurocentrist myth that is surreptitiously restored through such a meta-narrative. Are Picasso and Breton the redeemers of art after 1914 rather than, say, Diego Rivera and Rabindranath Tagore? To get at the possible degree of truth in the story, I suggest, requires that we both "trans-europeanize" but also de-romanticize and amplify it further. For what is generated in the wake of imperialism's first and subsequent global crises is not an international aesthetic culture *per se*; pre-imperialist, not to mention pre-capitalist societies had all spawned their own. Rather it is an experience of *aesthetic form itself* as "international." Standard conceptions of the avant-garde comprehend this new formal emphasis, but are too parochial in constructing its domain. Imperialism, as the conjunctural, national-theoretical entity posited here, splits off from each other, seemingly forever, the national-cultural paternity of art and its *formal* principle. The latter no longer thinks it needs the former in order to reproduce itself and take on empirical contents. A "revolutionary" world *aesthetic*—as opposed to a tradition, canon or culture—stands forth as the poetics of the new (anti-)imperialist internationalism, both proletarian and all-purpose liberal-humanist, and binds together items as apparently antinomial as surrealism and Zhdanovite socialist realism, *Birth of a Nation* and *The Battleship Potemkin*, Bauhaus and Brechtian epic theater, etc. All conceive of and even (re)produce themselves as instances of a *Weltliteratur* different from the one envisioned by Goethe and even, perhaps, by Marx and Engels. For a "world" that could mobilize, destroy and re-invent entire nations in the course of months or weeks now no longer paused to seek its universal forms of reflection in particular national histories and experiences. Only aesthetic forms, shorn of culture—montage, *ostranenje*, didactic formulas, style itself—could keep pace. Needless to say, even this "world," trans-European as it was, retained and reproduced, as we shall see in a moment, its extra-universal, distinctly national margins. But after 1914/1917 the new nationalities and nationalisms drawn into its wake would be spared the pre-imperialist illusion of themselves as, on historico-philosophical principles, "peoples without history."

III. Colonialism

A. The "Bandung era"

The new imperialist order that unsettles the traditional forms of bourgeois national consciousness in the upheavals of 1914/1917 emerges from World

War II fundamentally intact. Here again we must guard against the tendency to confuse the rise and fall of terminologies with true epochal transformations. Postcolonialism may, in the end, enjoy more than a trivial degree of historical referentiality, but "post-imperialism"—a term that someone somewhere has probably considered coining—still refers, if not to something even worse, only to a historical possibility.

But the "national question" that had posed itself in radically new ways in the wake of 1914/1917 acquires a still different historical meaning and urgency after World War II. For economic and political reasons too complex to be discussed in detail here, the "Allied" colonial empires that had emerged victorious from World War I (Britain, France and the USA) as well as those of the "Axis" (Germany, Japan and Italy) that had sought to (re)establish themselves in direct challenge to Allied Supremacy begin a steady decline and disintegration after 1945. This disintegration is not, to be sure, a voluntary affair, as the example of Vietnam in 1945—liberated from Japan by the Viet Minh only to have the British, with tacit US backing, hand it back to the French using French former POWs and even re-armed Japanese POWs[15]— suffices to show. Starting in 1947 with the independence of India and Pakistan a great period of decolonization begins, ending only in the early 1970s with the liberation of Portugal's remaining colonies in Africa. Following the historical accounts of Samir Amin and Aijaz Ahmad,[16] I will refer to this conjuncture in what follows as the "Bandung era," in slightly anachronistic allusion to the conference of newly independent Asian and African nations held in Indonesia ten years after the end of World War II. As Ahmad has argued in an especially clarifying essay,[17] it is at Bandung that the new national bourgeoisies of what common parlance will henceforth refer to as the "third world" publically consecrate their emergence as new players in world politics. The most prominent third world statesmen in attendance—Nehru, Nasser and Sukarno, with Tito as the sole European interloper and Zhou Enlai the somewhat anxiously tolerated guest of honor—personify a politics of "oppressed nations" that both guards its left flank against the potentially more radical, revolutionary anti-imperialism of third world peasants and workers but also its right against any attempt by the new imperialist hegemon—the United States—to restrict the third world state's limited national—and capitalist—autonomy.

Not all third world nationalisms conform to the Bandung prototype, of course. The China that, in the course of liberating itself from Japanese imperialism, carries out what is arguably the third great social revolution of the modern era stands in a qualitatively different, effectively exteriorized relation to the neo-imperialist world system. This remains so, however much its subsequently counter-revolutionary evolution (not to be confused with any sacrifice of *nationalist* militancy) may now induce us to forget it. China's unique historical development after 1949 has made it, especially in the wake of the collapse of Soviet-modelled socialism and the passing of the Bandung era, one of the great blindspots of postcolonial theory. The Korean, Cuban, Vietnamese, and perhaps also the shorter lived Luso-African revolutions must also be regarded as relatively exceptional in this context.

At the other extreme are the decolonizations that—perhaps because so relatively little was at stake strategically and economically—generate only momentary and superficial nationalist movements and ideologies. One thinks, for example, of certain former British colonies in the West Indies and former French ones in sub-Saharan Africa. But the national-political entity consecrated at Bandung—both actual and ideological—typifies the new historical juncture here under discussion for the following reason: it presupposes the now definitive historical failure of anti-imperialism to take the form of a strategic alliance of metropolitan and third world labor against capital as such, hence the decline, for the then foreseeable future, of "proletarian internationalism." The nationalism of Bandung rests on the *de facto* anti-imperialist alliance, that, in the final analysis, is to take its place: that of third world labor (primarily agrarian at first) and third world capital, under the latter's effective hegemony. An objective assessment of the enormously varied and rich cultural and intellectual output corresponding to this conjuncture—what we might now think of as the canon of third world cultural nationalism—presupposes comprehension of this fundamental historical and political factor, both as constraint and yet also as a deepening of the *trans-europeanization* signalled by the initial onset of imperialist crisis. By the time the Bandung era comes to its more or less agreed upon close in the 1970s, the ascendancy of the new third world, bourgeois-led states will have come to seem more ambiguous, setting the stage historically for the radical doubts concerning national liberation that are typical of most "postcolonial" theory and criticism. But here too a material genealogy of postcolonialism cannot afford historical embarrassments. The "oppressed nations" of the Bandung era remain, on the most fundamental level, the politico-strategic object of struggle forged out of the first imperialist conjuncture. What is different now is how the new, local political reality of class in ex-colonial nations such as India, Algeria, Vietnam or Ghana—a reality that either places a fledgling but "really existing" national bourgeoisie in a position of hegemony within the national setting or that makes the creation of such a class the implicit, structural goal of national liberation struggle—reflects itself in what we might term a *re-essentialized*, or even *de-europeanized* national space or imaginary. To emancipate the nation now appears to be something more than to de-link it from the chains of imperialist domination, *more* (if not, precisely *other*) than a question of relative class power. It is to attain national *sovereignty*, a *telos* in relation to which categories such as the *popular* and *culture* naturally predominate over those of class, capital or labor.

B. Fanon

Turning now to the question of the the theory associated with this new conjunctural reality, we find a broad variation, at first sight confused, of loosely theoretical discourses corresponding to the no less varied reality of anti-colonial and national liberation movements stretching across three decades and the better part of the planet. Theory, too, in a sense, reverts to a "national" form, unable to coalesce in a Lenin in the way the theoretical question of imperialism had, out of what now comes to seem an abstract and utopian universalism of class. Mao Zedong, Ho Chi Minh, Gandhi, Nehru, George Padmore, Nkrumah, Nasser, W.E.B. DuBois, Amilcar Cabral, Che Guevara, Walter Rodney, etc. are the names by which this eclectic theory, in variant degrees of elaboration, is first known. Even the so-called "Three Worlds theory", as Ahmad has shown in the above-cited study, breaks down into at least three variants—Bandung or "Non-Aligned," Khrushchevite-Soviet and Maoist—none of which can claim anything like the critical-analytical rigor of Lenin's *Imperialism*.

Still, certain instances of this more particularistic, nation-bound "theory" have now shown a capacity to outlive the nationalist movements as part of which they were initially formulated and thus to offer, in more historically and regionally mediated form, a general reflection on the decolonizing/national liberation process. The theoretical works of Mao Zedong are the first to come to mind here. "Maoism," is, to be sure, a self-conscious continuation of the already universalizing theory of "Marxism-Leninism," and what was, for many years, its enormous authority within not only communist but nationalist circles reflects what we have already noted as the historically exceptional status of China in the Bandung era. The precipitous collapse of this authority after the 1970s with only a few exceptions (e.g. the Shining Path insurgency in 1980s Peru or the New People's Army in a somewhat earlier period in the Philippines) reflects the no less rapid demotion of Mao to mere national figurehead in the People's Republic itself. This is no reason at all for neglecting the works of Mao Zedong, something no truly serious student of "postcolonial studies" can possibly afford. But in works such as the "Talks at the Ya'nan Conference on Literature and Art," delivered in the early 1940s under Japanese occupation, there is, admittedly, an ironic absence of *theoretical*—if not practical—concern for the "national question."[18] For Mao, the national self-identity and integrity of China is already an axiom; the only question is the strategic, even tactical one of how to liberate it from the Japanese imperialist yoke—something that, let it not be forgotten, the movement led by him went on over a protracted period to do with shattering results for postwar imperialism.

Far less epoch-making in their own right, but continuously and even increasingly resonant for contemporary intellectual and "postcolonial" sensibilities are the critical writings of, *inter alia*, a W.E.B. DuBois, a C.L.R. James or the Peruvian Marxist and nationalist José Carlos Mariátegui. James' classic history of the Haitian revolution, *The Black Jacobins*, for example, written in the 1930s with a prophetic eye trained on imminent nationalist upheavals in Africa, remains a theoretical reflection of first importance on the national, anti-colonial question.[19] But the one name that seems a virtually inevitable reference in the search for theoretical crystallizations of the national liberation epoch is that of Frantz Fanon. In *Black Skins, White Masks*, but above all in *The Wretched of the Earth*, Fanon, a black Martinican who devoted his French training in medicine and psychiatry to the Algerian anti-colonial revolution, gives to the Bandung conjuncture (whose final outcome he did not live to see) its most synthesizing, and, at the same time, most self-questioning and prophetic theoretical reflection.[20] Without ceasing to insist on the struggle for *national* liberation from colonial domination as a precondition for the *social* emancipation of the third world, Fanon presses the plebeian, if not precisely class critique of the third world national bourgeoisie almost to the limits of "third worldist" doctrine. His account of the transformation of pan-Africanist political leadership in the late 1950s from a catalytic into a regressive force that, after independence, "serves to immobilize the people," already anticipates the degeneration of African states into the corrupt, neo-colonized instruments of IMF and World Bank diktats many have become today.[21] The fact that *The Wretched of the Earth* still speaks so forcefully to the social experience of contemporary "postcolonial" politics, despite the no less complete political degeneration of the independent Algerian state to which Fanon directed all his energies is to be explained, I think, by this refusal to credit the third world national bourgeoisie (a class that was, in Fanon's words, "good for nothing"[22] with being more than a momentarily strategic ally on the road to a popular sovereignty loosely identified as "socialist." True, Fanon is not a Marxist, a point he clarifies with characteristic directness when he writes, e.g., that

> When you examine at close quarters the colonial context, it is evident that what parcels out the world is to begin with the fact of belonging or not belonging to a given race, a given species. In the colonies the economic substructure is also a superstructure. The cause is the consequence; you are rich because you are white, you are white because you are rich. This is why Marxist analysis should always be slightly stretched every time we have to do with the colonial problem.[23]

The immediate political realities of the Cold War, including northern ("socialist" and otherwise) labor's *de facto* abandonment of nations such as Algeria to the racist brutalities of French colonialism, appear to Fanon to disprove the universalist claims of Marxism, to unmask it, even, as a theory inevitably vulnerable to a West-centered stigmatism. Race has, in the end, prevailed over class in Fanon's third world, a fact that does not, however, lead him to a politics of racial identity but rather to a politics of "national consciousness" as the only rational means of averting the primitive, racially "Manichaean" forms of anti-colonial awakening. The inevitable violence of decolonization escapes a descent back into pathological forms only if it can be directed outwards at the (neo-)colonizer from a *sovereign* subject, fully national (as against ethnic or tribal) in its make-up. The national is the necessary prelude (perhaps a kind of collective Oedipal stage?) to the social, in which form it sheds its adolescent particularisms. As Fanon writes, again in "The Pitfalls of National Consciousness,"

> A bourgeoisie that provides nationalism alone as food for the masses fails in its mission and gets caught up in a whole series of mishaps. But if nationalism is not made explicit, if it is not enriched and deepened by a very rapid transformation into a consciousness of social and political needs, in other words into humanism, it leads up a blind alley. [24]

It is, of course, difficult to read Fanon today without a good measure of skepticism regarding the very possibility of this "rapid transformation." The broad array of nationalist and third-worldist movements that more or less consciously adopted Fanon's call to "national consciousness" often look, from a "postcolonial" standpoint, to have been precisely the "blind alleys" he warned against. Upheld by what he had witnessed in the early years of the Algerian national liberation struggle, Fanon's evident belief that an increasingly popularized national consciousness would burst free of its bourgeois limitations now looks impossibly voluntaristic—a belief, in his own terms, in the capacity of "superstructure" to become "substructure." History in the post-Bandung era has, to say the least, not been kind to this notion. Still, Fanon succeeds here in posing a problem that the Leninist, politico-strategic approach to the national question too easily passes over: if the nation is simply a form or an arena within which the class-based conflict of capital vs. labor unfolds (a conflict, recall, pitting "oppressor" against "oppressed" nations) must not this form itself, however de-mystified or "de-essentialized," have its subjective side? If class must, for its political realization, mediate itself as nation, must not class *consciousness* do likewise? Can the nation become an outpost, a barricade from which to oppose imperialism if those it "interpellates" persist in the colonial psycho-pathology of seeing themselves as simply inferior versions of a Western (or "Northern") master-subject?

Fanon himself seems to have formulated this question in literally psychiatric terms, whence his consistent emphasis on the violent formation of national consciousness as if virtually a form of collective therapy for the psychoses of colonized subjects. (See the final section of *The Wretched of the*

Earth, "Colonial War and Mental Disorders.") But in being recast from a more subjective standpoint, does not the "national question" become in fact the question of national *culture* itself as precisely that sphere within which a "national consciousness" makes the concrete transition from purely objective political theory and strategy to the more subjective level of mass, everday experience? Once again, *The Wretched of the Earth* reads, here in "On National Culture," like anything but an anachronism. Fanon's familiar dialectical breakdown of the evolution of cultural nationalist intellectuals into the three phases of assimilationism, exoticism and, finally, authentic nationalism should placate, up to a point, even the most fervent anti-"essentialist."[25] As the mere "stock of particulars," the "outer garment" of "custom" national culture remains trapped in its reified form, caught in a purely reflexive relationship with the Western, colonizing "civilization" it had once merely aspired to assimilate.[26] National culture only fully realizes its latent possibilities as that "zone of occult instability" that traces in its own movement that of the "people" itself in its self-activity and constant self-creation.[27] The theory of a true "national intellectual" who "addresses his own people"[28] may, like the general idea of a "rapid transformation" of national into social (class) consciousness, arouse suspicion nowadays, but here, it seems to me, Fanon has history a good deal more firmly on his side. For while the third world nationalism of the Bandung era may now be fairly judged, from the perspective of labor, to have been a political failure, its cultural history cannot be so dismissed. Do we not have in literary and artistic figures and movements, from Achebe, Mahfouz and Neruda to Cuban popular music to contemporary Chinese film something like the fulfillment of the dialectic that for Fanon culminated in the "national intellectual"? And can any future strategy of "postcolonial" (post)national liberation possibly afford not to steep itself in this tradition?[29]

C. "National allegory"

To attempt, now, to define a "poetics" of the nation corresponding to the Bandung conjuncture admittedly carries with it grave risks of over generalization. Few critics or literary historians possess the breadth of reading and knowledge required even to begin to determine whether such defintion is a valid exercise at all, and I am certainly not one of these few. One thinks inevitably here, again, of the controversy over Fredric Jameson's "Third World Literature in the Era of Multinational Capitalism,"[30] particularly in the wake of Ahmad's studied and aggressive criticism of this essay for what was reputedly its invention of a grandly mythological abstraction called . . . "third world literature."[31] Jameson's claim to have detected a latent "national allegory" in certain writings (e.g. those of China's Lu Hsun) then re-read as metonymies for a "third world literature" remains, nevertheless, one of the most prominent definitions of a cultural-nationalist poetics, and is at least a practical point of departure here for what is no more than a speculative exercise. As readers of the essay will recall, the analysis that underlies the "national allegory" theory has to do with the opposition of public and private spheres. Briefly, the social being corresponding to a fully reified capitalist modernity tends to assume purely private forms; that corresponding to the still incompletely, and perhaps never to be fully "modernized" third world national economies and polities does not. This is not to say that third world experience is therefore always *public* in form, but rather that a firm separation between public and private is much more difficult to institute and maintain. The private is always on the point of becoming the public, and thus it is, according to Jameson's reasoning, that the relation of the third world individual to the sphere of national life as a whole forces a break or leap in which the individual or private "destiny" takes on a directly, publically "national" dimension.[32] This subsumption of the particular by the general, and not, as would be the case in the metropolitan bourgeois novel, the reverse, is what Jameson chooses to call "allegory."

The potential for error here, to my thinking, lies in the *a priori* reduction of every individual instance of "third world literature" to such a latent national allegory. But it seems to me correct to regard this allegorizing process as a *structural tendency* in the narrative forms of "peripheral" modernities—a tendency that may, in many instances, never amount to *more* than an abstract possibility. If it can be allowed that the third world nation itself exists, on one plane at least, only as an abstract possibility—as a volatile and unstable form of social self-identity resting on the already volatile and unstable "Bandung" alliance of third world capital and labor— then it follows that attempts to represent this nation, to portray it in a narrative or symbolic medium, will reflect this abstraction within the formal elements of the medium itself.

Not all "third world literature" necessarily undertakes such a form of *national* representation, however, and, indeed, it may be just as typical of the narrative of "developing nations" to *refuse* the "nation" as such an abstract, so to speak, *thematic a priori*. The greatest works of "third world" cinema, from Satyajit Ray's *Apu Trilogy* to Ousmane Sembene's *Xala* to the Brazilian "Cinema Novo" of Pereira dos Santos, Guerra and Rocha, supersede national-allegorical interpretation—or submit to it only as a non-cinematic, dogmatic afterthought. In a Latin American context, I also think here, for example, of the earlier, urban novels of the Peruvian author Mario Vargas Llosa. In *Time of the Hero* (*La ciudad y los perros*) and *Conversation in the Cathedral* for instance, there can be noted an almost conscious decision to create *only* characters whose national-allegorical representativity is so complicated and ironized as to be made virtually impossible. "Peru" in these narratives has become an abstract postulate, or "thematic *a priori*," only in the negative sense of having been *ruled out* as the ultimate, positive

meaning of any personal or social emancipation. "¿En qué momento," asks
the protagonist of *Conversation in the Cathedral* in its opening pages, "se
jodió el Perú?" "When did Peru get fucked up?" True, Vargas Llosa is,
already in the 1960s, skeptical of cultural-nationalist formulas, for reasons
that at first draw him leftwards towards socialism but that, as his own class
and ideological limitations catch up with him, degenerate into rationales
for reactionary neo-liberalism. Yet *Conversation in the Cathedral* is every bit as
"third world" a fiction as the earlier, indigenist and much more allegorizable fictions of José María Arguedas, Peru's other great literary figure of the
fifties and sixties.

The point here is not to launch into the inevitably futile and reductionist
attempt to derive ever more authentic canons of third world literature, but
rather to note how, for an author such as Vargas Llosa, "national allegory"
makes itself felt *structurally* as just that form of representation that must be
consciously avoided if certain more socially realistic representations are to
become possible. And yet Vargas Llosa's heroes and villains are, in fact, *not*
the privatized monads of metropolitan hyper-modernity; their destinies
unfold precisely on that ever-shifting dividing line between the public and
the private that offsets any clean reproduction of national subjectivities (see
Chapter 11). What these novels resist as false is the final, allegorical solution of dissolving this problematic form of indviduality into the single, self-
identical substance of the "nation." But "Peru" remains no less the "thematic
a priori" here, if only because it must be consciously and abstractly *negated*
as the *positive* content of individual experience if that experience itself is to
become fully representable.[33]

The "re-essentialized" third world nation, that is, calls forth a narrative
or symbolic process of self-representation that need not be reducible to
allegory but that may be obliged to supplement this represenation, even,
perhaps, to interrupt or stop it if it should fail to acknowledge the
"thematic *a priori*." We can see the result of such a supplementary or
ruptural representation not only as outright allegory but also as purely
lyrical expression. Think, here, of the Caribbean poetry of negritude and
more particularly of the way an Aimé Césaire, René Depestre, Nicolás
Guillén or Luis Palés Matos evoke "Africa" as a poetic presence. In Guillén's
"My Last Name," for example, the poet reconstructs the past scene in
which his anonymous Dahoman or Congolese ancestor had his African
name blotted out by a Cuban "notary's ink" and a Spanish one ("Guillén")
inserted.[34] The history of colonization in its most brutal form is disclosed
in the seemingly innocuous fixity and transparency of a few letters on an
identity card. But when "My Last Name" comes to invoke the ancestral
homeland—the "nation" on its re-essentialized plane—the images Guillén
draws upon are of monkeys, spears, rhinoceroses and baobabs. "Africa"—
which is what, after all, motivates and foregrounds the brilliant historical
meditation on naming—is a place appearing to lack historical or social

specifity, a purely lyrical, even mythical presence. The nation, too, in effect, is only a "name." It is, to cite Césaire's words in the *Discourse on Colonialism* that place of "profound being" to be found "*beneath* [the] social being" of colonial and neo-colonial life.[35] Of course, it is the history of the "middle passage" itself that has placed *objective* limits on the poet's historical imagination in "My Last Name." But the need to gaze back at an effectively un-representable ancestral nation—which is simultaneously, for Guillén, the forward gaze into a Cuba freed of its colonialist-racist legacies—cannot wait for history to settle accounts. Here the nation ("Africa," negritude, a black Cuba) must take on a directly representational, symbolic presence, even if it means representation as merely a place of monkeys and baobabs. More, then, than a "thematic *a priori*," the nation that colonialism has either suppressed or called forth in defiance (or both) generates a species of *ethno-teleology*, a goal to be reached (or recovered) outside History proper.

Lest it be thought that such "ethno-teleologies" result invariably in aesthetic compromises, however, consider, finally, the work of the famed, post-revolutionary Mexican muralists Diego Rivera, David Siqueiros and José Clemente Orozco. In addition to virtually re-creating the modern iconography of Mexican nationalism with monumental images of pre-Columbian cities, modern workers and peasant guerrillas, the great murals of the 1920s, '30s and '40s have withstood the crises of that nationalism far better than the state that once subsidized them. In their painterly, but also public-architectural presentation (what Walter Benjamin termed the "tactile") they conserve, somehow, the revolutionary social energies that generated them. Rivera's Zapata looks as defiant of NAFTA as he does of Carranza and erstwhile neo-colonial elites. By the 1930s, moreover, the work of the muralists had become an international—even "revolutionary aesthetic"—style in its own right, profoundly influencing the work of depression era North American painters. (In whose hands, admittedly, the painting of national allegories becomes a rather more doubtful affair—think of the work of Thomas Hart Benton or of the young Jackson Pollock.) The mythical, "ethno-teleological" content of the Mexican murals is as transparent as ever. But the mass character, the virtually structural popularity of these "artworks" leaves them permeable to that "zone of occult instability" that for Fanon conserved the formula for a de-europeanized but also *de-bourgeoisified* "national consciousness."

IV. Postcolonialism

A. *"Globalization"*

A "material genealogy" of postcolonialism is, to reiterate the point upon which we began, complicated by the disparity between its generative principle—the sweeping history that the term invokes, if often unintentionally—and the narrow, intramural sphere in which postcolonialism is talked about and practiced. To fully reconstruct such a genealogy would require us to go on at considerable length about "Commonwealth Studies," "Colonial Discourse Analysis" simposia, competing postcolonial antho-logies, Australian academic clearing-houses and the like. I take as given here a readerly consensus that there is no time for this—but also that the hypermediated relationship of postcolonialism to secular realities, if carefully abbreviated, will allow us to make some important connections in what follows. In the small world within which "postcolonial studies" circulate we are now accustomed to speak in the same breath of Bhabha and Fanon, Said and Walter Rodney (i.e. the reader and the read), when a single step outside its walls suffices for these pairings to seem quizzical, and another for them to become incomprehensible. But the fact that relatively few read the reader does not *ipso facto* invalidate the reading nor prevent its genealogical investigation and assessment.

To reiterate further: at some point over the last two and a half decades the same small but significant class of intellectuals that had learned in the 1960s to say "third world" became more hesitant about saying it. "Postcolonial," a term with far more ambiguous political resonances, fits this hesitation much better and, beginning in the early 1980s, gradually replaced "third world," at least in some contexts. (A similar story could be recounted about "cultural studies" as a euphemistic substitution for "Marxist literary criticism" and even "Critical Theory.") The question for us here is what major historical shift prompted this minor terminological one (among others) and how such a shift affected conceptions, both popular and intellectual, of the entity that is still really at issue here: the nation.

Sticking to the schema employed so far, my answer is to propose a general, if highly uneven crisis of "third worldist" or national-liberationist ideology stemming in turn from the progressive collapse of the strategic class and national alliance of third world bourgeoisie and third world labor underwriting this ideology. The more narrowly conjunctural indices of this crisis are many, and it would be difficult to single out any one as more epochal or synthesizing: the overthrow of the Allende regime in Chile in 1973; the fairly rapid economic decline and marketization of "socialist" Vietnam after its final defeat of US and US-backed forces in the mid 1970s; the same nation's border war with "socialist" China a few years later; the increasingly counter-revolutionary direction taken in the People's Republic itself after the triumph of the Deng Xiaoping faction of the Chinese Communist Party; the Islamic Revolution in Iran in 1979; the eventual con-tainment and defeat by the US and its local clients of popular insurgent power in El Salvador and Nicaragua; the collapse of the USSR and its former satellites in the late 1980s and early 1990s, a fact of enormous and disastrous consequences for radical-nationalist regimes from Luso- and North Africa to Cuba; the US invasions of Grenada and Panama; the Persian Gulf War, etc.

It is neither easy nor very safe to speculate about the underlying causes of a crisis that is still very much in process, but these are clearly enough economic as well as political in nature. And the economic theory of choice these days, along an astonishingly broad spectrum from right to left, is that the various attempts of "developing nations" to industrialize without sacrificing national autonomy have succumbed to a new reality of "globalization," a reality in which the sheer scope of market space and activity exceeds the efforts of any but the wealthiest and most powerful nation-states to contain or control them. In most cases the "theory" of globalization functions as a mere apology for US, Western European and Japanese dominance of the world market, belying the fact that the crisis that has all but destroyed nationalized economic regimes in the third (and former "second") world, is *itself* global in dimension, and (as recent— 1998—developments in East Asia, dramatize) dire in its implications for the global hegemons as well.

But apologetics aside, there is little to debate concerning the failure of the economic model more or less vaguely adumbrated by the third world statesmen who had gathered at Bandung in 1955. Perhaps one can point to exceptions here: China, India, South Korea, maybe Brazil and South Africa—although, as this is written, the economic crisis that has shattered the capitalist myth of the "Pacific Tigers" has made the Chinese and even the Japanese "miracles" seem suddenly doubtful. Following the reasoning of political economists such as Robert Kurz, it seems to me plausible to speak of a general "collapse" of what Kurz terms "recuperative modernization" (*nachholende Modernisierung*) from Mexico to the (post-)USSR.[36] In the poorest nations of the third world, where the process of primitive accumulation of capital had yet to be completed, the sheer magnitude of the organic composition of capital (that is, the ratio of "constant" capital such as plant and infrastructure to "variable" capital, such as wages and labor costs) required within the current global process of valorization for such accumulation to occur makes it a practical and increasingly acknowledged impossibility. In the "sub-imperial" economies of China, India, Mexico, Brazil, etc. as well as in the newly "privatized" markets of Russia and Eastern Europe, the rapid selling-off of state-controlled industries—i.e. of the legacy of "Bandung" and "really existing socialism"—is supposed to free up capital for more productive utilization. But "privatization" as often as not is tantamount to a looting spree by financial speculators, signalling in fact the *destruction* of the previously accumulated stocks.[37]

The general truth arguably emerging from these particulars of crisis is that the third world national bourgeoisies have, almost without exception, failed as agents of a national modernization that—whether avowedly capitalist, "socialist," or, in that most exotic of Khrushchevite euphemisms, "non-capitalist" —was to to bring either a gradual or a revolutionary social emancipation in its wake. To attribute this failure to the inexorability of "globalization" is valid only if we grasp the latter phenomenon in *its* profoundly contradictory reality as a "law" of capitalist development that in fact restricts the very possibility of such development to a constantly narrowing and shrinking base of accumulation. It is not just Nikes and Coke that penetrate all corners of the planet but the negative, often catastrophic effects of "national" and regional capitalist crises themselves. Thus the economic, social "failure" of bourgeois-led national liberation in the third world (a "failure" that, we must still recall, has *not* been uniform and that has a flip-side in certain unequivocally progressive changes, especially in areas such as culture) can only be morally condemned if it is first laid at the doorstep of the current beneficiaries and mouthpieces of "globalization" in its guise as the neo-liberal panacea now waved in the faces of immiserated third word labor.

But failure is failure. In this context one inevitably comes back to Fanon's astonishingly prophetic insights in *The Wretched of the Earth*, where he had warned that the "incapacity of the national middle class to rationalize popular action"—something he clearly understood as a consequence of this class's fundamental incapacity as an agent of development and accumulation—would lead to the "retrogression" in which "the nation is passed over for the race, and the tribe is preferred to the state."[38] (Fanon's "Bandung," third-worldist outlook is still detectably in force in his simultaneous call for this class to "repudiate its own nature" and "make itself the willing slave of that revolutionary capital which is the people," a demonstration of faith that is the dialectical other of his scathing condemnation of this same class for its weakness and identification with Western bourgeois decadence.[39] But even here the contemporary realities of "globalization" seem almost immanent in his very choice of words, e.g. his dismissal of the third world bourgeoisie for "beginning at the end" of bourgeois civilization in the West. This is, in more strictly political-economic terms, precisely Kurz's argument:[40] that local, neo-national attempts to complete the phase of primitive accumulation are doomed by "beginning at the end" of global capitalism's own history of expansionary accumulation.)

Is it not precisely this "retrogression," this failure of "national" to transform itself into "social consciousness," that now unfolds from the Islamic and Hindu demagogies in Western and Southern Asia to the inter-ethnic and, so to speak, hypo-bourgeois wars in Africa and on the immediate southern and eastern flanks of metropolitan Europe? Fanon's insight is in fact needed here to complete the picture of what the "trans-european" nation as a social, political ideal is now becoming in the course of "globalization" : an institutional/ideological entity that, precisely because it has been rendered inoperative as a site for the accumulation and control of capital, seeks to compensate for this in undergoing a radical *re-particularization* verging, in the most extreme cases (e.g. Afghanistan, Serbia) on a *de-secularization*. In a strange sense, the earlier, imperialist conjuncture appears to have returned: events such as the rapid collapse of the Soviet bloc, and now the even swifter decimation of East Asian capitalist economies such as Indonesia produce a sense of impending global transformation—utopian and catastrophic by turns—for the cognition of which the framework of national consciousness can supply no real vantage point. Where are the strategically "weakest links" to be found now? Seemingly everywhere—has not the hour of the truly "wretched of the earth" come at last? And yet "retrogression" is the near-universal phenomenon. As Asian, African, East European and Latin American markets threaten to disappear and vast new migrations of unutilizable "human capital" pour out of these regions towards the shrinking bases of accumulating wealth, one begins to speculate that the "weakest" has become, in fact, the strongest, and perhaps soon to be only remaining "link" : the neo-imperial metropolis itself.

B. Said/Spivak

Suppose now one were to attempt to construct, as a kind of thought experiment, a phenomenology of the nation in its present, conjunctural reality. As just what sort of mental object, or experience, would it present itself to a contemporary critical consciousness, the further objective configuration of which we will leave, for now, unspecified? We might begin with the comparative observation that as an object for a Leninist and a third-worldist consciousness, the oppressed nation was endowed with a quality of "historical spatiality": the nation is experienced as a site for a fundamentally unitary, self-contained process of social and historical development. In the "Leninist" instance such spatiality was, in its most general manifestation, already global and not national, but the nation lodged itself discreetly here as a sort of fold within global space, a place one could be inside of without losing sight of the larger enclosure—even, in certain cases, a privileged vantage point from which to experience the spatial connections between all such folds. In short, a "weak link." It is this fold that closes onto itself, becoming coterminous with historical spatiality, in third-worldist or cultural-nationalist consciousness. Or to be still more precise: third worldism (as the enumerative logic of 1, 2, 3 obviously implies) splits this spatiality into two (or, supposedly, three) opposed spheres. The mechanical, "Manichaean" delusion afflicting such a consciousness—for the transcendental standpoint of phenomenology stipulates that space remains unitary in its essence—is invariably sensed, but only prompts further reflection from an exceptional, dialectical intelligence on the order of Fanon, who simply locates the "universal" historical sphere *within* the particular and seemingly narrower one of "national consciousness," claiming thereby to transform both.

These phenomenological forms of the nation evidently continue to play some experiential role in contemporary social consciousness, for which nations in their most immediate, common-sensical self-presentation are, after all, just aggregated, geographical units strung like beads, not linked together in a chain or (except in war) faced off in "Manichaean" pairs. But the "globalized"/"re-particularized" nation described above, as a site for the *dis*accumulation of capital and the production of migrancy, as a market increasingly without commodities or consumers, traversed by anti-modern, quasi-fascistic fits of religious identity formation and unravelled along ethnic and tribal lines, seems more and more to be a space emptied of any historical self-relation, not a "people without history" but yet not the place where "people" and "history" meet any longer. "Globalized" nation space is not the perfectly flattened surface of neo-liberal "Ends of History." (Even Fukuyama, we recall, acknowledged that there would probably always be "Albanias" and "Burkina Fasos."[41]) Colonizer and colonized, oppressor and oppressed, "man" and ethnic (female) "other", rich and poor: these are, perhaps more than ever, the visible fissures in the "world" that encloses us. But where does the concrete, historical space of their overcoming, the "historical spatiality" of *emancipation* begin? A *phenomenology* of the nation seems now utterly incapable of answering this question. It presents us with the elements of an emancipatory dialectic, but not with their unifying law of motion, making them seem, finally, as I have described them in the chapter immediately following, "incommensurable."

But this apparent emptying out of the nation as a *historically* emancipatory space has not, at least on the *phenomenological* level, enforced a reconciliation of critical consciousness with "really existing" globalization. For one might concede the actuality of the latter as a kind of total system and yet still—following in the philosophical vein of a Nietzsche, for example—posit an opposing principle outside this, or any, system. Metropolitan critical consciousness, at least of the academic kind, has for a generation or more been intimate with a modern variation of such anti-systemic critique in the form of poststructuralism. Suppose the globally dominant system could be likened to "discourse" in the Foucauldian sense. This would enable one to account for the seeming absence of the nation as "historical spatiality," given that the elements of a discursive system bear only a structural, not spatial or temporal relation to that system. Add to this the idea, intellectually popularized by theorists such as Foucault and Derrida, that, while strictly speaking nothing can be outside a discursive system, every such system has built into it an anti-systemic principle, a law of "*différance*" or a self-reproducing gap that continuously threatens to undermine it. Suppose further that the "nation" or its equivalent for contemporary anti-colonialism and anti-imperialism were this sort of anti-systemic principle—would not, then, the tables be turned, or at least turnable, on "globalization" ?

The reader may have recognized by now the general theoretical orientation of Edward Said's *Orientalism*, the work from which virtually all contemporary postcolonial theory ultimately derives.[42] The "discourse" named in its title is one that has, purportedly since the time of Aeschylus, constructed the Orient not as a "free subject of thought and action" but as a mere effect, internal to this discourse, and justifying "in advance" the Western colonization of the East.[43] In an incorporation of the Foucault of *Discipline and Punish* Said also equates orientalism with a "power/know-ledge" for which the Western cognition of a simulacrum called, say, "Egypt" is always already inseparable from the colonization and domination of the real Egypt. Thus "discourse" (orientalism) and a secular, historical reality (the Western colonization of the East) are, while not formally collapsed into each other, nevertheless indistinguishable from the standpoint of their object. They are two facets of a single, encompassing system that itself never comes to know or truthfully represent the "other" against which it is arrayed. Gaining the standpoint of this object would, if possible, be tantamount to subverting the "discourse" that—if we follow strictly the logic of *Orientalism*'s Foucauldian conception—conditions the possibility of the object's colonization.

There is, it is true, a more "worldly," philosophically more "humanist" cast to *Orientalism* as well, for it is a carefully researched work that devotes less time to poststructuralist theorizing than to the focused criticism, loosely historicist in methodology, of a highly specific, empirically "dis-cursive" object: the tradition of eighteenth- and nineteenth-century Western "orientalist" scholarship. Since publishing *Orientalism*, Said has consistently and publically identified himself with that most historical, extra-discursive movement called Palestinian national liberation, in its decades-long conflict with Zionist nationalism and annexationism. And, however doubtful his real intellectual debt to it, Said would certainly be the last to dissociate himself from the intellectual legacy of "Bandung." Moreover, he concludes his book with a measured advocacy of newer purveyors of orientalist scholarship (e.g. Clifford Geertz) "perfectly capable of freeing themselves from the old ideological straitjackets."[44]

But these aspects of *Orientalism* are not what gradually converted it into the harbinger, if not the paradigm, of postcolonial theory. By invoking a poststructuralist conception of discourse rather than, say, a historical-materialist theory of ideology as the governing category for anti-colonialist critique, Said had hit upon a way of salvaging from the post-Bandung crisis of national consciousness (on the level of what we have characterized here as its "phenomenology") a kind of transcendental advantage. As, so to speak, a "globalism" without space and time, "discourse" endows its "other" with, in principle, the same, indeterminate status. The "nation"—the "real," unrepresentable, unknowable "Orient" —acquires automatically subversive potential simply by virtue of its logical exteriority.

As noted, Said himself pulls back from this thought and renders, in the end, a more cautious, but less radical judgment on an orientalism whose "other" may just be a more enlightened, ideologically less "strait-jacketed" orientalist. As a result, *Orientalism* is severely weakened as a theoretically "postcolonial" statement, citing Nietzsche and proclaiming the discursive construction of truth at one moment and denouncing the falsifications of orientalists such as Lane or Gibb in the next, as if unaware of any inconsistency. It has fallen to another, founding text of postcolonial theory—Gayatri Chakravorty Spivak's "Can the Subaltern Speak?"—to push beyond *Orientalism*'s "humanist" limitations and propose in theoretically less ambiguous terms a "discursive"—more precisely a "textualist"—form of anti-colonial/anti-imperialist subversion.[45] In this critical essay—one of the last decade's most widely cited and yet most frequently misconstrued[46]—Spivak executes a Derridean move on Said's Foucauldian reading of colonialism as "discursive practice." The latter now becomes a "social text," an englobing, systemic presence of Western imperialism that obviates *Orientalism*'s vacillation—ideological misrepresentation or "power/knowledge" construct?—on the question of discursive truth content. "Imperialism," as understood by Spivak, does not merely monopolize the power to represent its "other"; *all* such representations have (always) already fallen under the aegis of the Western "Subject." With an implacability that Spivak will mollify in later writings, Foucault himself is rebuked for eliding the "epistemic violence" of the imperialist social text even as he (together with Deleuze) denounces those intellectuals who claim to "represent" the masses: for the self-absenting (Western) intellectual too easily conceals the still more primordial absence of the third world "subaltern," whose "speech" not even the Nietzschean anarchism of "power/knowledge" can hear.

"In the semioses of the social text, elaborations of insurgency *stand in the place* of the 'utterance.' The 'sender'—'the peasant' [aka the subaltern]—is marked only as a pointer to an *irretrievable* consciousness."[47] There can be, from this standpoint, no correcting for "orientalist" misrepresentation, nor even a substitution—"Eastern" for "Western"—of "discursive practices." Such changes would, at best, only make room within the "Subject" for a third world intellectual, or class (or gender) elite, still banishing the "subaltern" to the far side of Spivak's epistemologically constructed "international division of labor." ("Can the Subaltern Speak?" makes no apologies for its post-"Bandung" anti-bourgeois radicalism—the substance of its otherwise rather puzzling affinity for what was, before Spivak's essay introduced them to a non-Indian public, still the distinctly non-poststructuralist orientation of Ranajit Guha and the Indian "Subaltern Studies" collective.[48]) As the social equivalent of "that inaccessible blankness circumscribed by an interpretable text"[49] the anti-imperialist deconstructor of the "Subject" would, in keeping with the "always already" of its own social/epistemic subjection, *already have performed* its task *before* this Subject could represent/re-subject it, before it could be heard to "speak."

From its place outside the global, historical space of representation (but within the "hybrid" space of "textuality") the subaltern *nation* would thus be able to take full, radical advantage of its phenomenological implosion. The sense of not knowing where or when the global system encounters the staging points of its own negation becomes evidence, so to speak, for the "textuality"—i.e. the self-negativity but *non-self-transparency*—of this system.

The question hovering over this explication, however, is just what real theoretical validity this sort of thinking has once the phenomenological "brackets" are removed and the postcolonial "thought experiment" is concluded. It will surprise no one by now if I confess to being deeply skeptical on this score. (I refer the reader to the following essays in this volume, especially chapters 2 and 4, for an explicit presentation of my own critical view of "discursive" and "textual" anti-imperialisms.) But in defense of postcolonial theory in what is, I think, Spivak's paradigmatic formulation, it might be argued that in fact nothing more than a "phenomenology" of the nation, or, in more contemporary parlance, a "reading" of its "text," is being advanced. Moreover, when, in a footnote to "Can the Subaltern Speak?", one reads that "in a certain way . . . the critique of imperialism is deconstruction as such. . . ."[50] it is possible to understand Spivak in (at least) two ways: as saying that we must look to Derrida as the true theorist of the "subaltern," or, conversely, that the subaltern, as real, potential agent of deconstruction, makes Derrida superfluous. I will leave this for now to other readers of "Can the Subaltern Speak?" to decide.

It would, in any case, be erroneous to discard, as some have, the postcolonialist "strategies" now most often denoted by reference to Bhabha's vocabulary of "ambivalence," "hybrids," "migrancy," the "in-between," etc. as being mere confabulations. The retreat from historical standards of thought and critique implicit in such "textualist" strategies responds, defensively or not, to a historical crisis of third-worldist nationalism that has left even the most historicizing oppositionalities in a condition of strategical uncertainty. The under- or anti-historicism of postcolonial theory is, ironically, true, up to a point, to its own historical subtext. And while it is wrong to conclude from the phenomenological shrinkage of national-historical space that existing nations themselves are no longer sites of emancipatory possibility (tell that to the Zapatistas, or to striking telephone workers in Puerto Rico) there is also a strong historical case to be made for the progressive re-configuring of "historical spatiality" along post-national, more transparently global axes. The so-called "third world-ization" of the metropolitan centers of global capital resulting from massive labor migrations and the intensifying immiseration of "native" working populations—a trend no one disputes—carries with it profound, if still under-theorized strategical implications.[51] To repeat our earlier, "post" - Leninist metaphor: all "links" increasingly coalesce into one, whose "weakness" grows in direct proportion. Urban rebellions such as the one that

erupted in 1992 Los Angeles after the Rodney King verdict was announced
are not, in fact, the social manifestations of Spivakian subalternity or
Bhaba-ite "hybridity," and postcolonialism could make no claim to function
as their virtual theory. But the postcolonial revision of nationalist
phenomenologies is clearly attuned to such new political developments,
however mystified it may remain about their underlying causes.

C. "Narration as nation"

What, finally, might we identify as a "poetics" of the "globalized" nation?
Thinking along the lines of the postcolonial theory just discussed, the
question itself becomes superfluous: for once it is in terms of "discourse" or
the "social text" that we pose the national question, the distinction between
politics and poetics is effectively erased. The power to represent the nation
is already the power to dominate it, while the power to contest this
representation—or to undermine the very logic of representation itself—
either preconditions the national-emancipatory act or, depending on one's
reading of postcolonial theory, stands in for it. Presupposed in the
nationalist poetics of the imperialist and colonialist conjunctures as discussed above, the distinction between the literary or even more generally
symbolic form of an object and its practical, secular reality loses force here,
at least *qua* the *nation* as secular object. In the vocabulary introduced by
Benedict Anderson's *Imagined Communities* and popularized by postcolonial
criticism, the "nation" is predicated in "narration."[52] But what in *Imagined
Communities* is still a sociological approach to the symbolic (shared, more or
less, in Jameson's theory of third world literature, see Chapter 12) quickly
slides into the anti-symbolism of the textualist insight: why suppose that, in
predicating the nation, narration ever stops narrating? What, after all, is
the line separating the two, except an authoritarian move towards closure
of what is in principle a limitless "chain" of narrative signifiers? Isn't it when
the narration stops—or *is* stopped—that the "oppressed" nation becomes,
itself, the "oppressor"? So, for example, Bhabha has reasoned in one of his
better-known essays, "DissemiNation" (see the following chapter).[53]

As we have observed of the postcolonial theory of Spivak and Said, such
formulas quickly verge on unreality outside a phenomenological or "semiotic" framing of the colonial relation. Perhaps, after all, a contemporary
"poetics" of the nation is what postcolonial theory has been assembling all
along, while thinking of itself as a politics. This is a good place to remind
ourselves again that "postcolonialism" is not itself the discourse of national
or global movements and formations but of a few odd hundred English
departments. Yet if we speculate as to what forms of national experience
and imaginary identification would correspond to the manifold and "de-
territorialized" national spaces of late capitalist globalism, the theory of
narrative as a primary constituent of nationality becomes more plausible.

To be Nicaraguan in Miami, or Algerian in Marseilles presumably requires a greater investment in symbolic processes than would be necessary in the course of daily life in Managua or Algiers. History, of course, is what continues to ground this symbolic compensation—the same history that has generated nations themselves and determined the configurations of the national cultures without which the symbolic process itself would become ephemeral and cease functioning. "Nation" is not ultimately reducible to "narration." But narration, arguably, simulates nation in our globalized, interchangeable "locations," now off just about everyone's "cognitive map," and about which stories cannot really be told.

A set of contemporary literatures and cultures (including film, video, music, etc.) already too broad and diverse for canonical abbreviation has now grown up on this new symbolic terrain, so that the "world" increasingly knows something of what it is to "negotiate" South Asian "identities" in London or about how West Indian history also takes place in Brooklyn. To call this manifold corpus, in whole or in part—e.g. the Stephen Frears/ Hanif Kureishi film *My Beautiful Laundrette* or Paule Marshall's *Brownstones, Brown Girl*—"postcolonial" clearly makes some sense, if only as a matter of terminological expediency. The danger, as critics of postcolonialism such as Ahmad have insisted on reminding us, is that this taxonomy may induce us to forget that, for example, not all nor even most Indian literature is written in English and marketed in *The New York Times Book Review*, or that, conversely, a reading of Morrison's *Beloved* in Chicago is not inter-changeable with its reading in Buenos Aires or, for that matter, in Johannesburg. The third world has long since crowded into the late imperial *fora*, but from there not even the most "hybrid" intelligentsias can see clear across the globe. More than a century of imperialism and colonialism, of national liberations, abdications and disintegrations, has sedimented out in a global cosmopolis in which literary and intellectual "migrants," once the objects of racial and colonialist exclusion and con-tempt, now enjoy some legitimacy, and even, in certain cases, immense authority. The old centers of empire, for generations now the objects of a "reverse" colonization by their own peripheries, have tolerated what Said has called "the voyage in."[54] "Postcolonialism" is among this history's results, and reflects the profound transformation of Eurocentrist intel-lectual culture that such history has made possible. Meanwhile, however, the global inequalities and structures of exploitation and oppression that have led to an ironic "trans-europeanization" of the center imprison unimaginable majorities in catastrophic existences for which even a word like "imperialism" seems too mild. The fortunes of "postcolonialism," along with just about everything else, are inscribed in the history this brute reality portends.

DetermiNation: Postcolonialism, Poststructuralism and the Problem of Ideology

What are the boundaries of "postcolonial studies"? And what are its theoretical and political dimensions? However one eventually answers these questions, at least one thing strikes me as certain: the questioner will have to consider very carefully what Aijaz Ahmad has had to say on the matter or be reduced either to intellectual irrelevance, to intellectual dishonesty, or to both. The essays comprising Ahmad's 1992 volume *In Theory*, including his already widely cited criticisms of Fredric Jameson's theory of third world literature as "national allegory", should, if nothing else, render the routine and un-self-critical usage of terms such as "postcolonial", "third world", etc. an embarrassment.[1] While in no sense denying the basic legitimacy and importance of "studying" the literature and culture of societies with a history of colonization, Ahmad has, to my mind, made it incontrovertibly clear that vital political questions already intrude as soon as one seeks to generalize these societies, or their literatures or cultures, under categorical or abstract headings such as "third world", "postcolonial," etc. Principal of these is the question of *class*. As an "ideology of already constituted states,"[2] "three worlds" theory de-emphasizes, even to the point of suppressing, the reality of class division and antagonism within social formations linked by their common subjugation within the global capitalist or imperialist system. Against the historical evidence that unfailingly discloses the complicity of these classes in reproducing its inequalities and brutalities, the emergent national bourgeoisies of the de-colonized world are, in effect, vouchsafed by "three worlds" theory as the revolutionary opposition to imperialism. "Third worldism", argues Ahmad, inflicts such a class blindness even on Marxists such as Fredric Jameson, who would scarcely allow themselves to lose sight of class division when assessing "their own" metropolitan social milieux. The category of the "postcolonial," with its privileging of (de-)colonization and the relation of colonizer to colonized as unifying factors *qua* a literary or cultural corpus, presents a similar risk, although here the overarching unity of colonialism or imperialism as *system* is at least logically entailed.

But the act of categorization prompts the class question in another sense as well: namely, *vis-à-vis* the *practitioner* of third world or postcolonial studies. Ahmad here points with the utmost candor at the fact staring "postcolonialism" in the face, though rarely taken very seriously: that the categories of third world and now of "postcolonial" literature are themselves virtually the products of metropolitan or "first world" institutions. It is, as Ahmad puts it, in the metropolitan university or publishing house that a work of literature is "first designated a Third World text."[3] And in one of the more provocative essays of *In Theory*, Ahmad sketches a social history of postcolonial studies as a product of the increasing, though not uncomplicated integration of intellectuals from Asia, Africa and Latin America into the North American and Western European intellectual and academic establishment.[4] Despite the latent cultural chauvinism of the metropolitan university—or perhaps as a defensive response to it—there "arises" within it "a small academic elite" of immigrants

> which knows it will not return, joins the faculty . . ., frequents the circuits of conferences and the university presses, and develops, often with the greatest degree of personal innocence and missionary zeal, quite considerable stakes in overvalorizing what has already been designated as "Third World Literature". . . .[5]

Ahmad, that is, has forceably put the question to postcolonial studies of its possible service as an *ideology* in which particular class interests—those of the postcolonial national bourgeoisies, of an intellectual petty bourgeoisie ensconced in metropolitan institutions, and, though perhaps in a less direct way, those of imperialism itself—may find ways to represent themselves as universal and disinterested. While the question of postcolonialism and ideology in itself neither obviates the lateral questions of "boundaries" (i.e. what is the *object* of postcolonial studies?) or of the *method(s)* such "studies" ought to utilize, it is clear that the effect of ignoring or suppressing it would only be to aid, even if unwittingly, in the reproduction of this (putative) ideology itself

What makes a consideration of Ahmad's critique of postcolonialism even more compelling is the fact that he locates poststructuralism squarely within its ideological field.[6] Here he confronts directly what must be one of the crucial issues in any critical or theoretical discussion of postcolonialism—namely, its demonstrable affinities for a philosophy that has declared itself the enemy of all notions of identity and "fixed" meaning, indeed—in its latest, "postmodern" strain—of any tendency for thought to ground itself in universal principles of whatever sort. This is not to suggest that all those who work in the area of postcolonialism necessarily adhere to such a philosophy. But the convergence here is surely more than an accidental one, and those whose might be tempted to explain it as simply a mimcry of the field's more celebrated figures—Gayatri Spivak, let us say, or Edward Said—would still have to account for this mimicry itself, since there are other, and anything but poststructuralist, models to choose from—a Fanon, or a C.L.R. James, for example, or, among more contemporary figures, a Roberto Schwarz. As someone with a regional concentration on Latin America and the Caribbean, I can attest that not even a gross familiarity with Derrida or Foucault, much less with Spivak or Said, is in any way a pre-requisite for the general belief in what we might term the *incommensurability* of colonizer and colonized, of center and margin, North and South, first and third worlds, etc. I think it is safe to say that broad variations of such a belief dominate the would-be "cutting edge" of postcolonial theory among Latin Americanists, as witness the work of intellectuals otherwise as diverse as Néstor García Canclini, Enrique Dussel, Mary Louise Pratt, Walter Mignolo, Rolena Adorno, Roberto González Echevarría, Antonio Benítez Rojo and many others.[7]

Ahmad proposes a historical explanation for this ideological affinity, centering on the decline of the Marxist wing of the anti-imperialist movement after the ascendant period punctuated by the Algerian and Vietnamese revolutions:

> When the degeneration of the Iranian state into clerical fascism became unmistakable, the last remaining illusion of Third Worldist cultural nationalism finally had to be abandoned. What, then, to replace it with? Socialism had already been renounced as the determinate name of imperialism's negation. Nationalism—the whole of it—also now went. This is the redoubled vacuum which, in the radicalized version of metropolitan literary theory, poststructuralism is now to fill.[8]

The insight expressed here—that of the "redoubled vacuum"—is, I think, crucial to a theoretical grasp of all contemporary cultural and intellectual developments, whether postcolonial or metropolitan. It is this insight that underlies Ahmad's sustained critique of Said's *Orientalism* and of Saidian critical thought in general, and renders it, at least to my mind, virtually irrefutable. Observing how *Orientalism* effectively serves the metropolitan and postcolonial radical intelligentsia as a "bridge" between cultural nation-alism and poststructuralist anti-nationalism, Ahmad connects the eclectic, "self-divided" quality of the work, its mythologizing fixation on that very "West," whose orientalist myth-making it seeks to de-bunk, to what is in effect Said's captivity within a double bind of both anti-nationalism *and* "post"-Marxism.

But as powerful as it is, I think this historical insight into the evident ideological convergence of postcolonialism and poststructuralism is never-theless a limited one. I see it as the starting point for an ideology critique that still faces the question of how and why, given the historical reality of the "redoubled vacuum," it is poststructuralism in particular that rushes in to fill it. Ahmad explains this ideological shift as essentially a consequence of what poststructuralism is *not*. Since it is axiomatic that poststructuralism must pronounce against all principles of identity, totality and universality, then, clearly enough, it will also pronounce against both nationalism and Marxism. What interests me, however, and what I mean to analyze in what follows, is how the dominant, poststructuralist strain of postcolonial theory discloses in the very course of its own conceptual procedures—that is, *immanently*—the material, historical determination exerted by the "redoubled vacuum." I thus appeal to Marx's (and Engels's) theory of ideology, not merely as the false universalization of particular class interests (although this is an essential aspect of the theory as a whole) but as a false or "inverted" consciousness of the historical reality which, on another, more subjective plane, it desires simply to evade. To use Roberto Schwarz's marvellously succinct phrase (worth a thousand Althusserianisms), ideology is thus grasped as a "necessary illusion well grounded in appearances."[9] As such a "necessary illusion," i.e. as reflecting, in its own conceptual immanence, the "redoubled vacuum," it seems to me that post-(structuralist)-colonialism reveals a more contradictory face than is suggested in Ahmad's exposé. I hasten to add that I share Ahmad's view of poststructuralism as ultimately "repressive and bourgeois."[10] But what makes it truly pernicious in this sense—what makes it *ideological* rather than merely a doctrinal curiosity—is its apparent *correspondence* to an objective circumstance that it does not falsify or invert *ab initio* but only as its final conceptual move. To cite, somewhat against the grain, Lenin's expression, postcolonialism takes "one step forward" so as to take "two steps back."

Before proceeding, however, I should clarify that to undertake such an ideology critique of postcolonialism is not to imply that theories of ideology are themselves necessarily unknown or extraneous to postcolonialism itself. It is sufficient to cite Spivak's now virtually canonical essay "Can the Subaltern Speak?" to refute any such implication.[11] Although the essay itself slightly predated the subsequent institutionalization of "postcolonial studies," it continues to supply a forceful argument for adopting the "postcolonial" standpoint of the third world "subaltern" as itself a site from which to undertake the critique of the most deep-seated ideologies of the European/colonizing "Subject." Indeed, it is the poststructuralist, anti-representationalist "politics" of Foucault and Deleuze at which Spivak directs the initial brunt of her "postcolonial" ideology critique. This critique then leads her back to the Marx of the *Eighteenth Brumaire*, a text from which Spivak claims to discover a conceptual nuance with which to frame a critical standpoint as wary of naively representationalist epistemologies as it is of the naively spontaneist, and profoundly ideological claims of radical poststructuralist intellectuals to have dispensed with a *politics* of representation *tout court*.

To come to terms with "Can the Subaltern Speak?" would require that one do full justice to its painstaking, if often rather refractory arguments. Some attempt at this is made in Chapter 4. But for the moment I would venture the observation that, notwithstanding the justice of its claims against the efforts of Foucault *et al.* to elide the contradictory relation of "interest" and "desire," an elision abetted indeed by the latter's failure to consider its implications for the third world, "Can the Subaltern Speak?" nevertheless returns, in the end, to the very same theoretical—and, as I hope to show, ideological—ground from which Foucault and Deleuze themselves set forth on their misguided quest for a politics without representation.

The "missing link" here is clearly Althusser, whose own deeply problematic, if frequently brandished theory of ideology as an unconscious, pre-subjective mechanism of subject formation—what I have elsewhere termed its *a priori* and dogmatic "ban on consciousness"[12]—informs Spivak's own formulations (see, e.g., her characterization of ideology as "subject-formations that micrologically and often erratically operate the interests that congeal the macrologies [of "exploitation in economics" and "domination in geopolitics"]"[13] and—here again see the following chapter—lends its characteristically tortured style of Marxological exegesis to Spivak's reading of the *Eighteenth Brumaire*. Althusser, having posited ideology, or the famed Ideological State Apparatuses (ISAs), as structures unavailable to consciousness, had to resort to philosophical subterfuges screened by grandiose invocations of the "class struggle" when pressed to explain how, then, one could ever hope or pretend to alter them. Spivak, for whom the non-"speaking", non-self-representing "subaltern" is finally to supply the Archimedean point from which the unfathomable rupture of the imperialist "social text" becomes theoretically possible, gives the initial impression of having side-stepped this problem. But thinking so hinges on an ability to credit the idea of a trans-representational, trans-conscious subject of history that would have to make its entrance from the "other" side of the international division of labor in exactly the same way that Althusser's structurally unthinkable subject of "class struggle" is required to emerge full grown from the Jovian-head of the unconscious. In the end, at least to my thinking, "Can the Subaltern Speak?", for all its genuine efforts to find the "postcolonial" locus from which to evade *both* ideology *and* consciousness/representation, walks backwards into the core ideologeme of the colonial-as-the-incommensurable that, as we shall see, governs the thinking of "postcolonialists" who are in every other respect Spivak's inferiors.

But to demonstrate more concretely what I mean here by an "immanent" critique of postcolonialist ideology, I want to examine the work of Homi K. Bhabha, in particular two essays, "Signs Taken for Wonders: Questions of Ambivalence and Authority under a Tree Outside Delhi, May 1817" and "DissemiNation: Time, Narrative, and the Margins of the

Modern Nation."[14] I select these not because they can in any sense claim to initiate the postcolonial/poststructuralist convergence nor because they have necessarily provided theoretical models for other postcolonial critics and theorists, but rather for their conceptual range and complexity. Such complexity often crosses the line into the willful obscurantism of Derridean jargon, making of Bhabha the perhaps less than ideal exhibit here. But it is also a sign of Bhabha's high degree of theoretical self-consciousness, of the fact that he remains aware of the many possible objections to what he is proposing, and attempts to fend off such moves by introducing ever subtler conceptual distinctions and nuances. In Bhabha we thus have a sort of high-resolution moving picture of postcolonialist ideology in its "immanent" state.

In "Signs," Bhabha begins by stating what has become one of the standard *aperçus* of postcolonial theory: that it is the colonial relation as such—here the English colonization of India—that first elicits in the colonizing power the need for a symbolic image of itself as a stable, continuous *national* identity.[15] In "Signs" it is the "English book" that typifies this process of reverse symbolization:

> As a signifier of authority the English book acquires its meaning *after* the traumatic scenario of colonial difference, cultural or racial, returns the eye of power to some prior, archaic image of identity. Paradoxically, however, such an image can neither be "original"—by virtue of the act of repetition that constructs it—nor "identical"—by virtue of the difference that defines it. Consequently, the colonial presence is always ambivalent, split between its appearance as original and authoritative and its articulation as repetition and difference.[16]

"Ambivalence," here, becomes Bhabha's own substitute locution for the orthodox Derridean concept of prior displacement (*Entstellung*), or the "double inscription," as formulated in *Dissemination*, a text to which Bhabha will repeatedly refer back. In bringing such a concept to bear on the colonial, however, Bhabha claims not merely to be borrowing a conveniently descriptive terminology but rather to have *discovered in the colonial relation itself* what is, as it were, a worldly and secular instance of *Entstellung*—an instance which, therefore, only Derridean or poststructuralist theory could adequately capture and convey. "It is this ambivalence that makes the boundaries of the colonial positionality—the division of self/other—and the question of colonial power—the differentiation of colonizer/colonized—different from both the Hegelian master/slave dialectic or the phenomenological projection of Otherness."[17]

But here a problem arises. For if the "ambivalence" of the "colonial presence" is, like Derrida's double inscription, the enabling condition for any possible act of "meaning" or "placement" (*Darstellung*), does this not confer on the "colonial presence" an *a priori*, transcendental necessity that, as worldly reality, it patently does not possess? Must we, in fact, be "always already" colonizer or colonized? Derrida might be content to have it so, but for Bhabha this seems an unacceptable conclusion. To the theorem of "ambivalence," therefore, must be added a corollary: that of the possibility of *resisting* the ambivalent presence of the colonial by virtue of an effect of this ambivalence itself, an effect that Bhabha terms "hybridity." It turns out that colonial power or "domination" can only be maintained through a process of "disavowing" its primordial "différance." Such a power relies on "rules of recognition" and "discriminatory identities" by means of which this "disavowal" is enforced: "I am English; you are Indian." To be English is to be not-Indian, and vice versa. But what of the Indian who *reads* or even *rewrites* the "English book," as in Bhabha's example of a group of Indian converts to Christianity who, to the horror of their English proselytizers, demand an "Indianized gospel"?[18] Here, all at once, the "discriminatory identities" become crossed, the "rules of recognition" break down, and we are presented with a *hybrid*. And it is *then*, through the proliferation of such hybridity, that a "strategic reversal of the process of domination through disavowal" becomes possible.[19] By exposing the originating "ambivalence" of colonial domination, hybridity "enables a form of *subversion* . . . that turns the discursive conditions of dominance into the grounds of inter-vention."[20] Through hybridity other "denied" knowledges (note the strategic entry of Foucault here) enter upon the dominant discourse and *estrange* the basis of its authority."[21] "When the words of the master become the site of hybridity . . . then we may not only read between the lines, but even seek to *change* the often coercive reality that they so lucidly contain."[22]

It will not, I think, have escaped the attention of the careful reader how the danger of circularity creeps into the reasoning here: the "colonial presence," it would appear, is to be "resisted," "subverted," "estranged" and even, perhaps, "changed" entirely through a practice of exposing it for what it really is and always was. Colonialism exposed is colonialism overcome; its doing *becomes* its undoing. After all, what is the "hybrid" but an unsuspected reflection, or return, of "ambivalence"? Are these not, in actuality, synonymous terms, whose only "difference" lies in the fact that an act of "disavowal," a veil rather than a transparency, has been, conveniently or inconveniently, placed between them?

These are questions that bear in important ways on the larger one of postcolonialist ideology, but for the moment I want to postpone that discussion and attempt a more generalized and abstract characterization of what Bhabha—and, I would suggest, a good deal of postcolonialist theory —is seeking to put forward here. There are, upon analysis, two quite distinct and, it would seem, *logically* unrelated truth claims being advanced in "Signs." The first is that the relation of colonizer to colonized, though manifestly unequal and transitive, does not refer us back to some original equality or unity of terms, but rather *hints* at a *primitive disunity*, an originating *incommensurability* as itself the prior condition of all existing relations of identity, including those internal to the nation itself as the supposed site of colonial power and authority. The first truth claim, that is, pertains to the question of the *ground* of the colonial relationship. The second truth being claimed here, however, pertains to a quite different question—that of an emancipatory, anti-colonial *agency*. According to "Signs," such agency resides in the spontaneous power of the *colonized* to make *visible* or *apparent* this same primitive disunity. Exposure of the ground is proposed as itself tantamount to, or at the very least as enabling, the undoing of its oppressive effects.

Thinking as a Marxist, or even simply as a materialist, one's first instinct here is to reject the second of these truth claims as blatantly "idealist." And such it surely is. Are we to believe that the mere act of turning the tables on a *discursive* authority will really liberate anyone from the "coercive reality" that stands behind it? Ahmad, together with many other Marxist critics of poststructuralism, from Perry Anderson to Eagleton, Dews, Bhaskar, Meiksins-Wood and others, might be summoned here to good purpose.[23] But to get at the ideological aspect of the postcolonialism/post-structuralism convergence here, at its deepest level, one must, as I see it, look not only to the transparent fantasmagoria of its second proposition, but to the tacit belief, clearly latent in "Signs," that the second proposition is *directly implied* in the first: that the ruptured ground *already*, somehow, in disclosing its own truth, works its own demise. We have just now remarked the fallacy involved in such reasoning. The crucial point *qua* ideology is that *it is this fallacy itself*, this peculiar circularity whereby "ambivalence" describes *both* the hidden *truth* of the colonial "presence" and—as the "hybrid"—the *power* to abolish it, that reflects the historical conjuncture described by Ahmad as the "redoubled vacuum." To try to spell this out more concretely: what I am suggesting is that the recourse of postcolonialist-poststructuralist theory to the first proposition—Bhabha's "ambivalence," or what I have termed the primitive disunity of identity relations—reflects *both* the generalized, historical crisis of the cultural nationalism of the "Bandung era" set forth by Ahmad *and* the desire to move beyond it. The governing impulse of postcolonialism, to this extent, is clearly one of hostility to national*ism*, in implicit recognition of its betrayal of those who once saw in it the emancipatory alternative to colonialism and imperialism. Here the postcolonial consciousness takes its "one step forward."

But what should be the next step—namely, the *class* critique of third-worldist cultural nationalism, leading to the principled and unambivalent repudiation of the postcolonial national bourgeoisies (even when self-proclaimed "socialists") as either leaders or allies in the struggle against imperialism—typically remains deferred.[24] Why? Clearly, a major factor here—and one to which Ahmad does not, perhaps, give quite its due—is the simultaneous and already well-advanced crisis of "actually existing socialism" itself, as marked, especially for postcolonial and third-world(ist) intellectuals, by the increasingly counter-revolutionary direction taken in China after the eventual defeat of the left-wing protagonists of the so-called Cultural Revolution in the early 1970s—what I have elsewhere referred to as the "ideological degeneration of class struggles."[25] If, as Ahmad puts it, "socialism had already been renounced" by the apostates of cultural nationalism, this plainly reactionary renunciation was still not entirely without its objective historical basis. And no less of a factor in this deferral, to be sure, is the typically petty bourgeois origin and "metropolitan location" of the postcolonial intelligentsia itself, as well as of its metropolitan sympathizers. With labor in general retreat, this intelligentsia, like others, knows with instinctive precision how far it can go before its own material interests become endangered. It is just here that Ahmad's sociological critique of the postcolonial intellectual comes most forcefully into play—not so much as an explanation of what this intellectual thinks, but of what, for him or her, is unthinkable.[26]

Acknowledging the disunity of the nation(al) as ground of radical political identity and solidarity, but hesitant before the global *unity of class* as the historically necessary alternative, the postcolonial consciousness then takes its "two steps back" into the second proposition, or the fantasmagoria of "ambivalence"-as-agency. To suppose, however, that poststructuralist doctrine somehow provokes or makes possible this move is, itself, to "stand things on their heads." Poststructuralism's ideological role here is rather to furnish the postcolonial consciousness with the concepts it needs to, in effect, rethink the oppressive reality of the "redoubled vacuum" as the mock liberation of the "double inscription"—that is, in so many words, simply to equate the *historical crisis* of cultural nationalism with the *fait accompli* of its transcendence.

But this grows too abstract. Let us look again to Homi Bhabha, in "DissemiNation" this time, to see how this particular ideological process unfolds. Bhabha's argument here, reduced to its basic propositions, is roughly as follows: *first*, that the nation, whatever may be its objective, socio-historical determination, takes shape in the consciousness of its "citizens" as a discourse, even a narrative. Bhabha speaks of the "cultural constitution of nationness as a form of social and textual affiliation."[27] (The casual conjunction of "social" and "textual," implying equal ontological weight, is characteristic of the reasoning here.) *Second*, that, as this narrative construction, the nation exhibits a "disjuncture" or split "between the continuist, accumulative temporality of the pedagogical, and the repetitious, recursive strategy of the performative."[28] That is, as something narrat**ED** to its "subjects"—as "pedagogical object"—the nation remains constant and self-identical through a "continuous, empty time," punctuating this time itself as both its origin and its *telos*. But as an active process of narrat**ING**, the nation enters a different time, that of the subjective and "performative"—since, after all, the "people" must retell or "perform" the story of the nation for its "affiliating" powers to function. Bhabha's *third* proposition, finally, is that within this disjunctive temporality, the time of "dissemiNation," the "nation-space" becomes a potential site for an emancipatory agency. Here, as one might expect, his reasoning becomes rather elusive. Referring to Raymond Williams' "crucial distinction between residual and emergent practices," Bhabha claims that "this disjunctive temporality of the nation would provide the appropriate time-frame for representing those residual and emergent meanings and practices that Williams locates in the margins of contemporary society."[29] The disjuncture of national-narrative time, in other words, is said to enable the narrator (and social agent?) to disjoin the nation's emancipatory elements from its oppressive ones.

It will not be difficult to recognize here in the newer attire of the "disjunctive" our old friend "ambivalence," as indeed, in the conceptual movement of "DissemiNation," the underlying, dual propositional structure of "Signs." The obvious difference, of course, is that here it is the national rather than the colonial "presence" that, once disclosed as "ambivalent," switches from oppressive ground of identity to the site from which to resist and even overcome all such oppressive power. The agency described as "hybridity" intrudes within the nation-space itself, whose "liminality" (i.e. "ambivalence," "disjuncture," etc.) "provides a place from which to speak both of, and as, the minority, the exilic, the marginal, and the emergent."[30]

For a counter-argument, one could do no better, here, than turn again to Ahmad, especially his relentless exposure of the myth of the exile-as-subversive in "Languages of Class" and in the long essay on Salman Rushdie. But what is particularly illuminating about the line of reasoning in "DissemiNation," given our speculative concern for the postcolonial consciousness as an inverse reflection of the historical crisis of cultural nationalism, is just the way in which Bhabha, in order to recast the nation-space as a site of internal, liberating displacement, must first *explicitly* retract this space from the *integral* temporality of *history*. "Historians transfixed on the event and origins of the nation never ask, and political theorists possessed of the 'modern' totalities of the nation . . . never pose [Bhabha appears to have Ernest Gellner specifically in mind here], the awkward question of the disjunctive representation of the social, in this double time of the nation."[31] Against this, Bhabha's emphasis on disjuncture "serves to displace the historicism that has dominated discussions of the nation as a cultural force."[32] But, turning the tables here, may we not likewise propose that the postcolonialist/poststructuralist critic, "transfixed" on the narrative, discursive aspects of the national, and "possessed" of the secrets of the national/colonial's amazing power to self-subvert, "never

asks," indeed, "never poses" the "awkward question" of the nation and
nationalism as the historical *product* (neither origin nor *telos*) of capitalism?
Bhabha's polemical *mise-en-scène* here would lead us to suppose that,
between the classical, orthodox, historicist *ideology* of nationalism *per se*, and
the anti-historicist discovery of the nation as the "liminality of cultural
modernity,"[33] *tertium non datur*. Historical time—as opposed to narrative
time—comes, by negative inference here, to be conceived as if foregrounded exclusively by the nation itself, hence as powerless to advance
beyond—or retreat behind—this ground. To get free of nationalist ideology
one must first get free of history itself.

It is further revealing how, despite the customary deconstructionist
invocation of "difference" (in whichever of its thousand and one alternative
locutions) as the cure for all bad things, a foundational category does
ultimately emerge in "DissemiNation" to supply the politically desirable
alternative to historicity: that of *culture*, or even of the *ethnic*. "The nation,"
says Bhabha "reveals in its ambivalent and vacillating representation, the
ethnography of its own historicity and opens up the possibility of other
narratives of the people and their difference."[34] Or, again, even more
suggestively:

> Once the liminality of the nation-space is established, and its "difference" is
> turned from the boundary "outside" to its finitude "within", the threat of
> cultural difference is no longer a problem of "other" people. It becomes a
> question of the otherness of the people-as-one. The national subject splits in
> the ethnographic perspective of culture's contemporaneity and provides both
> a theoretical position and a narrative authority for marginal voices or
> minority discourse.[35]

The "otherness of the people-as-one"—a better motto for the official,
liberal version of multi-culturalism would be difficult to imagine. The
notion seems to be that once we finally recognize that the "nation" is just a
ready-made construction, patched together out of the desires and voices of
a variety of "ethnographic" subjects, then the oppressive logic of national*ism* will magically vanish. But, even assuming this to be true, how is this
"liminality" to be "established" if it remains in the interest of the nation's
"pedagogues" to keep it secret? And if, somehow, we were to overthrow the
"pedagogues," what point would there be any longer in "performing" this
nation, say, and not another? Or why not "perform" something entirely
unlike the nation? Moreover, the question goes begging as to just why the
"ethnographic perspective" is any less a "narrative" and a "cultural construction" (with its own "pedagogical" and "performative" temporalities)
than the nation is. Thus what good would it do us to "split" the "national
subject" into "ethnographic" ones, unless there is something more
benevolent about the "narrative authority" of the "ethnographic" over and

against that of the national? (And that is a promise rather difficult to credit in the days of the warring micro-nationalities and ethnicities spilling all across the post-Soviet and postcolonial nation-spaces.) In any case, what Bhabha offers us here is, so to speak, not a historical alternative to cultural nationalism, but cultural nationalism as itself an alternative to history—cultural nationalism, only here with the "national"—or "ethnographic"—itself conveniently cleansed of its *historical*, hence of its *class* determination.

Let me try, now, to synthesize what has been said so far: if post-colonialism, as a theoretical consciousness, inverts the historical crisis of cultural nationalism, lifting the nation out of its historical determinate-ness altogether (and, as a possible final step, substituting a mechanism of *cultural* determination) then poststructuralism serves this ideological practice by supplying it with a set of conceptual moves ("play" or "game" might be the better words) with which to recast this indeterminacy ("ambivalence," etc.) as an emancipatory drama with radical stakes and players. Agency, however, becomes a fiction if there is nothing determinate to act *upon*, if the agenda is already determined in advance by the agent. ("Freedom"—to use Engels's more traditional vocabulary—"is the recognition of necessity.") What poststructuralism does is to set the scene in such a way—by subtly or not so subtly rewriting the social as the textual, the practical as the discursive, etc.—that this fiction, for the naming of which it offers a vocabulary as limitless as it is pointless, can appear to be something real.

In Bhabha's case, this process of plotting out a semiotic, narrative or simply cultural detour around the present historical "impasse"[36] assumes a considerable degree of theoretical abstraction, requiring of the reader a patience for the aporias of high poststructuralism that he or she, of course, may not be able or willing to summon. But, as noted earlier, the post-colonial ideology, while liable to such complication, can take other, less "rigorous", more traditional and accessible forms.

Consider the example of Said himself in *Culture and Imperialism*. Here we are presented with what appears, at least, to be a solidly historicist treatment of the postcolonial, a "history of the imperial adventure rendered in cultural terms."[37] No escape into the "disjunctive temporality" of narrative here, but, rather, what itself promises to be the narrative of an objective, real-time set of events.

But this historical narrative itself turns out to be strangely impoverished and abstract, informed by none of the theoretical insights that such a "history of the imperial adventure" might be expected to rely upon. Of course, *Culture and Imperialism* consists mainly of a series of textual commentaries, foregrounded more by a conventional sense of *literary* history than anything else, but for a treatise that focuses so centrally on the nineteenth century, it is remarkable how *pre*-nineteenth century *Culture and Imperialism* seems, from a historico-philosophical point of view. Nothing, here, even of Hegel, much less of Marx. Listen, for example, to Said discussing the need to "set . . . art in the global, earthly context":

> Territory and possessions are at stake, geography and power. Everything about human history is rooted in the earth, which has meant that we must think about habitation, but it has also meant that people have planned to *have* more territory and therefore must do something about its indigenous residents. At some very basic level, imperialism means thinking about, settling on, controlling land that you do not possess, that is distant, that is lived on and owned by others.[38]

That imperialism, "at some very basic level," concerns "territory" may surely be granted—but *Culture and Imperialism* never advances beyond this level. In an almost physiocratic reprise, Said commits the double anachronism here of projecting feudal and early capitalist notions of landed property both backwards onto epochs that knew nothing of "territory" or "ownership" in the sense he gives it (the Taino/Arawak tribespeople encountered by Columbus at the time of his first American landfall would have been surprised indeed to know that they "owned" any "territory" at all), and forward onto a stage of historical development whose imperial elites have long since come to marshal their "power" for the "possession," not of "territory," but of an "immense accumulation of commodities," labor power chief among them. The result is that imperialism—that entity whose cultural history Said has promised to tell—is emptied at the beginning of any historical concreteness. The class determination of "territory" and "possession" effectively drops out here. Instead we are presented with a "focus on actual contests over land and the land's people," with a "kind of geographical inquiry into historical experience."[39] This sounds intriguing, but in practice it reduces imperialism itself to a kind of geography, an unequal distribution of "possession"— or "sovereignty"—over a pre-existing map of "territories." It thus comes as no surprise that the history of this "imperialism"—and of the "resistance" to it—is virtually oblivious to both the Russian and the Chinese Revolutions, arguably the two most signal acts of "resistance" to imperialism in the twentieth century. In a book replete with invocations of Gramsci, Fanon, Nkrumah, C.L.R. James, etc., a book that claims repeatedly to stand on the shoulders of the great anti-colonial leaders and visionaries of the third world, it is to be noted that the name of Mao Zedong does not receive, unless I am mistaken, a single mention. And that, whatever one's sympathies or antipathies towards Maoism, is an omission that surely says as much about the Saidian view of imperialism as the entire text of *Culture and Imperialism* itself.

Given such an oddly anachronistic theory of imperialism, it becomes more difficult to be confident of what Said will have to say about its "culture." To take just one brief example here: in the first chapter of *Culture and Imperialism* Said sets out to illustrate how "the processes of imperialism occurred beyond the level of economic laws and political decisions" through a brief discussion of Dickens' *Dombey and Son*, a novel in which the author satirizes the "world is my oyster" mentality of the British merchant class in the 1840s.[40] Said notes how this very satirization itself "ultimately depends on the tried and true discourses of imperial trade."[41] Dickens' criticism of this class may appear genuine, but "one must also ask, how *could* Dombey think that the universe, and the whole of time, was his to trade in?" [42] Although Said is careful not to deny the "value" of novels such as *Dombey and Son* "as works of art," the sense of his comment here is that Dickens, as himself a product of British "imperial culture," could not have been in a position to portray it in a genuinely critical light. If his character could think the whole world his, must not Dickens have at least entertained a similar thought? But how to explain then even just the *appearance* of criticism here? The truth that Said seems forced, by his own conceptual framework, to pass over is that Dickens could be profoundly critical of imperialist culture and yet also reproduce key aspects of it at the same time. To grasp this, however, requires a *class* analysis of this imperialist culture—a grasp of its internal contradictions—as well as some notion of how the realist novel as a genre made possible this contradictory, limited, but nevertheless valid and historically progressive form of social criticism. To draw the full theoretical connection between culture and imperialism, that is, one first needs a theory of imperialism that reflects it in its real, historically concrete dimensions and movement.[43] By basing his own theory of imperialism too narrowly on concepts such as "territory" and "overseas trade," Said cannot adequately account for the contradictory aspects of a *Dombey and Son*. And, in a certain sense, his own critique of imperialism comes to seem more eclectic and morally abstract, even, than that of Dickens himself.

But the important question for us here is *why* this anachronism and theoretical impoverishment, affecting what is otherwise a work of profound erudition and unassailable ethical convictions? And the answer, I think, is that, as with Bhabha's anti-historicist rewriting of the nation as narration, Said's resort to a pre-economic, territorial concept of imperialism reflects what is, in the final analysis, an intellectual retreat before the historical crisis of cultural nationalism and of the politics of national liberation. Let it be clearly stipulated here that Said, in *Culture and Imperialism*, is careful to disavow cultural nationalism on *ethical* grounds, and that this disavowal is fully principled and sincere. Nor can it be denied that *Culture and Imperialism*, on one level at least, reasons out of an awareness of this crisis as historically inescapable. "Gone," writes Said,

> are the binary oppositions dear to the nationalist and imperialist enterprises.
> Instead we begin to sense that old authority cannot simply be replaced by new

authority, but that new alignments made across borders, types, nations, and essences are rapidly coming into view, and it is those new alignments that now provoke and challenge the fundamentally static notion of *identity* that has been the core of cultural thought during the epoch of imperialism.[44]

But note that the collapse of nationalism's "binary oppositions"—the disclosure of the nation's essential "ambivalence" and disunity as ground— still leads, not (forward) into a new, historical unity of *class*, but (as it were, laterally) into "new alignments" "across . . . nations," whose danger to imperialism is no more than to "challenge" a "*notion*." Again, as with Bhabha, registering the historical *truth* of crisis can only prompt the postcolonial consciousness to create the historical *fiction*—the fantasma- goria—of an emancipatory agency.

Ahmad has pointed out how Said's loosely poststructuralist celebration of postcolonial "difference" and hybridity—what Said elsewhere in *Culture and Imperialism* refers to as the "contrapuntal"—essentially becomes a celebration of the postcolonial intellectual him- or herself (fighting "behind the lines" in the metropolitan theater) as the true hero of cultural anti- imperialism. This becomes clear in passages such as the following:

> In a totally new way in Western culture, the interventions of non-European artists and scholars cannot be dismissed or silenced, and these interventions are not only an integral part of a political movement, but in many ways the movement's *successfully* guiding imagination, intellectual and figurative energy reseeing and rethinking the terrain common to whites and non- whites.[45]

The ease with which such pronouncements can become self-serving and elitist is transparent. But if one may take issue with Ahmad to this very slight extent here, it does seem to me that there is something undeniably accurate in Said's observation of a cultural shift within the metropolis (the so-called "voyage in"). This, even if, in classically ideological fashion, Said over-inflates this new cultural and intellectual phenomenon with the power, *eo ipso*, to lead the masses into battle with imperialism. The underlying truth here, I would suggest, is that, although it has succumbed to a "reflux" of imperialism and has failed to deliver on its implicit promise of social emancipation for the masses on the imperialist periphery, many of whom now suffer greater oppression perhaps than at any point in the past, the historical epoch of national liberation struggles—the so-called "Bandung era"—*has* changed the cultural and intellectual landscape irrevocably for the better. Our own moment would seem to present us with the intensely contradictory reality of what might be termed "cultural revolution without social revolution." As to how permanent this cultural "revolution" is, one cannot be sure. The widespread contemporary desire for multiculturalist reforms and for the rooting out of "Eurocentric" bias in metropolitan institutions, politically ambivalent though it often may be, suggests that the clock is not likely to be turned back without some resistance. Said exaggerates the importance of these cultural advances, but that does not mean they should not be defended without compromise.

So soon, however, as these *cultural* advances substitute themselves for the *political* and *social* ends of anti-imperialism, we enter the ideological thicket of what I would term "cultural politics," with the emphasis on "cultural." Much of contemporary postcolonial theory seems to me to fit this description. If it is to steer clear of cultural politics, postcolonial theory must not only disavow the reactionary political logic of cultural nationalism, but break with it on its deeper, philosophical and theoretical levels as well. Poststructuralism cannot produce this break, but only continuously defer it.

Poverties of Nation: *The Ends of the Earth*, "Monetary Subjects Without Money" and Postcolonial Theory

I

The significant turn over the last decade or so from tacitly nation-centered to "postnational" literary and cultural studies is a fact as pointless to ignore or dismiss as it is easy to convert into a mythology. The upsurge of critical discourse on questions of hybridity, migrancy, diaspora, borders, etc. does not warrant, as is sometimes thoughtlessly claimed, the summary disposal of the national as a critical, or literary-historical category.[1] And the "theoretical" extravagances often uttered in the same breath that evokes the postnational—especially the mock-radical cult of the exile or migrant-as-*a priori*-subversive—are almost a reasonable excuse for taking one's intellectual exit cue at the first hint of the jargons in which they are packaged. But worse than investing utopian energies in an imagined politics of the "in-between" would be to throw out, along with postnationalism's prevalent, mystificatory forms of self-understanding, the historical and more immediately conjunctural and political changes expressed in this trend as such. For while the realities of migrancy and diaspora are not new—indeed, what could be older?—the pervasive sense that, jargons notwithstanding, these realities have come more and more to *typify* the contemporary experience even of dominant "nationalities" themselves is of a recent—and material— genealogy.

My view, as expounded in the previous chapter, is that this sudden and seemingly ontological collapse of nation-centeredness possesses a universal and perfectly discreet historical foreground in the collapse of the anti-colonial, national liberation movements that decisively shaped the epoch— the so-called "Bandung era" —stretching from the end of World War II to, at the latest, the fall of Soviet-style socialism, ca. 1989.[2] The question of what caused this collapse is as commanding as it is open-ended, and would take us far wide of our immediately critical mark in the present essay. (To answer reflexively, with the dominant wing of the institutionally sanctioned intelligentsia, "globalization," does little except confuse matters.) But we can perhaps get by here by observing that, although economic in the final analysis, the social failure of the national liberation project, in both its "socialist" and non-"socialist" instances, is already misapprehended if it is equated with an unconditional "success" of the formerly colonizing, henceforth globally imperializing centers of capital accumulation. As Robert Kurz has asserted (in an argument to which we shall return below in more detail) the effective failure of the third (and "second") world's nationalist modernization projects, whether carried out or not in the name of an ideology of cultural nationalism, results from a deepening, global crisis of capital accumulation and capitalist reproduction that, in the *very process* of shifting the social burden of the crisis onto the once "newly industrializing" economies, also marks its own increasing incapacity to exploit this fact to advantage in expanding the basis of accumulation as a whole.[3] That is, the breakdown of the national-liberationist (and "socialist") models of development (Kurz's "collapse of modernization") is, arguably, not to be compensated by some new phase of capitalist expansion and growth in the global economy, as the naive, or disinforming celebrants of "globalization" will have it. The attempt to carry out a "recuperative modernization" (Kurz's "*nachholende Modernisierung*") internally flawed as it may have been, could not withstand and was in fact the first to fall victim to the present global crisis of capitalism. Thus the "nation" as the theoretical centerpiece—and utopian imaginary—of national liberation doctrine suffers not only a dethronement but also a species of historical or dialectical curse: the "liberated" nation seems to point to no emancipatory nor even any ameliorative opening beyond itself—the philosophically sanctioned universal history that gave it ultimate meaning having, seemingly, "ended" along with it. ("*Soviel Ende war nie*."—"Never were there so many ends.", as Kurz begins *Der Kollaps der Modernisierung*.)

It is this supplemental cancellation of historical consciousness, this particular "end of History" that, as I see it, is required in order to account for the strongly ideological affinities of poststructuralist or "textualist"— i.e. constitutively anti-historicist—radicalisms for the postnational and "postcolonial." The "ludic" politics of poststructuralism (to borrow Teresa Ebert's chillingly accurate term[4]) appear, at the last moment, to rescue a seemingly failed historical project by rescuing it in turn from any historically grounded category of emancipation whatsoever. Analogously, the sense that the postnational is also the entry into the "posthistorical" foregrounds, I suggest, the sudden emergence of a postnational "subject-position" as a focal point for utopian projection and investment. The "end," or suspension, of a nation-centered temporality clearly has its spatial equivalent in the perpetual displacement of "dissemiNation, etc."

But for all of its mythical proclivities, the critical and philosophical thinking that gathers under the aegis of the postnational at least preserves an *ethical* sympathy with anti-colonialism and anti-imperialism. One might suspect in certain instances that this is no more than a rhetorical pose, but the fact that the pose is felt to be necessary reiterates the point. Between a critical text such as *Orientalism*, say, and *The Location of Culture* this sympathetic bond becomes a good deal less emphatic, but no one swearing by either text does so out a conscious loyalty to, for instance, the rationales of an IMF austerity plan. "Postcolonial" theory may be no less deserving of a rigorously historical materialist critique for all that; but even such a critique senses that it can appeal, in the last analysis, to certain commonly held values.[5]

The importance of such a common ethical perspective stands out much more sharply when one considers the other sorts of ideological fallings-out and about-faces that are being occasioned by the "postnational" historical crisis—and that often go unnoticed by the radical readers and humanists that gravitate to the "postcolonial." For the changes undergone as the older, romanticizing "third worldism" recoils from its own "end of History" can also follow a trajectory far more sinister and dystopian than post-colonialism's.

I have in mind, in this context, the recent, widely sold and discussed book by Robert D. Kaplan, *The Ends of the Earth: a Journey at the Dawn of the Twenty First Century*.[6] Kaplan, who writes on "travel and foreign affairs" had gained considerable notoriety in February, 1994 with the publication in the *Atlantic Monthly* of what was to be a section of *The Ends of the Earth* entitled "The Coming Anarchy." In the latter he had warned "Western" govern-ments and lending agencies of an impending social collapse in the poorest parts of the third world, especially sub-Saharan Africa. Along with other mainstream media "experts" like David Rieff and such praetorian academics as Samuel P. Huntington,[7] Kaplan has been granted a kind of secular pulpit from which to survey the dangers and "threats to security" that are now felt to loom out of the post-Cold War shadows.[8] Limiting my remarks to the first section of *The Ends of the Earth*, in which the author recounts his travels in West Africa, I want briefly to consider certain peculiarities of Kaplan's book that both distance it ethically but also, less obviously, link it ideologically to the "postnational" trend discussed above.

II

In his chapter entitled "Along the Gulf of Guinea," Kaplan interrupts the narrative of his journey from Togo across the border into Ghana to discuss a historical controversy: whether the European slavers who preyed on the coastal region through which he is travelling had initiated the slave-trade or merely assumed a commanding role in a practice already long in existence in the tribal kingdoms of Ashanti, Dahomey and Yoruba. Citing both Roland Oliver's *The African Experience* and Basil Davidson's *Africa in History*, Kaplan somewhat reluctantly concedes the latter's argument that the international slave trade begun in the sixteenth and seventeenth centuries by Iberian, Dutch and English merchants already marked the start of Africa's colonial subjugation to the European metropolis—and hence that a historically decisive change occurs as a result. Slavery, in the end, simply cannot be blamed on Africa itself—to what seems to be the mild regret of the author of *The Ends of the Earth*.

But even so, Kaplan asserts, slavery was not the "greatest burden inflicted on Africa by the Europeans. . . ."[9] This, rather, was the "political map, with its scores of countries, each identified by the color of its imperial master. . . ."[10] European responsibility for the slave trade, as, overall, for Africa's colonial victimization, may be a fact, but "cartography *created facts* by ordering the way we look at Africa and the rest of the world."[11] Citing Benedict Anderson's *Imagined Communities*, Kaplan finds in maps the "totalizing, classificatory grid" that can (in Kaplan's words) "make possible such questionable concepts as the Ivory Coast, Guinea, Sierra Leone, Togo and Nigeria. . . ."[12] And now, with the ancillary fact-creating of such things as national census-takings and museums, Africa itself had been "artificially reconceived" [13] —and this time by Africans themselves.

The Ends of the Earth, that is, offers up a "theory" of nationhood quite familiar to the adepts of "postcolonial studies"—the nation as narration, invention, fiction or "imagined community"—but does so for argumentative and ideological ends quite unfamiliar in this same context.[14] For contemporary postcolonial critics on the order of an Anderson, Bhabha or García Canclini, the fictive or narrational foundations of nationhood assume theoretical importance out of an intellectual, and perhaps also political impetus to burst, or de-"essentialize" the national myth, to glimpse, in however utopian and historically idealized a fashion, a form of polity cleansed of nationhood's frightening pathologies. In Kaplan's case, however, the nation—at least in its West African form—denotes an "artificiality" in relation to the truly "foundational" realities of tribe, terrain and climate. Sensing the nation as "fictive" does not, in Kaplan's account of West Africa, lead to the purportedly radical and enabling insight into the fictiveness or "liminality" of all forms of national and cultural identity— what might be termed the comedy of the postnational—but rather to the "tragedy" of nations that are not and never were "an organic outgrowth of geography and ethnicity."[15] To become merely a "narration," for *The Ends of the Earth*, is the greatest misfortune of nations—for it bespeaks the latter's loss of that which grounds "real" nations, that which, in fact, grounds all "narratives" as such—Nature itself.

And Nature, it seems, has a cultural, even a historical debt to collect. *The Ends of the Earth* blatantly avows its naturalism, proclaiming in its opening pages that the end of the twentieth century has become "a time when politics are increasingly shaped by the physical environment." "A brief moment marked by the Industrial Revolution, which gave humankind a chance to defend itself somewhat from nature, may be closing."[16] Here the double, even triple meaning of the book's title itself becomes starkly apparent—for it is not a "world," or even a "globe" across which Kaplan charts his pilgrim's course, but an "earth" whose "ends" (or extremes) offer a glimpse of an approaching apocalypse that it had perhaps been the "ends" (the *telos*) of the "earth" all along to inflict. "My goal," explains Kaplan, "was to see humanity in each locale as literally an outgrowth of the terrain and climate in which it was fated to live."[17] And Africa is the place to start—Africa, "alas, the inescapable center" in which our species was biologically destined to find its origin and in which, or so Kaplan hints repeatedly, it may have already begun its slide, propelled by uncontrolled population growth and new "luxuriating" viruses, into extinction. Africa, the "hottest" and, thus not accidentally, per Kaplan, the "poorest"[18] region of the world, is "nature writ large." [19]

Kaplan's "scientific" sources for this freely acknowledged "neo-Malthusianism" will be obscure to postcolonialists, but include, above all, Thomas Homer-Dixon, a University of Toronto academic who propounds a "physical-social" (as against a "social-social") theory trained on "the security aspects of the environment."[20] Kaplan sets apart Homer-Dixon (along with collaborators Daniel Deudney and Vaclav Smil) from outright "neo-Malthusians" of the Paul Erlich, "life-boat ethics" variety; from "neo-classical" economics, with its belief in the limitless growth theoretically possible under free market conditions; and from "distributionists" (such as Amartya Sen) who blame the West for "exploiting the third world and devouring the planet's resources."[21] Homer-Dixon's "physical-social" theory accepts the fundamental neo-classical faith in "human ingenuity" but doubts that such ingenuity (in Kaplan's gloss) "materialize[s] automatically" and speculates that "some societies are more ingenious than others."[22] ". . . [I]ngenuity," agrees *The Ends of the Earth*, "is never evenly distributed." A "deficient social ingenuity" is perhaps the root cause of Africa's accelerating surrender to a Malthusian Nature—for "what good are new Western vaccines in an anarchic African country where health clinics are constantly being vandalized or having their electricity cut?"[23]

The Ends of the Earth is rather more generous in the quotient of "social ingenuity" it assigns to India and China, areas that, unlike Africa, have at least embarked on "industrial revolutions" of their own. But it is not imprecise, I think, to identify Kaplan's intellectual and "theoretical" affinities as "eco-fascist." Kaplan cannot quite permit himself to embrace the blatantly racializing Eurocentrism of his most favored literary authorities and progenitors, above all Richard Burton, Joseph Conrad and Graham Greene. For example, he very cautiously defends Conrad's *The Nigger of the Narcissus* by posing the question of its putative racism to an African cleric in Sierra Leone, who stoutly defends the novel as "progressive for its time." [24] Burton's racially slanted account of Liberia is cited, together with Basil

Davidson's disparagements of Burton, but Kaplan comes indirectly to the former's defense by questioning whether postcolonial Liberia today is not worse off than it was when Burton visited in 1862. [25] Kaplan is still too much the post-Vietnam intellectual not to disguise his Eurocentrism. But the peculiar logic of his position reveals just what separates him from the Victorian-colonialist racism of a Burton or Conrad. For the latter, African "inferiority," however deep-seated it was presupposed to be, still appealed to the white European's responsibility to undertake a paternal act of "civilization" through direct colonization. It denoted a seeming natural-historical imbalance, which it was Europe's providential destiny to correct. For *The Ends of the Earth*, it signifies merely that even this ethically dubious effort was perhaps "naturally" doomed from the start. Burton's patronizing Eurocentrism was, Kaplan implies, wasted on Africa. Conrad's virtue is that, according to *The Ends of the Earth*, he wrote strictly from what he, in the "impregnability" of his "personal experience," "saw heard and felt."[26] Claiming the same, monadic and directly empirical authority for his own narrative, Kaplan "sees" an environmentally produced "anarchy" that nothing—neither the national liberation movements themselves, nor even the European colonizers whom they overcame and expelled—can or could have staved off. Greene's *The Heart of the Matter*, which *The Ends of the Earth* evokes in its account of Freeport, Sierra Leone, suggests to Kaplan how the guilt of the novel's hero (a British colonial police official) over an adulterous affair may have been all that could preserve his last few ties to "civilization" in an "evil," naturally corrupting place. (In the tropical heat, people are more likely to take their clothes off.) It seems never to have occurred to Kaplan that, for all of Greene's conservativism and racial cynicism, the inexorable corruption portrayed in *The Heart of the Matter* might disclose some "organic" connection to the nature of the colonial system itself. Such matters have now, at the "ends of the earth," become irrelevant, or so it seems. Thus understood, Kaplan's tale of postnational, eco-fascist vagabondage reaches perhaps its most astonishing climax in its story of a passage through civil-war-ravaged Liberia. The surrounding tropical forests, with their absence of "crisp borders," denote, "rather than a particular country . . . merely a particular place on the planet." "It seemed to me that the myths that might emerge from such a landscape were either too local (connected with tribe) or too general (connected with the earth) to sustain nationhood."[27] How, then, explain the civil war itself? What were the opposed sides killing each other for, if not for possession of a state, a nation? Kaplan cannot say, for "there was no economy here, nothing. . . ."[28] "It occurred to me that, perhaps, the forest has made the war in Liberia," confesses Kaplan. And yet he has seen nothing to make this theory credible, no "factual basis"—"merely a traveler's intuition."[29]

In *Imperial Eyes*, her critical study of eighteenth- and nineteenth-century European travel writing on Africa and Latin America, Mary Louise Pratt sums up this literature neatly as one that "narrates place and describes people."[30] One could ask for no more extreme an instance of this perverse form of myth than Kaplan's "the forest had made the war . . . ." Africans, it now appears, can no longer be conceded even that minimal degree of historical agency entailed in making war on each other. Nature, in its re-absorption of the short-lived African nation-state, its collapsing of the nation's very mythic underpinnings back into what Kaplan, without argument, presumes to be its spontaneous cultural generativity (but how do myths "emerge" from landscapes?) is left as the only historical player capable of action in this meta-narrative. At once hero and villain, it mocks even the Western efforts to act in the place of Africa's postnational, re-barbarized subjects. "The Slave Coast was ready to be recolonized, if only the Portuguese, the Dutch and the English would agree to come back with their money,"[31] but, of course, they're not coming back, not just because without the "Soviet threat there is nothing [in Africa] to interest them,"[32] but because even the agency of colonization must meet with some minimally social or cultural substance in order to realize itself. Burton, Stanley, even Cecil Rhodes could still believe in an African Nature of Enlightenment lineaments, one that would cede to "civilizing" efforts if strenuously and patiently enough applied. But the Nature of Kaplan and Homer-Dixon, the Nature that "made the war in Liberia," is the Nature of Hobbes, not of Montesquieu or Locke, much less of Rousseau. In its Malthusian absolutism and vengefulness, it ceases, even, to be Darwinian, unless the supposed self-annihilation of social order ("anarchy") can be somehow thought of as a form of adaptation.

In any event, *The Ends of the Earth* makes for a macabre demonstration of how the mythical underside of the postnational bonds as readily with new hybrids of eco-fascism as it does with postcolonialism or poststructuralism. The latter, in their "comic" discovery of the narrative, discursive or just simply cultural constructed-ness of "nation" and other deceptively naturalized or "essentialized" givens of social existence, find themselves not only on the far side of admittedly oppressive forms of identity, but of history as well—what I have elsewhere (see chapter 5) termed the "textualist fallacy." "Culture" becomes the newly pertinent sphere of agency, leaving one to speculate in endlessly metaphysical gyrations just how the construct**ED** is to do the construct**ING**. But such aporias at least leave culture in a relatively innocuous condition of abstract relativity. What happens when this same de-historicizing fallacy reads "culture" in an absolutized, re-"essentialized" mode as, finally, the *responsibility* of its constructed subjects is evident in Kaplan's eco-fascist postnationalism. (The "end was nigh," he concludes after his sojourn in the fictive, cursed "nation" of Sierra Leone, in the "failed battle" to "equalize cultures around the world."[33]) "Nature" is how the constructed is to do the constructing—or de-constructing. And Nature has determined that certain of us undergo a particularly ruthless and "personally experienced" form of deconstruction.

III

I shall reiterate, here, a point made earlier: that there are important tactical reasons for drawing a line between the "ludic" postnationalism that has recently dominated the "growth sector" in much literary and cultural studies and the much more toxic variety represented in *The Ends of the Earth*. But this is not to say that the former can in any way be adopted as the latter's corrective, or even palliative replacement. The strategic absence in Kaplan's dismal and reactionary vision of the postcolonial is not any orthodoxly deconstructive logic of the "other"—not "dissemiNation" as the antidote to Nature—but the full, contemporary historical reality of global capitalism itself.

I want to conclude this reading of Kaplan's text in the manner of an ideology critique by sketching in, however crudely and abstractly, this absence—something that leads me again to Kurz's *Der Kollaps der Modernisierung*. I am far from well versed in current political-economic research, especially as relates to Africa, but I do think that Kurz's theory of what he terms the "postcatastrophic" societies of the third and formerly second worlds (with the first in some ways already visibly on the post-catastrophic horizon) provides a uniquely illuminating standpoint from which to undertake the historical and dialectical exposé of the eco- or neo-fascist "postcolonialism" of *The Ends of the Earth*.

I will have to be concise here, but Kurz's central theoretical insight or claim is easily summarized: it holds that, in the wake of the most recent scientific and technical revolution in capitalist production (its "*Verwissen-schaftlichung*") the degree of capital intensity (Marx's "organic composition of capital") has become so great as to limit the very ability of capital to absorb labor power and overall productive capacity except in a constantly diminishing ratio. Capitalism becomes, in Kurz's phrase, "*ausbeutungs-unfähig*"—"unable to exploit": "the total global mass of productively exploited abstract labor, as a result of the permanently increasing level of the productive forces, declines *absolutely* for the first time in the history of capitalism."[34] Such enormously enhanced productivity, that is, leads not only to a classic crisis of over-production in which existing world markets are unable to absorb the increased flow of commodities, but to a general crisis of social reproduction in which the labor power of millions, if not billions, of newly proletarianized residents of the South and East becomes superfluous to the economic needs of capital. "Human beings are cut off from the the capitalist conditions placed on the satisfaction of their needs."[35] "Postcatastrophic" societies arise "that are bound to the global circulation of money by only the thinnest of threads."[36] Efforts to initiate a rapid process of "primitive accumulation" of capital, whether made under the banners of Soviet-style socialism or third-worldist national liberation—the revolutionary drive to what Kurz terms a "recuperative modernization"—

could not but ultimately come to grief, since "the level attained by the enormous stocks of capital in the West, a level presupposed if any further growth is to result, is no longer attainable—within the existing commodity logic—in other regions of the world."[37] "Such constant increases in productivity, increases that exceed the bounds of comprehension of commodity production, cannot but react with catastrophic force on any recuperative processes of primitive accumulation."[38] Ripped from their traditional village or tribal social economies and herded into the new, gargantuan urban slums of the third world—where they were to have become the new, global proletariat—an enormous mass, literally billions of human beings find themselves in the limbo of "*Geldsubjekten—aber ohne Geld*"—"monetary subjects, but without money."[39]

The resulting collapse of the postcolonial political and economic institutions that had arisen in the course of now abandoned strategies of capitalist modernization leads to the "*sekundäre Barbarei*" of civil and ethnic wars and their accompanying "Ersatz" ideologies of religious and tribal fundamentalisms and virulent neo- and sub-nationalisms.[40] That is, the very same historical dialectic that, in its initial stages, had produced the modern nation-state as a center for the accumulation of capital and for the erection and administration of a generalized system of commodity exchange, having reached (at least in Kurz's view) its terminal crisis, now works in turn to undermine and destroy the nation-state at its weakest points.

This is the *immediate* reality recorded by Kaplan in his street-level travels through Liberia, the Ivory Coast, Egypt, Turkey, etc., with only a knap-sack on his back but with Burton and Conrad—and Homer-Dixon—heavy in his thoughts: a reality whose paradox it is to have been historically and culturally generated but "naturally," even "environmentally" condemned to extinction. With a few melancholic regrets, but inevitably, given his entrapment in the purely immediate, fragmentary forms of appearance of the "post-catastrophic" world order, Kaplan reverts to the inveterate dualities of a Western, European "civilization" versus a naturalized "barbarism," leaving the nation hovering somewhere in between. The "end of History," at least in the third world, (but, if we are not careful to contain the spread of "anarchy," perhaps in our own backyards as well[41]) is the final, doomed return to Nature. But, held up against Kurz's theory of the post-catastrophic, Kaplan's eco-fascist naturalism discloses itself as the exact, ideological inversion of the reality he "personally experiences." It is not "the forest" that makes civil war in Liberia—or Rwanda, Zaire, etc.—but "monetary subjects without money," i.e. human beings, whose agriculturally and village-based "natural" economies now having been violently and summarily uprooted and undermined, find themselves marooned in an absolute and unremittingly *historical* space of "modernity" that seems to lead neither forwards nor backwards. It is the historical space of "*sekundäre Barbarei*"—and no one more truly if indirectly embodies its spirit than

Kaplan himself, along with his likenesses among the ranks of late-imperial and retro-colonial shills.

In conclusion, however, there is no reason to credit postcolonial theory with having superseded this same grotesque mystification. While it rests on an adamant prohibition of Kaplan's retro-colonial nostalgias, post-colonialism's purely cultural and discursive radicalism, its celebration of postnational hybridities as if nationalism were no more than a question of subject-positions, offers not the slightest critical purchase on the all too real immediacies narrated by Kaplan. Where *The Ends of the Earth* attributes the social catastrophe of a progressively non-reproductive global capitalism to "natural" factors external to its logic, postcolonial theory misreads this logic itself, as if the globalized exchange of culture and identities were not bound to the same acutely dysfunctional system that merely replaces older, bad forms of cultural-nationalist "essentialisms" with newer, ever more sinister ones. Postcolonialism forgets, or never grasps, that the flip-side of "hybridity" "diasporic consciousness," etc. is the postcatastrophic holocaust of "monetary subjects without money."

Marxism, Postcolonialism and
The Eighteenth Brumaire

I. Points of Departure

What is nowadays perceived as the mutual antagonism of Marxism and postcolonialism rests, in fact, on a rather more intimate and disparate relationship than may be supposed, even by a well-meaning intention to mediate between the two. Although postcolonialism in its presently domestic/institutionalized form has no doubt contributed to the fashionable dismissal of Marxism as a "discourse" reducible to its "Western" and/or "modern(ist)" origins, postcolonialism's own genealogy as an instance of "theory" or even just as a strategy of "reading" can, in a roundabout way, be traced back to Marxism itself. Of course, there is a sense in which all contemporary "theory" with social implications can be shown to bear a necessary, if tensile relationship to the thought of Marx, at least if one accepts the view expressed by Sartre in *Search for a Method* that a "going beyond Marxism" will be "at best, only the rediscovery of a thought already contained in the philosophy which one believes he has gone beyond."[1]

But what I refer to here is something more discreet: the sense, which postcolonialism inherits directly from poststructuralism, that Marxism can be purged of its "Hegelian" birthmarks and incorporated successfully within the same critical spirit that animates the poststructuralist critique of the sign. Althusser, Deleuze and Guattari, Laclau and Mouffe's *Hegemony and Socialist Strategy*, even the latter-day Derridean "Marxism" of *Specters of Marx* are all as much the forebears and tutors of postcolonialism as are DuBois, Gandhi, Fanon, Antonius or other "third world," anti-colonial avatars. One is sometimes inclined to believe that, in fact, postcolonialism as currently practiced has a great deal more to do with the reception of French "theory" in places like the United States, Britain, Canada and Australia than it does with the realities of cultural decolonization or the international division of labor. Like poststructuralism, postcolonialism as a theoretical and critical project is non-Marxist, but it does not frame itself—as does, say, Popperian neo-positivism—*directly* as an anti-Marxism. Rather, it erects itself on a Marx *as read*—by Althusser, above all, and then subsequently by a Laclau or a Stuart Hall, etc. At a minimum, postcolonialism bears an archeological relation to a Marx that, to follow Foucault's familiar thesis, hovers, along with Freud, over all "theory" itself as a "discursive practice heterogeneous to its ulterior transformations."[2] If one is to pose even the theoretical possibility that a Marxist criticism might, in Jamesonian fashion, make room for the putatively valid insights or discoveries of postcolonial studies within its mediated totality, post-colonialism will first have to be traced back to the point in its own intellectual genesis at which the thought of Marx *in its unity* appears to it as a "point of departure," to be either embraced or refused. Not Marx as "text," or even as "discursive practice," but Marx as *method*, as a necessary relation of theory and practice, must first be so positioned as to be able to "speak" to the postcolonial critic.

In the last analysis, such a genealogical encounter would require a working back out and beyond the older, arch-debates occasioned by the structuralist and poststructuralist claims to (post-)Marxisms of their own, beginning with the problem of Althusserianism itself. This obviously cannot be fully rehearsed or even sketched in here, but I want to attempt a possible short cut by way of an unusually discrete textual constellation: the explicit citation (and, in the latter case, subsequent exegesis) of a particular phrase from Marx's *The Eighteenth Brumaire of Louis Bonaparte* in two Ur-texts of postcolonialism: Said's *Orientalism* and Spivak's "Can the Subaltern Speak?"

II. *The Eighteenth Brumaire* as Orientalism

Still arguably postcolonialism's *fons et origo*, *Orientalism* probably also heralds the Marxism/postcolonialism schism by demoting Marx himself to the rank of just another Western orientalist. Scarcely a page into its introduction, Marx is named, along with Aeschylus, Dante and Victor Hugo, as a purveyor of a "style of thought based upon an ontological and epistemo-logical distinction made between 'Orient' and . . . . 'Occident.'"[3] Said later concedes an "exceptional" status to Marx, given Marx's explicit protests in his journalism of the 1850s against the depredations of British colonialism in India. But Marx's simultaneous approval of the objectively "revolution-ary" impact of colonialization on "Oriental despotism," despite the former's cruelty and greed, shows his view of India in the end to be "perfectly fitted . . . to a standard Orientalist undertaking."[4] Aijaz Ahmad, in a now celebrated polemic, has called attention to the the distortions and deceits woven into Said's dismissal of Marx. Ahmad points out, for example, that much of the anti-colonial historiography produced in India itself agrees, substantively, with Marx's assessment, despite and without ignoring its over-lay of nineteenth-century Eurocentrism—thus making ironic "orientalists" of a Mukhia or a Namboodripad. And what, Ahmad asks, to make of Marx's analogously "tragic" view of the destruction of the European peasantry as part of the inevitable transition from European feudalism to capitalism? Does this make Marx a "capitalist"?[5]

Taking most of its cues on Marx from the Foucault of *The Order of Things*, *Orientalism* is undoubtedly the source for much of the more spontaneous aversion to Marxism evident in contemporary postcolonialist circles. But it is telling that despite its Foucauldian haste to consign Marx to an obsolete and West-centered "episteme," the text of Marx itself remains a kind of literary authority for *Orientalism*, at least in one instance. I mean, of course, the phrase from the concluding section of *The Eighteenth Brumaire*, written in reference to the French "small peasant proprietors" (*Parzellenbauern*) who were, in Marx's view, the social class *politically* "represented" by the dictatorship of Napoleon III: "They cannot represent themselves; they must be represented."[6] The first citation (in the original German) follows on a section of the introduction to *Orientalism* in which Said clarifies his interest in Orientalist "representations" *as* representation, i.e. as separate from the question of the "correctness" or truth of representations. "The exteriority of the representation is always governed by some version of the truism that if the Orient could represent itself, it would; since it cannot, the representation does the job, for the West, and *faute de mieux*, for the poor Orient. 'Sie können sich nicht vertreten, sie müssen vertreten werden,' as Marx wrote in *The Eighteenth Brumaire*."[7] The same phrase is cited a second time in *Orientalism*'s final chapter as Said remarks on the unabashedly Cold War logic that came to govern even the study of oriental languages such as Arabic in the United States. After quoting the Cold War propaganda "analyst" Harold Laswell at length—to the effect that the modern propagandist, concerned to uphold the imperial order, must eschew democratic notions and recognize that "men" are not "the best judges of their interests"[8]—Said allows that modern orientalists may now put on a "liberal veneer" and encourage a humane study of Orientals based on an abstract "mutual understanding." "To this end [says the liberal orientalism] it is always better to let them [Orientals] speak for themselves, to represent themselves (even though underlying this fiction stands Marx's phrase— with which Laswell is in agreement—for Louis Napoleon: 'They cannot represent themselves; they must be represented.')"[9]

To anyone even loosely familiar with the text of *The Eighteenth Brumaire*, *Orientalism*'s manner of citing it must appear odd—and, indeed, very much in keeping with the scant knowledge of its source alleged in Ahmad's polemic. Although it is difficult to be sure here, the citation appears to accuse Marx of *approving* this unilateral, coercive form of representation, almost implying that Marx had "Orientals" and not nineteenth-century French peasants in mind when he wrote it—or that one was, for him, as good as the other. The waters are even further clouded when *Orientalism* claims the citation as Marx's "phrase . . . for Louis Napoleon," rather than for the *Parzellenbauern* who had been his electoral and demagogic base of support. Indeed, the somewhat confused thinking that elicits the quotation almost seems to rest on an outright identification of Marx with Louis Napoleon himself, as if Marx not only regarded French peasants as properly deprived of the right to "represent themselves" but had even recommended their direct subjugation to the Bonapartist state as the "best judge of their interests." After all, it is, says Said, a phrase "with which Laswell is in agreement"! And finally there is the fact, as Spivak was subsequently to observe in another context (much more on this below) that "represent" translates the German verb "*vertreten*" and not, as Said's citation of it implies, "*darstellen*."

Perhaps, after all, this is unfair, and *Orientalism's* passing citation of the *The Eighteenth Brumaire*, incidental at best to the book's general thesis, is merely a rhetorical display without metonymically critical or interpretive intent. Said is hardly the first person to quote Marx against or in indifference to the grain of Marx's own viewpoint. *The Eighteenth Brumaire*, in particular, is a veritable mine of quotable, all-purpose phrases, most famously its opening lines—". . . the first time as tragedy, the second time as farce . . . ."—which William F. Buckley might find occasion to cite as readily as Malcolm X. Given both *Orientalism's* stated suspicions and limited knowledge of Marx, it is reasonable to read its citation of him as both muddled and less than just. Still, outside its original context, the phrase does at least suit Said's generally rhetorical purposes.

III. "They can be represented; they must not represent themselves."

But both rhetoric and interpretive validity aside, what this particular moment of citation itself discloses is a common metaphoric and conceptual node within which both Marxism and postcolonialism encounter each other as, in principle, commensurable "theories": namely, representation itself as a subject/object relation in which epistemology and history, "knowledge" and "power," appear to become fused.

It is with a heightened awareness of this nodal point, and, indeed, with a seemingly greater attention to the text of Marx that Gayatri Spivak comes herself to cite the same phrase from *The Eighteenth Brumaire* in "Can the Subaltern Speak?".[10] Here, its readers will recall, the occasion is a taking of issue with "Intellectuals and Power," a 1970s "conversation" between Foucault and Deleuze in which all pretensions of radical intellectuals to "represent" the workers' struggle are abjured, and a "diffuse," de-centered strategy, clearly *sans* party or "revolutionary vanguard," is proclaimed. In short, emancipation, theorized in a manner consistent with Foucault's well-known "power/knowledge" formulae for a "microphysics of power" and "specific intellectuals," can and must take place independently of "representation."

Spivak rebukes such a neo-spontaneism for failing—here in its Deleuzian collapsing of interest and desire—to problematize its own metropolitan outlook, and thus of leaving what she terms the "epistemic violence" of imperialism essentially intact, despite overt gestures of anti-elitism. Have not Foucault and Deleuze too conveniently forgotten a history of Western victories for the oppressed that have left a non-Western, super oppressed "Other" in chains? What can a politics freed of representation mean for this — "subaltern" — Other, if in fact it had *already* been relegated to the status of something non-representable?

Marx's phrase comes back into play here for its greater caution in observing something like this gap within "representation" itself. *The Eighteenth Brumaire*'s word for the "political," seemingly subject-less and unfree "representation" of the *Parzellenbauern* is "Vertretung" (implying a "rhetoric-as-persuasion") and not the "economic," as well as epistemological "Darstellung" ("rhetoric-as-trope"). By now Spivak's argument—political, exegetical and philological all at once—has taken on a density and an indirectness that has confounded many a reading, but the detectable inference here is that the Western intellectual or "Subject" has been positioned in relation to the "subaltern" much as, in Marx's estimation, Louis Bonaparte had positioned himself in relation to the *Parzellenbauern*: the "Subject's" power to "represent" (*vertreten*), resting on the powerlessness of the "Other" to self-represent in this sense, is cloaked in a philosopheme of representation (*Darstellung*) that is, in principle, free, unaffected by power relations. The "freedom" of the *Parzellenbauer/* subaltern to "represent itself" (*sich darstellen*) in, say, an "idée napoléonienne" or a Foucauldian program for "micropolitics" is the ideology, the unfreedom of its *Vertretung*, its being-represented in subjection to an intransitive "executive power." Taking, perhaps, some liberty with the intertextuality set in place by Spivak's citation of the *The Eighteenth Brumaire*, one might read "Can the Subaltern Speak?" as a catachrestic rewriting of the latter in the following, precise way:

"They cannot represent themselves; they must be represented" [*"Sie können sich nicht vertreten, sie müssen vertreten werden"*] becomes,

A. **from the standpoint of the Western imperial "Subject"**: *"They can represent themselves [Sie können sich **darstellen**]; [but] they must be represented"* [[*aber*] *sie müssen vertreten werden*];

B. **while from the standpoint of the "subaltern" it is re-written as:** *"[Since] we can be represented", [therefore] we must not represent ourselves."* [*"[Da] wir **vertreten** werden können, so müssen wir uns nicht **darstellen**"*];

The intellectual, even if "sympathetic" à la Foucault and Deleuze, "dissimulates" his or her own complicity in the continuous "constitut[ion] of the colonial subject as Other"[11] by "conflating" the two senses of representation, disguising the "epistemic violence" wreaked on the Other as something remediable on the level of *Darstellung*. This remains so even, and perhaps especially *when* such conflation is followed by a quasi-anarchist disavowal of all representational mediations as unnecessary impediments to emancipation. For this Other as "subaltern," it becomes vital, then, to refuse the *Darstellung*, the "staging of the world in representation"[12] in which its Otherness for "power" is constituted, if the reality of its own colonial/imperial *Vertretung* is not itself to be concealed. And we owe this insight into the "complicity of *vertreten* and *darstellen*, their identity-in-difference as the place of practice"[13] not to Heidegger or Derrida, nor, even, to Althusser, but to Marx himself, a Marx "obliged to construct models of a divided and dislocated subject,"[14] a Marx with "cautious respect for the nascent critique of individual and collective subjective agency" for whom "the projects of class consciousness and the transformation of consciousness are discontinuous . . . ."[15]

IV. *Parzellenbauern* of the world, unite!

One has, indeed, left the Foucauldian Marx of *Orientalism* far behind here— far enough, in fact, to make of Marx a kind of ally of the postcolonial subaltern against a "West-centered" Foucault! Marx himself is claimed as virtually a "strategic essentialist" standing in the way of the surreptious re-essentializing of the S/subject and Other that is replicated in even the most fervent, metropolitan poststructuralist advocacy of "*différance*." For all its forbidding density and excentricity, it is in "Can the Subaltern Speak?" and not in *Orientalism* that postcolonialism actually undertakes to *read* Marx into its own conceptual operations, to subsume it rather than to simply abjure it as "Eurocentist" or "essentialist" *tout court*. Where *Orientalism*, deeply ambivalent towards Marx, seems not to know whether it cites *The Eighteenth Brumaire* as the source of an insight potentially critical of orientalism or as just the latter's discursive symptom, "Can the Subaltern Speak?" understands the crucial importance to a possible "Marxist" postcolonialism of representation as *philosopheme* and seems already to have calculated a method for siphoning off the whole of Marx through a phrase— "They cannot represent themselves, etc."— with a plausibly metonymic connection to it. Two chains of equivalencies are allusively invoked — (1) Napoleon III=the Western intellectual= the Subject; and (2) the *Parzellenbauern*=class *per se*=the "subaltern." These, so long as the insight into the discontinuity of *Vertretung/Darstellung* can be likewise read back *a posteriori* or "symptomatically" into Marx's text as well, make of the citation itself a virtual palimpsest.

But to even a moderately circumspect reader of *The Eighteenth Brumaire* Spivak's extrapolations from this phrase will quickly come to seem doubtful. While of some philological interest, the *Vertretung/Darstellung* distinction cannot be cited as evidence, one way or the other, for a Marx "obliged to construct models of a divided and dislocated subject whose parts are not continuous or coherent with each other."[16] From the standpoint of the *unity* of Marx's thinking in *The Eighteenth Brumaire*—the standpoint to which I aspire throughout—this is to commit the fallacy of collapsing the text's theoretical content onto the level of a purely lexical set of distinctions. Moreover, it implies the unlikely notion that Marx had construed, in the relation of the *Parzellenbauern* to their representative/*Vertreter*, Napoleon III, a *generalized* relation of class *per se* to its political forms or modes of representation. In fact, not even the peasants themselves as a class are held to this rule. "The point should be clearly understood," states *The Eighteenth Brumaire* not even a page after its disparaging diagnosis of the *Parzellen-bauern*, that

> the Bonaparte dynasty represents the conservative, not the revolutionary peasant: the peasant who wants to consolidate the condition of his social existence, the smallholding, not the peasant who strikes out beyond it. It does not represent the country people who want to overthrow the old order by their own energies, in alliance with the towns, but the precise opposite, those who are gloomily enclosed within this old order and want to see themselves and their smallholdings saved and given preferential treatment by the Empire. It represents the peasant's superstition, not his enlighten-ment; his prejudice, not his judgement; his past, not his future; his modern Vendée, not his modern Cevennes. [17]

True, Marx's word for "represent" here is not *vertreten* but *repräsentieren*, but "Can the Subaltern Speak?", sensibly, thinks better of arguing here that yet another mode of representation, distinct from *Vertretung*, is brought into play. Louis Bonaparte's power to represent (*vertreten/repräsentieren*) the *Parzellenbauern* does not, as "Can the Subaltern Speak?" infers, rest on a non-identity of "desire and interest", or a crisis of subjective/collective agency as something intrinsic to *all* class difference but on something specific to *this* class—the *Parzellenbauern*—under given historical conditions. These are historical conditions that, in an earlier conjuncture, when the first Napoleon had completed the anti-feudal revolution that had given them their *Parzellen*, determined a *relative* identity of interest and desire, of *Vertreter* and *Vertreten*, and that, in a possible future, might again allow for a conscious class agency as the peasants "find their natural ally and leader in the *urban proletariat*, whose task is to overthrow the bourgeois order."[18]

It is telling, indeed, that "Can the Subaltern Speak?," in its haste to make of Marx a precursor for the deconstruction of the subject-as-agent, excludes entirely from consideration *The Eighteenth Brumaire*'s richly elaborated, differential analysis of class agency in the case of the two hegemonic, *socially* representative classes, bourgeoisie and proletariat. No faithful reader of *The Eighteenth Brumaire*, Spivak included, could speculate as to its "critique of the subjectivity of a collective agency" without calling to mind the passage in the opening section of the text in which Marx contrasts "bourgeois revolutions, such as those of the eighteenth century" to "proletarian revolutions, such as those of the nineteenth." The former "outdo each other in dramatic effects" but are "short-lived" and followed by a "long period of regret" (*"ein langer Katzenjammer"*) in which past heroics are reduced to the everyday drudgery of bourgeois existence. The latter, by contrast "constantly engage in self-criticism and in repeated interruptions of their own course," retreating before their Antaeus-likened opponent "until the situation is created in which any retreat is impossible, and the conditions themselves cry out: '*Hic Rhodus, hic salta!*'" [19] And here, too, a single chiasmus—from an immediately preceding and equally memorable passage of *The Eighteenth Brumaire*—crystallizes the dialectic in question: "Previously the phrase transcended the content; here the content transcends the phrase."[20] (*"Dort ging die Phrase über den Inhalt, hier geht der Inhalt über die Phrase hinaus."*) None of the *The Eighteenth Brumaire*'s various lexemes for "representation" are present here on the surface of the text, but the concept itself is surely at work. Unlike the *Parzellenbauern*, both bourgeoisie and proletariat *can*, it seems, "represent themselves." For *both* an "identity of interests" clearly *does* "produce a feeling of community, national links" and "a political organization." For the bourgeoisie as collective subject/agent, however, self-representation is only accidentally— "ecstatically"— a real self-knowledge and self-activity. The self-representation "works" in the sense that it enables a momentary, accidental identity of class subject and class agent. But this identity—this *"sich vertreten"* which is also a *"sich darstellen"*—disintegrates as soon as its (historical) work is accomplished. The "phrase transcended (*hinausgehen*) the content" here denotes a surplus of representation that is perfectly compatible with a form of class agency, but that has its reverse side in a *deficit of consciousness* in relation to "content." Bourgeois self-represen-tation, as *The Eighteenth Brumaire* evokes it in an allusive, allegorical language of "phrases," "masks," and "ghosts," is, in short, its "false consciousness" as a class. The *Parzellenbauern*, too, in a self-representation limited to an *alienated "sich darstellen,"* exhibits a false consciousness of its own material, class existence. But if, as Lukács puts it in *History and Class Consciousness*, "consciousness and self-interest . . . are mutually incompatible"[21] in the case of the small-holding peasantry, in the case of the bourgeoisie such incompatiblity is *itself*, for a determined historical moment, compatible with a hegemonic relation to society denied to the *Parzellenbauern*.

Yet the proletariat—to follow through with this reading of *The Eighteenth Brumaire*—does *not* thereupon resolve the bourgeois surplus of representation in favor of a merger or identity of "phrase and content." Rather it *subsumes* within its own *self*-representation the contingent, seemingly irrational and "ecstatic" quality of "bourgeois revolution." Representation now no longer stands between class subject and class agency, screening the first from the second; it discloses itself as simply the *self*-mediation of a class consciousness in whose formal make-up consciousness and agency, desire and interest, *Vertretung* and *Darstellung* already *objectively* coincide. "Content," in "transcending" the "phrase," reveals the phrase itself as merely a moment of content, inseparable from the latter's dialectical law of development. Representation itself no longer appears as an unmediated cleavage or "discontinuity" of subject and object leaving history to one side or the other, but as consubstantial with history as a unified, yet contradictory process of ceaseless self-mediation. To again refer to *History and Class Consciousness*—a work still unsurpassed, in my view, as a "reading" of Marx—the superiority of proletarian to bourgeois class consciousness does not subsist in any non-contradictoriness but rather in the fact that the contradiction that constitutes the structural limit to bourgeois consciousness becomes for the proletariat an *object* of consciousness.[22]

The point of all this, contra "Can the Subaltern Speak?," is that the divergence of *Vertretung* and *Darstellung* is not constitutive, nor even "symptomatic" of class but is *itself* relative to class difference as Marx theorizes it. It can only appear to mark a "discontinuity of class consciousness and the transformation of consciousness" if we read the *Parzellenbauern* as a metonymy for class as such, or, in more general terms, if we abstract representation from consciousness, enforcing an initial separation between the two to which neither *The Eighteenth Brumaire* nor Marx's thinking as a whole conforms—and which the latter arguably supersedes. Both *Vertretung* and *Darstellung* as distinct, opposing moments of representation—as well as representation itself in its formal separation of subject and object, representation as non-identity—become, in Marx, sublated moments within the more concrete category of consciousness as both class-determined and as historically immanent — as "in and for itself."

IV. The (postcolonial) desire called . . . Marx?

Still there is, it is true, nothing sacrosanct about the literal and integral text of Marx, nor even about the conceptual system it reflects—and nothing to prove, *a priori*, that "Can the Subaltern Speak?" might not be right about the inherent "discontinuity" of class self-interest and consciousness that it, in my view, falsely reads into this text. The downright strange thing about this essay—made even stranger by the fact of its own rapid elevation to near-legendary, "textual" status—is that it would think of advancing a theory of class consciousness infused by the aporias of "representation" (as understood in, say, Derrida) in deference to the authority of a work that can rather easily be shown to resist, if not refute such a notion. What could motivate such a reading? What "desire"—now perhaps genealogically carried over into postcolonialism as an established trend—could be at work here? It would only beg this question, in the end, to point to Spivak's debt, however critical, to Althusser — my candidate as the all-time world record-holder for confabulations and misreadings of Marx [23]—or to liken "Can the Subaltern Speak?" to kindred, post-Althusserian and "secular post-structuralist" exegeses of Marx, among them *Hegemony and Socialist Strategy*, the *Anti-Oedipus* and even Derrida's *Specters of Marx*, which owes something of its own citational, Heideggerian/hermeneuticist relation to Marx as "text" to Spivak's earlier foray into this shadowy territory. In a sense Foucault was right about Marxism as discursive practice at least rhetorically: a citation from Marx can be found—or "spun" —so as to prove virtually anything, from history as the "spectral" to the need to divide Poland. And protesting, "orthodox" counter-exegeses—of the sort in which I myself have just indulged—may ultimately be rather futile gestures. To answer, here, the question of "desire" (or "interest"), we need to think more carefully not just about the current rhetorical uses and abuses of Marx, but about what precise sorts of cross-passages and subterfuges historical actuality has itself opened up to radical "desire" in Marx's text. If postcolonialism can be shown, after "Can the Subaltern Speak?," to rest on a discernible misreading of Marx, this genealogical result will only retain its interest—and the opportunity of a commensuration be preserved— if it can be further shown how the thought, or system of Marxism, as subject to the same desire, might come to re-read, or re-write itself.

Let us, to simplify matters, consider yet again the passage from *The Eighteenth Brumaire*— " . . . now the content transcends the phrase"— written over, as it were, by Spivak's citation—"They cannot represent themselves . . . ." (In the spirit of "Can the Subaltern Speak?", we might, clumsily, re-write it too as "then the representations transcended what was represented; now what is to be represented transcends the representations.") Here, to reiterate, Marx formulates a dialectical inversion in which the aporetic, "discontinuous" movement of representation, its constantly renewed surplus or deficit, re-appears as subsumed in a historical relation of *internalized* difference (eighteenth century vs. nineteenth century, past vs. present) that is, moreover, determined as a class (conscious) difference: bourgeois vs. proletarian, or, even better, vs. "social" revolution. The non-identity of representation, once concretized socially and historically, no longer posits a pure identity as its "other" but rather a dialectical reversal, or *Aufhebung*. Representation as proper to a consciousness in-itself (a "false consciousness") becomes representation as proper to a consciousness raised to the level of the "in-and-for-itself"—not, therefore, a "true" consciousness, but a consciousness that (as "act") "overthrows the objective form of its object."[24]

One understands nothing of *The Eighteenth Brumaire*—and, in essence, nothing of Marx—if this dialectic of the "*an und für sich*," straight out of Marx's own sublating, critical embrace of Hegel, is missed or obfuscated. "Can the Subaltern Speak?," which, alas, has its Marxism straight from Althusser (and in *that*, at any rate, cedes the advantage to *Orientalism*) may thus, in the end, plead innocent to the charge of misreading, as one cannot, technically, misread what is *already* a misreading.

But one's understanding, one's "reading" of Marx on this point must also concede the extreme vulnerability of the theory of a *class*—that is, a *historicized* —consciousness "in and for itself" (Lukács's proletariat as "identical subject/object of history") to its own historicity when history-as-present itself appears, perversely, to withhold what it also promises. "The content transcends the phrase"—Marx writes these words, putting the verb "*hinausgehen*" in the present tense, in 1851 or so. Revolution— a "revolution of the nineteenth century"—is understood to be imminent. A century and a half later, at the end of a twentieth century that at various moments imagined Marx's prophecy fulfilled, the words are still electrifying, but they cannot shake the ironic reading that would question whether they too have not become a mere "phrase," and the deeds of the (perhaps false) prophets who uttered them a new "nightmare weighing on the brains of the living." Perhaps, in fact, the "situation" in which "any retreat is impossible" has not yet been—or is only now being—"created." But, even if so, must not we, as the twenty-first century readers of a nineteenth century call to arms, inexorably come to think of a "content going beyond the phrase", of a class "in and for itself," as a prophecy turned wishful thinking, as a revolutionary perlocution reduced to no more really than a constantly resurfacing "desire" ? And if such is, for better or worse, the "desire" inscribing *The Eighteenth Brumaire*, must we not allow that, all else aside, it is a desire shared by "Can the Subaltern Speak?" — and perhaps by postcolonialism as a whole?

Read in this light, Spivak's pseudo-exegesis—in fact, a move to reverse the thrust of Marx's reasoning by collapsing history back into a textualized "representation" —begins to seem almost a gesture of orthodoxy, at least in the sense of a reader's loyalty to a literal text. The desire for the "content" to "transcend" the "phrase" need not simply relent because history gives the appearance—to Marxists and postcolonialists alike—of having fallen back once and for all "behind its point of departure," back into an eternal re-enactment of "bourgeois revolution" as surplus of representation. One has only to read the second half of the dialectical chiasmus differently—to interpret the present-ness of "*hinausgehen*" ("*Dort ging . . . hier geht . . . hinaus*") not as denoting imminence but as a sign of Eternal Return, as the present-ness of the "always already"—and the desire for transcendence will appear to *itself* as realized. In this way, Marx's verdict on the *Parzellenbauern* as so to speak, beneath self-representation does more than write over, palimpsest-like, the remainder of *The Eighteenth Brumaire*, including its opening invocations of a revolutionary eschatology. The reverse subsumption of "content" back into representation, of the prophetic and perlocutionary back into the aporia of *Vertretung/Darstellung*, obeys the urge to rescue, at least as *affect*, the possibility of a *hinausgehen*. What if, in "transcending the phrase," "content" were disclosed not as immanent to history as a rational-dialectical unfolding, but to representation, to the "phrase" itself—as a "content" existing not on the outer, historical circumference of subject/object non-identity but on its inner, infra-representational threshold, in that "inaccessible blankness circumscribed by an interpretable text."[25] One would not need to cast off Marx, as urged by a Foucauldian poststructuralism or postcolonialism, but simply to read a text like *The Eighteenth Brumaire* from back to front, from representational "discontinuity" *back* to class–consciousness, from *Parzellenbauern back* to bourgeoisie and proletariat. Does not, after all, a class that is a "simple addition of amorphous magnitudes" living in abject subordination to an "executive power" that it is free to "represent" (*darstellen*) however it likes so long as it consents to its own subordination (*Vertretung*); a class that holds on to its own small scrap of private property under the illusion that a permanent and progressive indebtedness is still a sign of ownership: does not such a class correspond on an empirical plane to today's "Western proletariat" as well? From both post-Social Democratic and post-Socialist outposts, it does in fact seem a long time, almost longer than anyone can remember, since the working class last "represented itself," and one could check off by the dozens the latter-day Napoleon IIIs who have made careers by "robbing" entire nations of *Parzellen*-proletarians of their wealth in the form of labor power so as to be able to "to give it back to them" in the form of tax-cuts and lottery tickets. [26] No doubt this is too cynical a view of today's "postmodern" proletariat, but it is a cynicism implied not only in "Can the Subaltern Speak?" but in a broad array of contemporary Marxist literature as well—the flip-side of the shared, increasingly unhistoricizable desire for a *hinausgehen*. And it goes some way towards explaining why a text such as "Can the Subaltern Speak?" could resonate so loudly among radical academics and even convince many of them of its rigorously Marxist credentials.

Very much in the manner of Althusser, who beckoned all to *Lire le Capital*—but only as a text that, as it turned out, never actually managed to say what it really meant—Spivak shows how the desire that Marxism come true compensates for an abandonment of its *method*—historical, dialectical and, in this, anathema to Spivak's deconstructionism—by clinging even more doggedly and with an almost obsessive philologism to its "text." This latter is not simply "misread"—as if a second, more careful reading would be enough to restore dialectical method and "discourse" to at least a relative unity. The "text" is read, as it were, *against* its own methodological content, as if the purportedly failed prophecy contained, hidden somewhere in its explicit wording, another, implicit prophecy, audible only in a gap between text and method, "phrase" and "content." The wider this gap the more closely one must scan and the more "theoretical" significance one must purport to find in the words themselves—at the level of the sentence or even of the lexeme. In the interstices of *Vertretung/Darstellung*, Spivak discovers the secret passage into a Marxism through the looking glass, a passage into what is almost an *alter*-history, a secularized and teleological "textuality" in which "content" can "transcend the phrase" because content was always itself only a phrase too.

In all of this "Can the Subaltern Speak?" conforms to a broader ideological/literary affiliation to Marx initiated by Althusser and refined in secular poststructuralisms and post-Marxisms from Laclau, Hall and Butler to much of today's standard issue Cultural Studies. Marx's systematic placement of class difference at the center of all seemingly transcendant questions (aesthetics, ethics, etc.) makes him, one now finds, a philosopher of "différance" as well—so long as one can drain all historical and dialectical substance out of "class" itself." Spivak's unique contribution to this effort was, of course, to equate the abstract, textualist notion of deconstruction with a principle of anti-colonial/anti-imperial subversion, to lift, via "representation," the textual out of the historical and re-map it onto the "postcolonial." The post-*historical* desire deposited in the text of *The Eighteenth Brumaire*, by means of an exegetical feignt, here became the new form for an older, "third-worldist" and "essentialist" desire (for the *nation* as prior to the social revolution) likewise conscious of having been betrayed by its own eschatology. The radical alternative to the *Parzellenbauer* becomes not the "revolutionary peasant," much less the proletariat, but the "subaltern" as itself a species of *Parzellenbauer* that trumps its oppressors by outflanking its would-be representation in the "imperialist social text," namely, by its "müssen sich nicht darstellen." And so it is that "subaltern", Gramsci's nuanced, but precisely class-analytical concept, comes to supply to a variant of poststructuralism a term able to solder within itself, medallion-like, the unalloyable metals of a historical agency and its textualist simulacrum, a term that, having once at least conveyed something of the uncanny subversiveness Spivak finds in Bhubaneswari Bhaduri's suicide one now hears used to qualify everything from hip-hop to middle-class Franco-Ontarians.

Here too, in fact, a "desire" already readable in *The Eighteenth Brumaire* is re-inscribed once more, and if "subaltern" serves the purpose of raising consciousness of the ethnic and gendered margins of the already super-exploited (or perhaps already "unexploitable") then its textualist origins may have since become moot. Yet the fact remains that the real, genealogical order of determinations is turned upside down if we think of postcolonialism or the "subaltern" as the "theoretical" emissaries of the third world to the court of Western theory, whether poststructuralist or Marxist. Postcolonialism's origins are, at base, those of secular post-structuralism as a whole. The "colonial" is here a variation on a "post" theme, which travels from about as far East or South as a line traced by the lecture circuits and book distribution networks of French poststructuralist "Theory." Marxism, on the other hand, for all its history of Eurocentrist handicaps, has a better claim than postcolonialism to carry a non-European passport, having for generations rooted itself in colonial and neo-colonial societies that never knew they were becoming postcolonial. But all told, the place where Marxism and postcolonialism might actually meet again is not one that either theory needs to travel very far to get to.

VI. Labor and the subaltern

To conclude, I want to propose that this is not the place of representation, nor even, at first, the place of politics, but that of *labor*—a theoretical category left implicit, for the most part, in *The Eighteenth Brumaire* and fundamentally excluded, except in immediate, empirical form, from post-colonial theory. The enormous interest of "political" works such as *The Eighteenth Brumaire* is that in them Marx sought to work out the concrete, even conjunctural implications of a critique of political economy already being formulated in works such as *The Poverty of Philosophy*. Labor in *The Eighteenth Brumaire* is mediated as politics through the category of class. It is the still primitive, under-socialized labor of the *Parzellenbauern* that ultimately determines its failure to become a class "for itself" and hence its reduction to a mere object of politics, of the class will of others. The labor of the proletariat, on the other hand (though here *The Eighteenth Brumaire* is curiously more parenthetical) is socialized labor in its highest form, and hence determines the historical potential of the proletariat to become a politically conscious class—not to "run" society but, come the revolution, to *become* (classless) society itself. Labor in *both* instances is in essence the abstract labor convertible to its value form in commodities, money and capital. But this fact is effectively occluded from consciousness in the case of the *Parzellenbauern* as a result of the illusion of private property ownership created by the mortgaged "smallholding" itself. Unlike the proletariat, the class of *Parzellenbauern* does not confront capital in its direct form as privatized means of production but indirectly in the form of its creditors. This same occlusion of class consciousness is expressed politically as support for Napoleon III.

In contrast to both, finally, the bourgeoisie, as owner or "bearer" of capital, owes its political efficacy as a class to its control of the labor of others. The irony—if not the "farce"—written into this form of "agency" is that, as such control assumes more and more automatic forms through the purely unconscious mechanism of exchange, "politics" itself is reduced to a question of guaranteeing the smooth functioning of this mechanism, making politics as a representational process—as a parliamentary or deliberative mechanism for the public play of competing interests—more and more superfluous. Only the periodic crises of capitalist accumulation and reproduction bring the political back into the foreground—but in ways that now may require the suppression of bourgeois parties and individuals in the "material" interest of the class as a whole.

For *The Eighteenth Brumaire*, however, class mediates between politics and its ultimate basis in the labor process not only on the level of the social totality but on that of the nation-state itself, of the "polis" of "political economy." Class relations are therefore political relations in another sense as well: as the variant relations to state power. "Class struggle" is rooted in labor as the prime, motion-giving factor of production itself, but its outcomes, its political history, take place within a state, or within a shifting, sometimes antagonistic, constellation of states.

But what if conditions became such as to allow for, or even to force the politicization of labor—its acquisition of conscious social agency through its becoming class—to take place simultaneously both inside and outside the state and inter-state arena? What if, to return to the terms of our earlier discussion of class consciousness in *The Eighteenth Brumaire* and "Can the Subaltern Speak?," it now becomes necessary to plot the immediately historical dialectic from the "in itself" to the "in and for itself" simultaneously on both sides of an "international division of labor"? The mediating role of class then becomes much more difficult to theorize, since the process through which class as structurally determined by labor and production *becomes* the class that possesses political, even revolutionary agency can no longer simply presuppose a given state power or national polity as the *agendum*, the object to be acted upon.

Marx does not ask this question in *The Eighteenth Brumaire*, for the good reason that, in the mid-nineteenth century, the globalized market and its international division of labor remained "a secondary sphere subordinated to national economics and enclosed by the latter's military and political forms of self-affirmation."[27] The transformation of the world market into the "immediate, functional space of economic subjects" and the dissolution of national economics by a "total system of commodity production"[28] is a possibility allowed for theoretically in the Marxism of *Capital* but only actualized—though this is obviously a controversial point for Marxists and non-Marxists alike—in the last two generations or so. From the perspective of "globalization," the need to re-think class and even labor itself in its political mediations and forms requires us to re-think as well the dialectical order of determinations in which labor's accession to self-consciousness, to the condition of a class-being for itself, grows negatively but *directly* out of its abstraction/commodification as "labor power."

This dialectic too foregrounds the "political" criticism and theory of *The Eighteenth Brumaire*. The stripping away from the laboring subject of every last human attribute, leaving only an abstractly quantifiable object subordinated to the mass of dead labor that is capital is not only conceived as the impending, universal "negation of the negation" in which the now totalized object that is labor exercises its prerogative to become a total subject. For *The Eighteenth Brumaire* it is an impending *political* outcome as well, a "post" -bourgeois revolution. Not just the self-reproductive power of capital as a universal social relation but the class rule of the bourgeoisie, as embodied in a state or system of states, reads its historical epitaph in the social self-consciousness bound to grow out of labor's ever more total reification.

The contemporary history of "really existing globalization," however, presents us with a new reality in which the commodification of labor in much of the "postcolonial" world is nearly simultaneous with its becoming unemployable for capital. If Kurz and others are right, and the continued accumulation and valorization of capital now rests on levels of labor productivity (and an organic composition of capital) so elevated as to render superfluous—"unexploitable"—the labor power of all but a dwindling number of individual laborers, then what comes into view is a dialectic in which labor bursts through its abstract form as labor power only to become, so to speak, a subject *alongside* the commodity fetish, not (or not yet) in place of it. The commodification of labor continues to operate as, simultaneously, its socialization, but within the new terms set by a globalized society that also simultaneously de-socializes a constantly increasing number of its members. This is the world inhabited, in Kurz's phrase, by *Geldsubjekten ohne Geld*, of impending *sekundär Barbarei*,[29] a world envisioned by the *Manifesto* as a scarcely thinkable "common ruin of the contending classes."

In this light, *The Eighteenth Brumaire*'s beckoning towards a social transformation "beyond" representation takes on a meaning as unsuspected, say, in Lenin's reading of it as in Spivak's. The "content" transcending the "phrase" reads off not just as the class interest of labor but as *labor itself*—a labor that may now be ceasing to count as labor in its commodity form.

How, then, does a labor both "globalized" and, as part of the same movement, conscious of itself only as a "thing" but *without* value, as outside a society that was to have given way to labor's own social dialectic, mediate itself as a politics? This, I suggest, is the question that now defines a space in which Marxism and postcolonialism might discover a set of common, or even just commensurable insights.

One of these might, after all, be the insight into the "subaltern" as a social and political subject unrepresentable (or "ungovernable") within accepted notions of politics. But "representation" would have to be rethought here as governed not by the logic of "textuality" but by that of the labor theory of value itself in order for the idea of the subaltern to take on any real theoretical substance.[30] As *Geldsubjekt ohne Geld*, the subaltern points to a historical limit intrinsic to the commodification/valorization of labor, a limit that postcolonialism was sometimes quick to glimpse, but which it glimpsed only, and if at all, in the mystified form of a "deconstructive case." Postcolonialism will, in the end, have nothing to say to Marxism, nor Marxism to it, until the debt to the "French ideology," to the legacy of "secular poststructuralism" is cancelled in full. No doubt Marxism has accounts to be settled as well, among these the loan of a secularized Protestant work ethic that, in Kurz's view, marked the ideological limits of a "Marxism of modernization" that the fall of Soviet socialism and the current global crisis of over-accumulation with its resulting devalorization of labor perhaps only now exposes fully. Whether the agency for revolutionary change under present conditions must still be sought at globalism's "weakest," now subalternized "links"; whether, in fact, the encroachments of "secondary barbarism" and the trend to pathological forms of rebellion such as religious fundamentalisms and ethnic particularisms (for these, too, are historical forms of the "subaltern") make all remaining hopes for emancipation from the margins baseless; whether, in the end, the very political form of revolution must now be entirely re-thought: these are all questions neither camp can evade if society is "to create for itself the revolutionary point of departure."

Roberto Schwarz: A Quiet (Brazilian) Revolution in Critical Theory

During July and August of 1995 I taught as a visiting professor at the University of São Paulo. The official subject of my course was "a teoria literaria e o 'postcolonial,'" under which rubric I had included readings not only by the "usual suspects" (Said, Jameson, Spivak, Bhabha, Fanon, Ngugi, *et al.*) but by a number of Latin American critics and theorists as well. I had never really doubted that my students at USP would be at least generally familiar with Said and Jameson, and I was certainly confirmed in this from the very first class. Even Bhabha was already widely known and cited by many of them, particularly those who were doing graduate work in English or Comparative Literature. What I was not prepared for, however, was the general lack of familiarity—thinly disguising, perhaps, something even more perplexing: a lack of concern—with the works of, for example, Mariátegui, Fernández Retamar, or Monsiváis. Part of this had to do, of course, with the considerable cultural and literary barriers that still separate Brazil from the rest of Spanish-speaking Latin America. All my Brazilian students certainly had profound involvement with their own national intellectual and literary-critical traditions, above all that of Antonio Candido, whom they regarded—no doubt, correctly—as the unquestioned founder of modern Brazilian literary studies. But to know Bhabha and not, say, Ángel Rama? This was a mild shock for me, and it complicated my already ironic position as a white, North American, male purveyor of "postcolonial theory" to Brazil even more so as I was now also converted into the inadvertent—and underqualified—ambassador of Peruvian, Cuban, Uruguayan and Mexican critical theorists as well. The lesson implicit in all of this, however, gradually became clear: the walls dividing Brazil from the rest of Latin America were the same as those dividing it, say, from India or China. They were not insuperable; they had a gate. And that gate was both single and universal: it was the Euro-North American metropolis. Bhabha had passed through it, and therefore was an acknowledged figure. Rama, the most prominent literary theorist and critic from Brazil's neighboring country, Uruguay, had not passed through it—or at least, had not, having entered the metropolis through it, passed out of it again—and was therefore a relative unknown. The "post" in "postcolonial," already subject to multiple and indefinitely limiting qualifiers, had suddenly become even more tenuous and ephemeral.

My experience in São Paulo nicely dramatizes, I think, the peculiar ambiguities that accompany any legitimate effort to promote greater intellectual intercourse and "dialogue" between the two Americas. For not only is there the chronic and familiar danger that Latin Americanism in the North and in Latin America itself may tend to become two separate entities, the former simply draining off the resources of the latter. There is likewise the problem that, even within Latin America itself, the familiar, still effectively neo-colonial structures of intellectual distribution and consumption tend to persist. As Latin Americanism becomes more and more of a "growth industry" in the North[1]—and as it finds itself getting absorbed into new "theoretical" waves such as postcolonialism—those who seek a genuine North/South dialogue must (to borrow Doris Sommer's *mot*) "proceed with caution."[2] By this I mean: one must avoid *not only* the flagrant intellectual opportunism and "cultural imperialism" of simply re-packaging the South for the ever-shifting intellectual consumer demands of the North, "theoretical" and otherwise; one must *also* avoid the less obviously false assumption that the South itself does not already participate, under its own steam, in this process.

The path towards real dialogue has to be sought in a careful and nuanced understanding of what—in a rigorously material sense—the real North/South relation is, and what patterns of intellectual traffic it makes both desirable and necessary. Much about this relation has changed in the wake of expanded and accelerated "globalization," but the fundamental economic and political inequality it entails, and that used to go by the name of "dependency," has only grown more complex and disguised, not less essential. It is an error to equate the surface trend toward greater integration with any sort of structural revolution. There is, for instance, much excitement and interest generated by the new, "hybrid" and "border" cultures within which, in effect, North and South begin to lose what were assumed to be their distinct contours.[3] The continuously self-displacing location of the "border" has, up to a point, become a new species of master metaphor or paradigm for Latin Americanism. But, salutary as this is in respect to older, "essentializing" paradigms of straight-faced Eurocentrism or cultural-nationalism, even the de-centering "border" perspective risks keeping the northern academy complacent in its imperial provincialism, distracting it from the possibility that the South, while not the locus of the absolutely subverting and authenticating "otherness" once attributed to it by an erstwhile "third worldism," might nevertheless be just as likely an incubator of critical-theoretical breakthroughs as the North. For, just as "globalization" does not automatically lead to the breaking down of all cultural and intellectual "trade" barriers and disparities (as my experience in São Paulo showed), neither does it necessarily equalize or de-center the particularities of national or regional intellectual cultures that go into producing "world-historical" ideas. A genuine dialogue with the South might, that is, have to start by re-authorizing the South not only to speak to us of itself but to speak to the North about *theory*—i.e. about *ourselves* as well—in *the very process* of speaking of itself.

It is this possibility that I want to explore in more detail by discussing the recent work of the Brazilian critic Roberto Schwarz, work in all respects central to my own. Although some of his most important work is now available in English,[4] Schwarz may not be the first name on the lips of northern Latin-Americanists and postcolonialists when queried about important Latin American critics. Even my students at USP, although they had all heard of Schwarz and had even read him on occasion, were surprised at my claims for his significance and thought of him mainly as an important Machado scholar and disciple of Candido. (He is, in fact, both of these as well.) But Schwarz's critical approach to problems of Brazilian culture and society have, in my view, profound if still relatively unexplored implications for Latin Americanism as a whole, and perhaps no less so for a theory of "postcolonial" culture and society. Indeed, as the title of my essay suggests, I think the careful extrapolation of Schwarz's core theoretical insights—that of "misplaced idea," for example—to other, not necessarily Brazilian contexts promises to lead us straight into certain of the most fundamental questions of critical theory as such, in particular that of the possibly changed structure of mediation linking the socio-historical totality to its political and cultural levels. This is not to argue that Schwarz can or should simply be lifted out of Brazil and installed as still another contemporary oracle of "Theory." In fact, it is just Schwarz's modest and scrupulous insistence on working out of and through the concrete Brazilian conditions that are his given intellectual and political circumstance, his ability to resist the urge to a jejune and abstract globalism, that—not so paradoxically, really—give to his critical departures their broader, global implications.

Schwarz, of course, belongs to a critical tradition that, as much as any other, makes good to transcend the barriers and disparities of a neo-colonialized intellectual culture. This is the tradition of Marxism. (The son of Austrian-born, left-wing Jewish refugees from the *Anschluss*, Schwarz might claim nearly as direct a descent from a Central European school of dialectical critique that includes Lukács, Adorno and the Frankfurt School as from Brazil or Latin America.) Until recently at least, no one would consider this as in any way an anomaly for a Latin American intellectual, Marxism, in one of its modes at least, being as commonsensically *Latin* American as it is stereotypically *un*(North)American. But Schwarz is also atypical in this context as well. I do not know how he would respond personally to the insinuation here, but, reading him, I am reminded of Lukács's well-known and still controversial claim in *History and Class Consciousness* to the effect that, even if all of Marx's historical and political theses were shown to be mistaken, it would be possible for a Marxist to concede such mistakes *without* conceding an orthodoxy that, as Lukács unequivocally states, "refers exclusively to method."[5] It strikes me that in Schwarz's contributions to a social and cultural theory of the (neo-/post-) colonial condition we find a set of ideas as challenging and disturbing to the dogmas of a Marxist "orthodoxy" of "theses"—dogmas no less familiar in Latin America than anywhere else—as they are rigorously orthodox to the dialectical method of Marx.

I cannot make a systematic case for these assertions here. But I think a more concrete insight into Schwarz's "quiet revolution" can be obtained by a brief, contrastive pair of citations, followed by some moderate comment-ary. Let me try to demonstrate:

Writing in *Outside in the Teaching Machine*, Gayatri Spivak responds to Benita Parry's criticisms of her positions as follows:

> Whatever the identitarian ethnicist claims of native or fundamental origin (implicit, for example, in Parry's exhortation to hear the voice of the native), the political claims that are most urgent in decolonized space are tacitly recognized as coded within the legacy of imperialism: nationhood, constitu-tionality, citizenship, democracy, even culturalism. Within the historical frame of exploration, colonization, decolonization—what is being reclaimed is a series of regulative political concepts, the *supposedly* authoritative narra-tive the production of which was written elsewhere, in the social formations of Western Europe. They are being reclaimed, indeed claimed, as concept-metaphors for which no historically adequate referent may be advanced from postcolonial space, yet that does not make the claims less important. A concept-metaphor without an adequate referent is a catachresis. These claims for founding catachreses also make postcoloniality a deconstructive case.[6]

In his recent article, "A Seminar on Marx," Schwarz, commenting here on the fundamental theoretical departure achieved in F.H. Cardoso's 1962 monograph, *Capitalismo e escravidão no Brasil meridional*, but in an indirect characterization of his own work as well, writes in what seems a remarkably similar vein:

> The most innovative implication, though, concerns the application of Euro-pean social categories (not excluding the Marxist ones) to Brazil and to the other former colonies, a procedure that induces error but is at the same time indispensable. Let us set aside criticism of the rote following of formulas, a just criticism but valid in the Old World as well as here. Our difficulty is more specific: in the countries that have emerged from colonization, the system of

historical categories shaped by European experience comes to function in a space with a *different but not an alien* ("diverso mas não alheio") sociological conjunction in which those categories neither apply properly nor can help but be applied; better, they circulate in counterfeit but are an obligatory reference and even tend toward a certain formalism. This space is *different* because colonization did not create societies similar to that of the mother country, nor did the subsequent international division of labor make them equal. But it is a space *of the same order*, for it too is controlled by the embracing dynamic of capital, whose developments give it a standard and define its guidelines. From a distance, the partial operativeness of European coordinates—a disconcerting, sui generis configuration, which requires the observer's differentiating astuteness—is a tangible effect of the modern world's tendencies, or of capitalism's uneven and combined developmente . . .[7]

"Concept metaphor for which no historically adequate referent can be advanced from postcolonial space"; "a space . . . in which those categories ['shaped by European experience'] neither apply properly nor can help but be applied." There seems no question that both Spivak and Schwarz are, at the outset, describing the same "space," the same, seemingly insoluble, historico-epistemological puzzle here. And Spivak's formal, discursively oriented term for this puzzle—"catachresis"—might serve both attempts to theorize it as a useful shorthand. Is not "catachresis" a reasonable alternate locution for "misplaced idea," i.e. in Schwarz's own (translated) words, "the dissonance between representations and what, upon consideration, we know to be their content"?[8] I emphasize this formal, abstract point of convergence between the deconstructionist Spivak and the Marxist Schwarz (an opposition that, of course, Spivak herself would not allow as final) as a way of stressing that those who, like myself, argue against the poststructuralist variant of postcolonial theory on historical-materialist grounds, must grant that, despite the mystification, some partial truth *is* run up against in theories of "catachresis," "hybridity," etc. There is a genuine problem to be grappled with here, and it will do no good simply to cast off as specious jargon something that earlier versions of third world cultural nationalism, often with a false consciousness and jargon of their own, tended to treat as a simple matter of "returning to the source." Aijaz Ahmad justly singles out this same passage from *Outside in the Teaching Machine* as evidence that Spivak unwittingly converges on the right-wing cultural nationalism of Hindu fundamentalists (who also insist that no "historically adequate referent" can be had in India for such "western" things as democracy and constitutionality).[9] But he thereby risks conveying a tacit belief that the exposure of the poststructuralist mystification obviates the need for a historical-materialist understanding of "catachresis."

It is precisely this latter understanding that Schwarz, more than anyone working today I think, has substantially clarified in essays such as "Misplaced

Ideas," "Nationalism by Elimination" and in the as yet untranslated work
appearing in the 1999 volume of essays, *Seqüências brasileiras*. [10] The central
insight running throughout is, rather than to think out the puzzle of
catachresis as ultimately resolvable on its own terms, to "stand" it instead
back on its "feet" and thus to grasp it as that precise form of "inverted
consciousness" corresponding to a concrete *mode of socio-economic being*—
"Brazil," for Schwarz—that *itself* constitutes the radical "difference" of the
"postcolonial space." The problem of catachresis—of imitation, of "misplaced ideas"—is a *false* one, and yet its very falsity obeys a social and
historical *necessity*.[11] The *solution* to such a necessarily false problem cannot
be to solve it on its own (false) terms; but nor can it be to reject the problem
out of hand, as if it were merely the result of a chance mistake or a lapse of
consciousness. The "return to the source" as a search for origins leads, as in
the peeling away of the skins of an onion, to nothing. But "one cannot
solve the problem by going to the opposite extreme. Philosophical
objections to the concept of orginality tend to regard as non-existent a real
problem, that it is absurd to dismiss."[12]

Schwarz, that is, simply brings the Marxian theory and critique of
ideology to bear on the catachrestic puzzle. But note that this conceptual
move, obvious as it may at first seem, requires that we think not just the
"idea" in its positive content but *also and equally* its accompanying effect of
"misplaced-ness" as ideological reflexes. The seemingly self-evident truths
of a nineteenth-century European liberalism—e.g. the right of the
individual to be judged on his or her own "merits" —become, in the setting
of a slavocratic Brazil, "ideologies to the second degree," "necessary illusions" no longer (as in "first degree" ideology, per Schwarz's wonderfully
succinct definition) "well grounded in appearances," but still grounded,
nonetheless, in the social, economic being of a ruling class so conditioned
by the extreme "social duality" of "its" national formation that it cannot
generate "ruling ideas" of its own.[13] "Favor" not "merit" decides the fate of
the individual, but if it were to acknowledge and defend this reality openly
and directly, the official, ruling consciousness would already be undermining its own exceedingly narrow basis for self-legitimation. It is because
of this, reasons Schwarz, that the "misplaced idea" much more readily lends
itself to its social, emancipatory critique: "widely felt to be a defect . . . this
system of displacement certainly did debase ideological life and diminished
the chances for genuine thought. However, it made for a scepticism in
matters of ideology which could be both thorough and effortless."[14]

But, in order to raise this critique itself to the highest level of theoretical
consciousness, one must carefully avoid falling back into the more
Eurocentrically Marxist procedure of representing the "ruling ideas" as if
the self-transparency and, so to speak, nation-centeredness of their
enveloping social space were automatically assured. The very social, class
space in which the ideological mechanism functions must never cease to be

thought of in its simultaneous condition of provisional self-integration *and* extrovertedness—"*diverso mas não alheio.*" That is, one must think critically by means of the already developed Marxian categories, but at the same time think *against* their own tendency to "catachresis" or "misplaced-ness" by working a social and economic reality never systematically addressed by Marx *back* into the categories themselves. For, if, as Marx writes, the categories of social and political-economic theory are themselves "but forms of being, conditions of existence" raised to the level of consciousness, then so too raised to consciousness must be the differential gap—social and historical, i.e. "material" in nature—that appears, on the superficial plane of ideology, merely to "misplace" them in relation to a "Brazilian" or "postcolonial" material being. It is in this way that I understand Schwarz when, commenting again on Cardoso's *Capitalismo e escravidão*, he notes that the "rather macabre dislocation" between concepts of productivity and capitalist economic rationality and the reality of the nineteenth-century Brazilian slave economy neither "disqualifies" these concepts nor is itself "insignificant." "Quite the contrary: then as now, discrepancies [the original Portuguese here is "*inadequações*" or "inadequations"] of this sort opened our eyes to the dark but decisive side of contemporary history, to its global side of unintended consequences that developed behind the backs of the principal parties."[15]

Returning to Spivak, I think it must be evident by now that in posing the question of postcoloniality in the terms of a relation of catachresis she rightly seeks to avoid the relapse into the nativist position apparently prescribed by Parry. But she does so only so as to take up an uncritical stance herself with respect to the *social and historical conditions* underlying catachresis as "ideology to the second degree." The abrupt assertion that postcoloniality, because it must always start out from the place of its own "founding catachreses," is therefore a "deconstructive case" marks, in fact, the precise place of Spivak's own—and much contemporary postcolonial theory's—failure to consider the postcolonial as a "case" for a critical *social* theory. True, there is no illusion here as to the possibility of solving the catachrestic puzzle *qua* puzzle, whether through a neo-third-worldist cultural essentialism or a surrender to Eurocentric "universals." And Spivak does not deny that claims for "democracy," etc. must still continue to be made from "postcolonial space," despite the absence of "historically adequate referents"—although just why this should be so is not explained. The uncritical turn here is not, to repeat, the pointing out of a historical inadequation of concepts, but the stubbornly and rather conventionally literary-formalist failure to attribute this inadequation to historical and social factors themselves, as if its explanation could only be sought in the abstract, formal content of the concepts or "concept-metaphors," or in their discursively structured field. Once this failure is in place, the turn to a supposed "politics" of deconstruction, in which, for example, the postcolonial plots to subvert Western imperialism itself by revealing the catachreses lying at its own foundations, or by exposing the West's transcendental need for a "subaltern" or "hybrid" other, etc., etc., strikes me as practically a matter of indifference. Once again we find ourselves on the fantasmagorical terrain of Bhabha's "ambivalence."[16] One might just as well believe in the propensity for imperialism to deconstruct itself.

It seems to me painfully typical of our present political and intellectual moment that the most theoretically impoverished aspects of "postcolonial studies" should now be aggressively exported from the metropolis to regions such as Latin America, while the genuinely thoughtful and rigorously theoretical work of a Roberto Schwarz still languishes in relative neglect outside of Brazil. Here, as I have already stressed, we see a certain colonialism still at work, not to mention a universal and unabated hostility to Marxist thought. Indeed, even Marxists sometimes have to learn to turn their faces to the South. Inducting Schwarz into the vanguard corps of metropolitan "Theory," however, while it would surely have many beneficial side effects, would ultimately be self-defeating. And in any case, it is not a likely scenario. The still predominantly poststructuralist literary-academic ambience that quickly finds a niche for a Néstor García Canclini or a Nelly Richard will find little to tempt it in works such as "Misplaced Ideas." Rather, it will have to be the northerner's job, Latin-Americanists and otherwise, to extrapolate and disseminate. What we need, to be precise, is not just to reproduce the theoretical space cleared by the work of Roberto Schwarz but to reproduce, for purposes of our own, local intellectual and cultural politics, the United States, say, as the conceptual equivalent of Schwarz's "Brazil." "Brazil," that is, neither as globalized simulacrum nor as endless catachresis, but as the space, "*diverso mas não alheio*," of our own millennial version of the mediated, concrete universal.

6

The "Hybrid" Fallacy, or, Culture and the Question of Historical Necessity

"Troubled by the spectres of an undefinable entity, "Mexicanness," the dominant classes renounce what is *sui generis* to demand the colonial right to hybridity."[1]

I. Borges's Ellipsis

In "The Argentine Writer and Tradition," one of his most celebrated essays, Borges questions the traditional view (as held, for example, by Leopoldo Lugones and Ricardo Rojas) that the only authentically Argentine literary tradition resides in the literature of the gauchesque, and that its classic text is this genre's best-known work, José Hernández's *Martín Fierro*.[2] While not denying the literary virtues of this particular tradition or the brilliance of *Martín Fierro*, Borges demonstrates with merciless logical clarity that to write, as did for example the poet Enrique Banchs, of nightingales (a species not found in Argentina) can be as much an expression of an Argentine national experience as to write of gauchos. Perhaps even more so, since, according to Borges, there is nothing *more* Argentine than to express oneself in what appears to be a "foreign" culture or idiom. The gaucho singer-poets or *payadores* themselves, after all, preferred the "universal" themes of love, death, the stars, etc. to the "local color" of the learned epics by gauchesque authors such as Ascasubi, Estanislao del Campo, Bartolomé Hidalgo and Hernández himself. As Borges (citing Edward Gibbon) reminds us, Mohammed himself saw no need to speak of camels in the *Q'uran* in order to prove its Arabic identity—and, according to Gibbon, not a single camel appears.

In the end, Borges affirms the idea of national tradition, but reserves the right—and perhaps even the special privilege—of Argentine writers to eschew the cult of local color and write of anything they choose. He even goes so far as to suggest that, like the Jewish and Irish intellectuals who found ways to convert their own marginalized—in effect, colonized—social status into a platform from which to write without paying homage to the dominant culture's official truths and heroes, Argentines might be in a position to do something similar for all of Western culture and civilization. Here Borges no doubt has himself particularly in mind.

But implicit in "The Argentine Writer and Tradition," even if Borges himself does not state it openly, is an idea that in recent years has come to characterize an entire current of literary and cultural theory under rubrics such as "postcolonial," "postnational," "hybridity," etc. This is that the so-called "essence" of a national culture purportedly expressed in a national literary tradition (e.g. the gauchesque) represents in fact a species of cherished, or "foundational" fiction, an "imagined community," etc. The nation, far from being the pre-existing, essential content of the narratives making up a tradition, is itself nothing but a narrative, a fiction, produced by, among others, these very fictional narratives themselves.

"The Argentine Writer and Tradition" argues with a wonderful clarity uncharacteristic of much present day "theory" what might more generally be referred to as the *fallacy of essentialism*, that is, the false idea that the nation or its "tradition," etc. is a fixed, free-standing and pre-existing content or "essence" —and that as such an essence, the nation bears a mechanical, transparently symbolic or allegorical relation to its literary or cultural forms of expression.

But Borges neglects a fundamental question here: granting that the gaucho as national icon, say, or the heroic figure of Martín Fierro himself are, on one level, sheer literary inventions, having, in principle, no more to do with the real lives of Argentines than nightingales, *what explains the evident ability of this particular literary invention*—and *not* nightingales, or, say, the upper-class, patrician heroes of José Mármol or Esteban Echeverría—*to function as a national symbol*? Or, in more general terms, why, if they are, in the end, purely arbitrary, do certain narratives, certain cultural forms, etc. serve to "found" or underwrite nationalist ideology while others do not?[3]

Once posed in this form, the theory of "nation as narration" is disclosed as a question of more than the purely speculative, metaphysical interest given it by Borges. It becomes a question of history, indeed, of the *historical determination* or *necessity* of cultural, narrative or symbolic forms of social experience and consciousness.

So, for example, one might argue that, its starkly allegorical dimension notwithstanding, *Martín Fierro* typifies a concrete, historical experience that takes in not only the gauchos themselves (if it in fact does so at all) but rural Argentine landowners, middle class intellectuals and even urban, immigrant proletarians who have never seen the pampas or ridden a horse. That is, the relation of *Martín Fierro* as narrative form to the underlying, *historical* experience of a particular "national" formation is not the trans- parent relation of a symbolic vessel to a pre-existing "essence," but *neither* is it the purely and abstractly contingent relation in which a narrative or fiction simply "invents" its own object. It is a relation, rather, into which, by a series of what are no doubt extraordinarily complex mediations, there enters an element of historical necessity.

From a more philosophical standpoint, the neglected category in Borges's metaphysical and speculative mode of reasoning shows itself to be the dialectical category of the *concrete universal*. In counterposing the cult of mere "local color" to the universal truths of world literature, Borges, for whom consciously dialectical thought appears to have been nothing short of allergenic, blithely cancels out the notion that the universal itself might assume "local," concrete forms. By "concrete" I refer here to the local or the particular in its own historical determinateness, universality and necessity, and more explicitly to the concept of the "nation" as itself such a determinate, historically necessary, universal form of social life and experience.

From this perspective, we can perceive in turn that the *fallacy of essentialism* is in fact merely replicated, not truly superseded, in much postcolonial theory, becoming what we might term a *fallacy of textuality*. In this instance the myth of an ahistorical, pre-existing national essence is simply replaced by the myth of a subject who "narrates" or "imagines," from a locus of evidently absolute, ahistorical contingency, the "nation" as "social text." The myth of the nation as "essence" is merely transposed into the myth of the nation as "essence"-constituting, narrative subject. A cultural "hybridity" takes the place of—to use Néstor García Canclini's terms—culture as national "patrimony."[4] But the logic that treats culture as, in principle, severed from all historical determinacy remains as firmly anchored as before.

II. Towards a Historical-Materialist Theory of Culture?

"Correcting" for "Borges's ellipsis" thus requires, to follow the above line of reasoning, that we pose the question of the nation and of national culture outside the terms of the essentialist/textualist fallacy, or—to use the term popularized by Lukács's *History and Class Consciousness*—outside the "antinomy" that frames the question as such.[5] This in turn would require that we grasp such an antinomy as *itself* the product of historical forces. But the question of the necessity of culture, of its historical determinateness, cannot be further explored, in my view, without a radical, even a somewhat ruthless interrogation of the category of "culture" itself. This is not the occasion to embark on such a questioning in any systematic manner, but the following remarks may at least help to foreground more local questions of cultural "hybridity."

As noted in chapter 3, it has become something of a commonplace to assert that history is entering a "post-national" age, and that nations and fixed national identities are being rendered obsolete. Contemporary events certainly suggest that there is some truth to this. The error is to suppose that with the possible historical crisis of the nation as a cultural form, the question of *culture as historically determinate*, as a historically possible and necessary form of emancipatory practice—that question that has rendered the national question itself so seemingly intractable and mysterious— is likewise superseded.

So as to further illuminate this problem, and thinking back here to chapter 4, consider yet another familiar passage from Marx's *Eighteenth Brumaire of Louis Bonaparte*: "Men make their own history, but not of their own free will; not under circumstances they themselves have chosen but under the given and inherited circumstances with which they are directly confronted."[6] One could argue that the germ of a Marxist understanding of culture is contained here in the phrase "the given and inherited circumstances with which they are directly confronted." It captures the sense in which culture is both the objective outcome, or determination, of history, but also the fact that—at least in the "pre-history" of class society—"men" experience culture not in its objective form as historically determined but as something "directly confronted" and "given." The historical determinacy of culture, if not its very historicity *per se*, is erased in its "experience" as such a "given."

However, in historical periods during which culture as "given" is constantly being undermined and altered—the "constantly revolutionized" world of capitalism described in the *Manifesto* in the famed passage, "All that is solid melts in air . . ."— the more habitualized perception of culture as a natural, fixed aspect of existence in general arguably tends to give way to what appears to be the diametrically opposed perception: "culture" no longer as inert "given" but as absolute contingency, even as a "construct," produced by (un)consciousness in its immediacy as a thinking, imagining, discoursing, narrating, etc. subject.[7]

All of this can be considered, in turn, as bearing on the question of national culture, on the "nation" as cultural form, etc. The historical forces that produce, over epochs and generations, nations and national cultures are effaced in the immediate, subjective consciousness or experience of nationality on the part of "national" subjects. Thus the nation is eternalized, mythologized, etc. But in a historical period such as our own, in which older nation-states themselves collapse, leading to new outbreaks of ethnic and national antagonism, and in which huge "national" populations migrate as labor flows across national borders, the constant overturnings and modifications of what had seemed for generations "given" generate the spontaneous impression of the nation as sheer fiction, as a historical form of culture or identity so mutable and unstable as to appear to be *nothing but* a formal construct, a quasi-absolute contingency of form, subject to perpetual reformulation by the "national" subjects themselves. It is this surface reality or appearance that, one might speculate, reflects itself in the sort of thinking typified by Benedict Anderson's *Imagined Communities* and in the "postcolonial theory" of a Bhabha or the "postmodern" ethnography of García Canclini.

But the crucial point for us here is that in *neither* case is the standpoint of sheer, ahistorical immediacy, of the "given"—the standpoint corresponding to the individual atom of modern bourgeois society—overcome. With specific reference to both cultural-nationalist and "postcolonial" theory, we can again recognize in this antinomy the sterile oscillation between cultural nationalism as a fallacy of *essentialism*, which understands the nation as an isolated, immediate *content*, possessing only a mechanical, transparent relation to its cultural form, to "postcolonialism" as a fallacy of *textualism*, which understands the nation as the mere illusion or "effect" of a content or essence, an illusion generated "always already" by the formal mechanisms of culture's narrative or "performative" codes. The nation remains the object of a thinking entrapped in the oscillation between two forms of "cultural" mythology: culture as empirical, inert "given" (as reified object) and culture as purely contingent, absolutely mutable "effect" of its encodings (as reified subject).

III. Mariátegui's Paradox

But so as to focus more narrowly on "hybridity" in relation to the foregoing, I want to turn for a moment to an earlier—"pre-postcolonial"?—Latin American engagement of the question: the early twentieth-century Peruvian Marxist, Jose Carlos Mariátegui's "Literature on Trial," the essay concluding his well-known *Seven Interpretive Essays on Peruvian Reality*.[8]

Towards the end of "Literature on Trial" one reads the following remark:

> A critic could commit no greater injustice than to condemn indigenist literature for its lack of authochthonous integrity or its use of artificial elements in interpretation and expression. Indigenist literature cannot give us a strictly authentic version of the Indian, for it must idealize and stylize him. Nor can it give us his soul. It is still a *mestizo* literature and as such is called indigenist rather than indigenous. If an indigenous literature finally appears, it will be when the Indians themselves are able to produce it.[9]

The distinction Mariátegui makes here seems simple enough, and it is a refreshing and salutary one in a period of stridently facile claims to ethnically pure standpoints and *loci* of expression. Without denying the fundamental right of an indigenous culture and society to act as its own most privileged interpreter and representative, Mariátegui nevertheless resists the exclusionary grant of aesthetic or cultural legitimacy to such self-representations alone. Non-native (*mestizo*) interpretations or expressions cannot avoid "idealizing" and "stylizing", but this quality of "artifice" can still claim the relative value of a historically necessary prelude to self-representation. The crucial factor here is the indigenist's foregrounding solidarity with the plight of indigenous society, a commitment to its struggle for social liberation. This, as Mariátegui carefully explains in "Literature on Trial", as well as in "The Problem of the Indian," is what distinguishes indigenism from a vulgarly romantic "Indianism", whose outward sympathy for the indigene is, nevertheless, premised on an acceptance of the economic and political structures that condemn the latter to an exploited and subordinate status.

But a closer and more critical examination of Mariátegui's thinking here will uncover something beyond the truism that those who live within or "come from" a particular culture know and can represent it more truthfully than those who observe it from the outside. For in broaching the question of representation *qua* a cultural or ethnic "other," Mariátegui lands himself squarely in a theoretical puzzle of sorts: even as "Literature on Trial" affirms the mediate ("idealizing" and "stylizing") limits of representation in relation to its object—limits that, in any but the most naively romantic conception, would be deemed an inevitable, necessary condition of representation as such—Mariátegui's essay envisions an eventual cancellation of such mediacy once the represented object itself takes up the activity of *self*-representation. Extraterritorial and "artificial" representations of an autochthonous "soul"—"*ánima*," in the original Spanish—merely await and prepare the ground for the moment when the "soul" can assume this task itself. But then the question becomes: what will determine or enable the "soul's" eventual capacity to self-represent if such a capacity is absent? And how has it been ascertained that such a "soul" is not ready *now* to "interpret and express" itself?

Mariátegui's evident vulnerability to such a line of theoretical and ethical questioning, his unhesitating willingness to recruit the "subaltern" into emancipatory projects that only *later*—but how and when?—become *self*-emancipatory, etc., is perhaps already enough to disqualify him, whether for good or for ill, as a "postcolonial" theorist. But as just noted, the move to "essentialize" and at the same time speak "for" (i.e. in place of) an indigenous "other" *itself* takes a paradoxical form in Mariátegui's indigenism inasmuch as it simply appends itself as a kind of prophecy to an already consciously activated theory of representation-as-mediatory with which it is logically at odds. Mariátegui's thinking, that is, *inverts* what one thinks of as the standard progression from a naive, romantic aesthetic of direct and immediate communion (a literature that "gives us" its, or a people's, "soul") to a more sophisticated and reflective aesthetic premised on a formally mediated—and perhaps *itself* "soul"-constituting—process of communication. Here it is the *latter* reality that appears as a necessary but somehow unfortunate *preliminary* to what will ultimately, *per hiatem irrationalem*, become a condition of *pre*-representational "autochthonous integrity." An aesthetic intuition that takes shape under the dialectical aegis of the concrete and the mediational—and that is clearly the outgrowth of Mariátegui's Hegelian (via Croce) and Marxist philosophical formation—

shifts abruptly onto the ground of a neo-romantic, and tendentially avant-garde theory of aesthetic experience as a moment of absolute "profane illumination."[10]

The same apparent paradox—something like the story of a return to a place one has never been to before—in fact surfaces throughout "Literature on Trial," at times even assuming a recognizably "Mariateguian" form of statement. "National literature in Peru, like Peruvian nationality itself," writes Mariátegui, "cannot renounce its Spanish ties."[11] The superb seventeenth-century chronicler of Incan and Spanish imperial feats and lore, the "Inca" Garcilaso de la Vega, is hailed by Mariátegui as "the first Peruvian," but "without ceasing to be Spanish." "Peru" or "Peruvianness" ("*peruanidad*") exists, but only as a formal, abstract postulate whose real content cannot shake off the non- and even anti-"*peruanidad*" (Spain) that lies at its origin. In effect, "Peru" itself can only be understood as a sort of paradox, more specifically as a form lacking its own organic content and which, if it is to compensate for this lack, must find a way to create this organic content out of its own formal, "artificial," inorganic being. (Schematically, "nation" or "N" denotes a relationship in which form, "F", gives rise to content, "C", or, $N = F \rightarrow C$.) In this sense, "Literature on Trial" can be considered as the paradoxical project for the writing of a Peruvian literary history that, properly speaking—i.e. as a *national* literature—does not yet truly exist.

But Mariátegui, even as he disposes of the liberal-romantic myth of "*peruanidad*," finds himself blocked en route to what should be its properly dialectical, viz., more radically historicized alternative. The nation, according to a broadly Hegelian purview, gives concrete form to a content—language, culture, manners and customs, etc.—that historically antecedes it. Form grows—historically— out of content, or, to revert to our schema, $N = C \rightarrow F$. But Peru appears to invert this dialectic, for here history has produced the abstract, rational form of the nation as a result of the nineteenth-century wars of independence without, as yet, having produced the content—"*peruanidad*"—that should have acted as its organic substratum. As in the case of literature, we are thus again confronted with the paradoxical necessity for form to create its own content, as it were, *ex nihilo*, or $N = F \rightarrow C$. Only now it is not only a national literature that must be synthesized by borrowing—or appropriating—the content of another (non-national) culture, but the nation as a whole that must "create" itself. And this in turn implies that the objective, historical "spirit" or *Volksgeist* that, in the Hegelian dialectic, takes on mediate, concrete form as the nation can somehow be *consciously*—i.e. subjectively—directed to this end. The dialectical appeal to history as the medium in which to reconcile the national project with the dictates of reason must find a place *outside history* if the dialectic itself is to achieve fruition. Because the history of Peru itself begins inorganically in an act of colonization, therefore it too—like the literature of indigenism—must set out from the plane of the *inorganic* if it is to become the object of an organic, autochthonous historical unfolding. The nation as the historically concrete must be historically "cemented"— "creating the new Peruvianness, using the Indian as its *historic cement*."[12]

How is this to be accomplished? Mariátegui's answer here, again, is to resort to a process of "idealizing and stylizing", i.e. to a politics of pure artifice or *myth*. "The nation itself," as Mariátegui remarks early on in "Literature on Trial", "is an abstraction, an allegory, a myth that does not correspond to a reality that can be scientifically defined."[13] Mariátegui initially intends this remark as a critique, materialist in spirit, of the nineteenth-century Romantic literary historicism in which, once severed from their dialectical context, the mystificatory tendencies already latent in the category of *Volksgeist* had solidified into an array of positivized national essences, each with its own official "history." As a "postcolonial," he occupies an especially advantageous position from which to detect the Romantic myth of nationhood, since the still very recent colonial begin-nings of Peru render transparent the historical constructed-ness ("allegory," "abstraction") of a "nation" that, for instance, in a Germany or Italy, more readily comes to persuade itself of its pre-historical origins in a Nordic vale of mists or in a Virgilian epic. Here, in fact, Mariátegui effectively anticipates a critical intuition—the "nation as narration"—that has become one of the trademarks of postcolonial theory.

But—and with this Mariátegui's affinities for postcolonialism end—those very same socio-historical conditions that have rendered the allegorical, abstract myth of the nation transparent to the anti-colonial intellectual are, for Mariátegui, conditions that demand an act of faith in the national myth itself. A historical content can, in theory at least, give rise to its own dialectically evolved form through a strictly non-conscious, spontaneous process, inasmuch as such a content—since it is itself a composite of dynamic and self-activating human practices, from material production to language—already possesses an intrinsic source of motion and develop-ment. A consciousness of this process arises, if at all, only after the fact. But the inverse of this—a historical form ("Peru") that can only complete and preserve itself by creating (or borrowing) its own synthetic content—starts from a condition of historical rupture and hypostasis and must therefore act *consciously* to infuse an external source of self-activating content into the pre-existing historical form. And since, in the case of Peru, this source lies in an indigenous, vestigially tribal society marginalized by the abstract, formal institutions of the nation and lacking any spontaneous need or interest in playing the historical role required of it, a way must be found to introduce this consciousness "from without." If, that is, the Indian is to serve as the nation's "historic cement" (or "foundation") then *someone* or *something* must lay the foundation, or position the fragments for "cement-ing." Hence the resort to myth, the form of conscious belief presumably most appropriate to a tribal culture. The "leap of faith" expressed in mythical belief is assigned the task of closing the historical abyss between form and content.

IV. The "Hybrid" Fallacy

Mariátegui's "paradox," then, is that, in trying to think through, in its "postcolonial" context, the question of national culture according to the dialectical category of the concrete universal ($N=C{\rightarrow}F$) he can only arrive at the opposite result: the evident necessity to posit or create a national-cultural content for a pre-existing national-cultural form, the need to "cement" or "found" the "concrete," or, $N=F{\rightarrow}C$.

Perhaps, in fact, this is no paradox at all, but simply the outcome of Mariátegui's own lingering "essentialism," his unwillingness to accept a Peru in which the duality, or heterogeneity of culture(s) would not or could not be resolved in an "autochthonous integrity" on the level of the nation itself. Reading "Literature on Trial" today it is indeed impossible not to be scandalized by Mariátegui's openly racializing denigration of Peru's Blacks and Asians, not to speak of a virtual silence on questions of gender and his failure to foresee the massive internal migration of Peru's indigenous peoples to Lima and other urban settings, where their own, purportedly organic and embryonically national culture would simply become one element of the multi-cultural mixture. Perhaps, after all, Borges was right, and Mariátegui's theoretical difficulties disappear as soon as the "hybridity" of, for example, an Argentine nightingale, or an urbanized indigene—at least in "postcolonial" regions such as Latin America—is accepted as both the preferable, and, in any case, the inevitable condition of culture.

Such, indeed, has become the thinking of many contemporary Latin Americanists, Néstor García Canclini prominent among them. In *Hybrid Cultures*,[14] García Canclini breaks ranks with those "modernizing" theories (e.g. developmentalism, dependency theory) that confront the "multi-temporal heterogeneity of each nation,"[15] the regions's "co-existing, multiple logics of development"[16]—i.e. "hybridity"—as problems to be overcome rather than what is in fact the necessary point of departure for any form of emancipatory theory and practice in Latin America. The phenomenon we have abbreviated as "$F{\rightarrow}C$," while signifying, for Mariátegui, culture's artificiality and colonial stigma, becomes, from García Canclini's "postmodern" standpoint, merely the formula for "hybridity" itself—a formula perhaps more accurately abbreviated as an open-ended "$F{\rightarrow}C{\rightarrow}F{\rightarrow}C{\rightarrow}$. . . .", emphasizing the true unfixity of culture, the fact that its authentic "content" is never anything more than a myth, exploded so soon as one cultural form encounters another, or so soon as such a form crosses the "border" of country and city, North and South, etc.

But even if his affirmative approach to hybridity has the advantage over Mariátegui's indigenism of avoiding the latter's national-cultural "essentialism" and its resulting retreat into a politics of myth, García Canclini merely trades the essentialist fallacy for the textualist. As constitutively—that is, after all, "essentially"—"hybrid," culture may indeed free itself of the national mystique, but only by its reversion to the purely descriptive, formal positivity—e.g. a merely symbolic realm of "meanings" — to which it is reduced in *Hybrid Cultures*. As "hybrid" rather than "autochthonous," Latin American culture purchases a higher degree of empirical plausibility, but at the cost of relinquishing even just the thought of its determinate, necessary relation to history as a process of emancipatory struggles, as *praxis*. García Canclini gets rid of the national myth, but the substitution of hybridity for nationality, or "patrimony," textualizes and thus trivializes culture as the object of a critical theory and practice.

Let me give an example here of what I mean. In chapter 7 of *Hybrid Cultures* ("Hybrid Cultures, Oblique Powers"), García Canclini takes up the question of the changed nature of historical memory in "postmodern" or hybridized cultures. He sees this change as exemplified in the new, popular-cultural reception of public monuments in places such as Mexico City, where the latter frequently are covered with graffiti and printed bills, or serve as the settings for political protests that both contradict but also transform the official or "patrimonial" cultural content of the monuments themselves. *Hybrid Cultures* features various photographs of monument sites in Mexico, two of them showing demonstrations (one composed of parents protesting their children's disappearance, another of feminists protesting in favor of abortion rights) in front of the Hemiciclo Juárez.[17] It is thus, explains García Canclini, that the "iconography of national traditions (Juárez) is used as a resource for struggling against those who, in the name of other traditions (those of Catholicism that condemn abortion), oppose modernity."[18] In just this sense, feminist protests, or graffiti painting or poster-pasting raids on public monuments demonstrate not merely a spirit of mass iconoclasm, but the "hybrid" logic of a (post)modern, urban culture in which the "meaning" of official icons is not only disdained but actively transformed. "Graffiti (like the posters and political events of the oppositions) express popular criticism of the imposed order."[19] This spontaneous impulse to hybridize them, shows, according to García Canclini, that the "monuments" have become "inadequate for expressing how the city moves. Is not the need to politically reinscribe monuments evidence of the distance between a state and a people, or between history and the present?"[20]

The simple answer to this is obviously yes, but what this in turn says to us regarding the relation of popular culture to national symbols is not itself so simple a matter. What *Hybrid Cultures* clearly infers about culture from this popular reinscription is its constant tendency to spill over the boundaries set for it by national institutions such as the state—its tendency to open up and inhabit the "distance" spoken of above.

But this is a limitless, theoretically infinite tendency. Suppose the social demands expressed in the cultural subversions of monuments such as the Hemiciclo Juárez were themselves realized in the form of a new law legalizing abortion, or even in a new, more democratic state. New monuments might then be created, and those who had formerly upheld the national authority of the old ones might then become the cultural subversives, the agents of "hybridity." (This is, in part, what has happened in the contemporary United States, as seen, to cite the most extreme example, in the 1996 bombing of the Federal Office Building in Oklahoma City.) There is, again, nothing false *per se* in the observation of this transgressive or "hybrid" tendency of culture, but the further, implied claim (shared by *Hybrid Cultures* with much of contemporary cultural studies, North and South) that "hybridity" has some intrinsically radical or emancipatory efficacy would require us to concede such an efficacy to a good many of the "oppositional" cultural practices of the neo-conservative and neo-fascist right in Europe and the United States. The point here—dramatized by pushing the idea of hybridity to admittedly near-absurd extremes—is that culture becomes severed from politics if it is conceived in strict, formal opposition to concrete, historically existing, or potential, social formations, among which are still to be included contemporary nation-states. Where the question of culture takes on real theoretical, critical substance is precisely where it becomes truly pertinent to the possibility of *closing* the "distance between state [although not, clearly, in its present form] and people, . . . history and the present." However "hybrid" it has grown in our currently "globalized" lifeworlds, culture must still be predicated on some real or possible social *unity* with an interest either in maintaining or transforming existing conditions. Otherwise, it becomes the emptiest of categories. The graffiti and guerrilla-style street actions that García Canclini points to here can clearly be considered in such a light as cultural practices that may contain within themselves, in an implicit or mediated form, some deeper social content expressing such a (perhaps only future, potential) unity. But the superficial fact of their "hybrid" relationship to the public monuments tells us virtually nothing about this. Again, it merely registers, as "theory," the empirically obvious, leaving unasked the question that Mariátegui at least was at pains to pose—how to think the relation of culture to nation (or even simply "location") in Latin America from a simultaneously historical and socially emancipatory perspective? The resort to concepts of "hybridity," "multi-temporality," "heterogeneity," etc. becomes sophistic unless it can show how these sub-national "temporalities," etc. connect up *necessarily* and *historically* with the question of the *negation* of the existing form of society.

In this context it is instructive to contrast García Canclini's "hybrid" cultural reading of national monuments in Mexico City with Carlos Monsiváis's profoundly historicized critique of the architecture of Tlatelolco and the public structures built for the 1968 Olympics, here in the context of his analysis of the student movement of that year:

> The political apparatus, whose anachronistic flag is summed up in and held aloft by President Gustavo Díaz Ordaz, concedes nothing under pressure . . . . The State is not flexible, and a tragic solution soon becomes inevitable. [. . .] Such inflexibility is expressed in architecture. The buildings in Tlatelolco are an extension of the reason of state: gigantic proportions must exorcise its inferiority complex and prove us to be the equals of any nation. What is expressed in the constructions built for the 1968 Olympic Games, and in the buildings of Tlatelolco? Let me venture a hypothesis: the will of Mexican leaders to elevate themselves over and above the realities of their time, as well as pointing to a psychology and morality (ideology) that are to be translated into massacres and mass imprisonment. Those who have offered to host the Olympics must protect it (if threatened) at all costs. [21]

Like García Canclini, Monsiváis points to the enormous gulf separating the nationalist ideology of public architecture and the actualities of national life on the street level. But for Monsiváis this cultural fissure within national experience is inseparable from the history that has produced it. Indeed, as analyzed in the wake of the events of 1968, the buildings of Tlatelolco are seen to have prophesied, in their specific form of monumentality, the slaughter that would later take place on their thresholds. The "nation" they had symbolized has now been rendered transparent to the other nation—that of the student rebels—that briefly held sway in the open space they enclosed, and whose suppression in 1968, however temporary, is shown by "High Contrast, Still Life" to have determined virtually everything—from politics to culture—that was to ensue in the subsequent generation. I am sure García Canclini would be the last to challenge Monsiváis's conjunctural reading of modern, post-Revolutionary Mexico, but it nevertheless must be noted here how secondary, and finally irrelevant, the idea of "hybridity" is to such a reading.

V. A "Postcolonial" Postscript: Culture and Necessity

But how, then, if "hybridity" affords only a trivial, pseudo-solution, to resolve "Mariátegui's paradox" of $N=F{\rightarrow}C$?

A fully developed response would exceed time and space limitations here, but, to elaborate further on the previous chapter, I would like to point to what I think is the answer by way of a further reference to the work of the Brazilian critic Roberto Schwarz. In his essay "The Importing of the

Novel into Brazil,"[22] Schwarz discusses the effect of a literary disparity—or, if one likes, "hybridity"—in the novels of the nineteenth-century Brazilian author José de Alencar when a "classical" Balzacian plot structure is superimposed on the social world of nineteenth-century, slavocratic Brazil. In novels such as *Senhora*, the "plot cannot become a formal mode of exploring the reality depicted."[23] "For some reason or other . . . the harsh moral dialectic of money is used to describe the gallantries of frivolous young men and women but does not affect the rich landowner, the businesman, the bourgeois mothers, or the poor governesses, whose lives are ordered by the laws of favour, or of brutality pure and simple." [24] According to Schwarz, it is the latter sorts of characters, included by Alencar ostensibly for their "local color," that inadvertently enable something like a real insight into the Brazilian reality of the times.

Schwarz further argues that it is only in the novels of Machado de Assis that the disparity between local reality and Balzacian/metropolitan literary form ceases to be a mere literary defect and becomes, rather, a "constructive principle" of the narrative itself. "[I]n order to produce a truthful novel one needs to use real material. [. . .] With Brazil being a dependent country, there needs to be a synthesis in which the distinguishing features of our inferior position in the emerging imperialist system appear in a regular fashion."[25] Such a synthesis becomes the point of departure for Machado, enabling "the ideological repetition of ideologies" characterizing Alencar to be "interrupted."[26] This, says Schwarz, represents a "complex variant of the so-called dialectic of form and content: our literary material only achieves sufficient density when it takes in, at the level of content, the unsuitability of the European form, without which we cannot be complete."[27]

Thinking again of our abbreviated notation for "Mariátegui's paradox," we might symbolize the Machadian dialectic remarked on by Schwarz as: "[F→C]→F." That is, the seeming paradox or "disparity" in which social forms pre-exist social contents is grasped as *itself* the "autochthonous," form-giving content of the Latin American, neo- or "post"-colonial social formation.

And here, I propose, we discover the solution to the seeming paradox itself. "Hybridity," or "F→C," must *itself* be grasped as a historical and a socio-economic condition *before* its cultural ramifications, its most obvious and superficial aspect, can be evaluated. "Hybridity" as a cultural process is not the problem to be overcome—to think so is Mariátegui's fundamental error. But neither can it be claimed as in any way a socially or politically meaningful, viz. *necessary* factor in the struggle for emancipation. That factor, clearly, is how to overcome the underlying social and economic reality of extreme class duality that generates the surface, cultural effect of "hybridity"—a duality Schwarz elsewhere describes as "forms of inequality so brutal that they lack the minimal reciprocity without which modern society can only appear artificial and 'imported' "[28] (While obviously not the only critic or theorist in Latin America to read the latter's cultural specificities back into its social and economic structure—as the example of Monsiváis has already shown—Schwarz is the first I am aware of to have systematically and rigorously carried over the fundamental insight of Latin American Marxist economics into the dialectical unity of capitalist modernity and "underdevelopment" into literary and cultural critique.)

Overcoming such "forms of inequality" may or may not, in the end, entail the liberation of the "postcolonial" nation *per se*—although it seems a good bet that it *will* entail the capturing and wielding of the state power of existing nations. And we can agree with theories of "hybridity" that by reverting to the old, cultural-nationalist essentialisms this struggle condemns itself to failure. But beyond this formal refusal of the essentialist fallacy, "hybridity" offers no purchase whatsoever on the emancipatory question itself. To cite Schwarz one last time: "the radicalism of an analysis that passes over efficient causes will become . . . delusive."[29]

Part II

Nation and Narration on a North/South Axis: Case Studies for a Regionally and Historically Grounded "Postcolonial" Studies

Cortázar and Postmodernity: New Interpretive Liabilities

I. Revenge of the "Lector Hembra"

"But he had ended up without words, without people, without things, and, potentially, of course, without readers."[1]

To write about Julio Cortázar requires, it seems, that one first re-read him. A commonplace, no doubt, but one that already says a good deal about the intellectual nature of the task itself. In one obvious sense this necessity to re-read is unavoidable, since, barring the appearance of previously unpublished material, the Cortazarian *opus* became a finite one in 1983. But having to re-read, for me at least, is a consequence of *not having read* Cortázar for a considerable length of time. I cannot state this as a fact *per se*, but I would guess that this preparatory need to "dust off" Cortázar is not just my peculiarity, but is shared by students, critics and general readers of Latin American literature at the turn of the century. Left out of this group, perhaps, are those who "specialize" in Cortázar and, of course, those reading him for the first time. But am I wrong in sensing that this latter cohort comprises a steadily dwindling number?

Where, then, to start this re-reading? *Hopscotch*: there could be no hesitation here. Other works—the short stories, in particular—hardly bear excluding, but to re-read Cortázar without re-reading *Hopscotch* would clearly be self-defeating. This is not necessarily because *Hopscotch* is, or is deemed, Cortázar's best or most important work. While this has tended to become the accepted wisdom among critics and literary historians, there is certainly a sizeable minority of Cortázar's readers who might dispute it.[2] But *magnum opus* or not, it was *Hopscotch*—published, now, some three and a half decades ago—that gained Cortázar entry into what is still that most exclusive and exalted of chambers in the modern Latin American literary canon: not just the "boom", but, as it were, its path-breaking and inaugural texts. Although, perhaps, less and less frequently read over the years, *Hopscotch*—along, of course, with *One Hundred Years of Solitude*—has lost nothing of its glamour as an *event* in what is still the dominant "grand récit" of Latin-American literary history. *Hopscotch* has become a literary monument that one may be forgiven for having to re-read, but that must never be omitted when administering the guided tour of canonical points of interest. Indeed—as sometimes has a way of happening in the course of negotiating the canon—the very habit of speaking of *Hopscotch* as a "classic" appears, somehow, to vouchsafe its non-reading.

Having re-read it, I think I know why this is: *Hopscotch* has a profoundly dated quality. It *reads* like the literary equivalent of, say, a rock-and-roll album cover from the same period: the "sixties" are written all over it, but in a way that produces (at least for a reader of my generation) embarrassment rather than nostalgia—much less an illumination. Through page after page of Cortázar's great *succès de scandale* I found it impossible to suppress the sensation that I was in the presence of a relic. The past was not in it; rather, this text *was* the past itself: that irrecoverable, irredeemable past-ness of something that once marched at the vanguard of fashion and taste, but that now, having been rapidly overtaken, forfeits the dignity of what is merely "old"—say, a table or even a radio from the same period. *Hopscotch* has become—to quote the novel itself—"like those objects, those boxes, those utensils that sometimes would turn up in storerooms . . . and whose use no one can explain anymore."[3]

To admit to such a reaction may be considered out of place here and will very possibly anger Cortázar specialists and connoisseurs, who might just as easily counter that this is not at all *their* experience when reading *Hopscotch*. Perhaps I am giving too much importance to my own literary idiosyncracies, but, again without having proof of the fact, I would wager that the impression I have described of extreme datedness—almost of archaism—is more than an accident of personal taste. Indeed, in its own particular way, the experience afforded by *re-reading Hopscotch* now, thirty or more years after its first appearance, may qualify as "postmodern". Without, necessarily, assuming a new literary identity as a postmodern textual or cultural specimen itself, *Hopscotch*, together with Cortazar's *opus* as a whole, becomes a highly discreet, readerly site for the production a species of postmodern *affect*: the unmistakable sensation of coming *after* what was *already* the hyper-modern—or what Roberto Schwarz has described as "that slightly passé air which surrounds the modernist desire to change everything with distance and nostalgia."[4] *Hopscotch* would have to have been, effectively, the last book in order to be read as seriously as it plainly desires us, in all its emphatic self-projection as "écriture," to read it. I would like to understand better why that is, and thus it is with an analysis and exploration of this, as yet, strictly spontaneous and intuitive sense of the postmodern that I propose to begin.

Where, then, to start? It seems to me that this can only be with *Hopscotch*'s particular narrative approach to sexuality and gender—what we might term its gender heroics. Even if the novel were in every other respect free of the more embarrassing marks of its late-modernist pretentiousness, this feature alone, I think, would be sufficient to unmask it as an archaism. I refer, here, not merely to the obvious ways in which it confines its female characters (La Maga and Talita, principally, but including the more peripheral characters of Babs and Gekrepten) within a symbolic narrative of masculine agency and feminine passivity—Cortázar's "bourgeois-romantic vision of women."[5] The fact that Oliveira, despite all his desperate longing for both a present and an absent La Maga, can never conceive her as anything but an objectification of his own mock-heroic soul-searchings, does not, after all, do much to set apart Cortázar's novel from what is, obviously enough, a long-standing literary and cultural-psycho-logical norm. What makes the aggressive masculinism of *Hopscotch* really egregious is not that it tacitly legitimates such a gender(ed) heroics but that it regards itself as being, for this very reason, at the vanguard of philosophical consciousness. "To rape is to explain." "Otherness lasts only as long as a woman lasts." [6] Betokened in charming maxims such as these (and there are many more) is not only a perpetuation of a patronizing and degrading view of women—which Cortázar shared with the general culture —but its conscious, pseudo-philosophical apology. I leave aside as spurious the possible defense of Cortázar here on the grounds that these are only the views of his protagonist Oliveira, and that the author surely meant them to be condemned [7]. Surely *nothing* in the novel is *meant*, in this blatant sense, to be condemned, or to be praised. But one does not have to read Oliveira as a public school role-model to understand that the spontaneous sympathies evoked, as a rule, in all heroic literature will have the effect of granting such a "philosophy" a legitimacy it might not otherwise be able to claim. I think it is bad faith on the reader's (and critic's) part to deny the obvious here: that Oliveira's idea of women is presented to us, his readers, as a reason to take him seriously, even as a reason to find him sexually enhanced. His "tragedy"—if it is one—is not that he regards La Maga, (and, in a wider sense, all women) as his own self-objectifications in the form of the "other," but rather that he must inevitably fail to merge with this object.[8] The full reality of how women are made to live as a result of such gender heroics (or anti-heroics) does not enter into the symbolic universe of *Hopscotch*.

If it did, the novel might be centered instead on the character of La Maga, whom we would then follow on her flight back to Montevideo, or accompany in what might also be her suicide, failed or successful. Speculating on such a would-be "feminist" *Hopscotch* may, in the end, be a pointless exercise, but it is hard, as one re-reads it, not to sense that this sort of narrative unfolding would have made for a much more compelling story. I suggest that there is something about us as readers now, something, perhaps, that subtends our more or less vague identity as "postmoderns," that makes the protagonism of an Oliveira seem increasingly unimportant, not to say irritating. By the same token, the thought of La Maga as heroine kindles a certain sympathetic interest that, as I read it, Cortázar fails to project or to anticipate within the novel. And this failure points to one of the great failings of the novel itself, when read in light of the demands placed on any work of literature by contemporary events themselves: Cortázar, writing in the late 1950s and early 1960s, simply did not perceive the real import or developing energy of the women's movement—arguably one of the most signal of modern "cultural revolutions." Cortázar's "modernity" plainly did not include feminism—which is part of the reason why, reading it now, it seems almost intolerably obsolete.

The second mark of *Hopscotch*'s archaism I want to remark on here is its purportedly non-linear structure, or the "hopscotch" itself. If *Hopscotch*'s sexist gender heroics produce its *ethical* embarrassment for the reader, then it is the gimmick of the hopscotch—of the novel which is really two, or an infinite number, of novels—that seems the most unmistakable signature of its *aesthetic* obsolescence. To be honest, I have forgotten whether in my first encounter with *Hopscotch* in the early 1970s I read "hopscotch" or "lector hembra" fashion—only that it was the excited talk of a novel that could be read in a non-linear order that had originally caught my interest. But in either case, re-reading *Hopscotch* in Cortázar's recommended, non-sequential order now produces (for me, at any rate) only a persistent sense of impatience and irritation. The much anticipated moment of synthesis or illumination simply never arrives. In the early 1970s the sheer will to have such an "experience" was perhaps great enough to overcome, or at least put off this disappointment, but not now, I think. For the hopscotch turns out to be really just a "conventionally" linear experience of plot-reading, broken up by a miscellany of clips and "Morelliana" of widely varying interest but never *formally* anything more than *interruptions*. Perhaps the only saving grace of the hopscotch is that it draws attention away from the schematism and poverty of the linear plot itself—the fact that so remarkably little actually happens in the novel of 56 chapters, much less in the 155-chapter version.[9] Of course, Cortázar—in his bid to produce a *nouveau roman* that would be the envy of his French contemporaries—is in good company here. My guess is that if people read *Hopscotch* little these days, they read the novels of Robbe-Grillet, Butor, Simon, Sollers, etc. even less. (The late Marguerite Duras may be the single important exception, at least insofar as the breathless, pseudo-profundity of the *nouveau roman* still echoes faintly in narratives such as *The Lover*.) But even a casual browse through, say, Robbe-Grillet's *Jealousy* is sufficient to experience what has become, now that the novelty has faded, the utter boredom of the aleatory, non-sequential narrative—the great, arid myth of the *coupage*, or, in the then oncoming structuralist enthusiasm, of the *combinatoire*. One appreci-ates more than ever, from this perspective, the fine poetic sagacity of

Borges, who, exhilarated by essentially the same dream of an infinite and labyrinthine narrative, understood its formal impossibility from the standpoint of the *reader* and chose instead to tell, repeatedly, only the *story* of this dream—and to tell it *briefly* and through carefully crafted, Poe-like plots that could not possibly be *less* aleatory or *more* linear. Cortázar's great blunder was thus, so to speak, not to have tried to imitate Borges, but to have written as though the Borgesian utopia could be consciously enacted.

What, if anything, salvages *Hopscotch* from the wreck of its own formal conception are the sporadic occasions on which it treats this aesthetic ironically. A supreme instance of this is chapter 23, or the Berthe Trépat episode—although one may wonder whether in this case the irony is not unintentional. Recall how Oliveira, in order to get out of the rain—or is it to get out of the pastiche of Sartre's *Nausea* with which the chapter begins?—ducks into the "Salle de la Géographie," where the pianist and composer Berthe Trépat is about to perform a triple-bill consisting of the "*Three Discontinuous Movements* of Rose Bob (première), the *Pavan for General Leclerc* by Alix Alix (first time for a civilian audience) and the *Delibes—Saint-Saëns Synthesis*, by Delibes, Saint-Saëns and Berthe Trépat."[10] This latter piece Trépat has composed—as Valentin, the master of ceremonies and Trépat's elderly, gay house-mate informs the audience—according to the principle of "prophetic syncretism." Cortázar's account of the concert, culminating in the performance of the "Synthesis," and over the course of which the already sparse and rag-tag audience dwindles down to one—Oliveira—is a minor *tour de force* of black comedy. "It was," writes Cortázar, "almost like a chapter out of Céline, and Oliveira felt himself incapable of thinking beyond the general atmosphere, beyond the useless and defeatist survival of such artistic activities among groups of people equally defeated and useless." [11] And the "prophetic syncretism," Cortázar continues, "was not long in revealing its secret": "three measures of *Le Rouet d'Omphale* were followed by four more from *Les Filles de Cadix*, then her left hand offered *Mon coeur s'ouvre à ta voix*, while the right one spasmodically interspersed the theme of the bells from *Lakmé*," etc.[12] There follows the incident for which this chapter is best known, as Oliveira, stricken with an inexplicable surge of affection for the aged, masculinized and grotesquely attired Trépat—a truly Célinesque rapture that will consummate itself erotically with the *clocharde* Emmanuelle at the close of the novel's first part—offers to accompany her home and is physically rebuffed when she takes his solicitations to be sexual. But is not the most striking aspect of this musical interlude the manner in which, for us as "postmodern" readers, it perfectly mimics the experience of reading *Hopscotch*? What better term than "prophetic syncretism" to describe the literary "theory" of Cortázar's novel itself? And has not the reader, ideally constructed by such "prophetic syncretism," become, like Trépat's audience, "defeated and useless"?

Perhaps this is a conscious self-parody on Cortázar's part. I am inclined to doubt this, but then neither, I admit, can it be considered purely fortuitous. For if Berthe Trépat becomes, here, an unexpected comic heroine of the "linear" novel, do we not find in Morelli her counterpart as concerns the "expendable" chapters of *Hopscotch*? It has long been a commonplace of *Hopscotch* interpretation that the character of Morelli serves Cortázar as a mouthpiece for his literary philosophy, especially as it touches on *Hopscotch* itself. But the crucial and perhaps overlooked point here is that, as Morelli's conception, this philosophy is ultimately unable to take itself seriously and becomes, like the "Delibes–Saint-Saëns Synthesis," the object of a certain postmodern laughter.

How so? The Morelli chapters are of three basic sorts: (1) those in which Morelli's metaphysical and literary dicta are presented directly to the reader: these generally bear the heading of "Morelliana" and are not marked as citations; (2) those in which some member of the Serpent Club cites a fragment of Morelli; and (3) chapters in which the members of the club directly propose various readings, intepretations and evaluations of Morelli's "works" (among these, evidently, his "novels", which do not appear in *Hopscotch*—unless, of course, *Hopscotch* is to be read as one of them). This latter set of chapters climaxes in the full-scale *disputatio* of chapter 99, as the disciples meet in Morelli's apartment after his death. (A possible fourth group here is the one chapter—154—in which Oliveira and Etienne visit Morelli himself in the hospital.) Read together, the first two series of chapters present us—in addition to a miscellany of metaphysical speculations that could just as well be Oliveira's—with the theory of a new novel, of which *Hopscotch* is perhaps the prototype. (Chapter 62, of course, is to give us *62: a Model Kit*.) This "new" novel is one in which, simply put, representation itself has been reduced to an absolute minimum, forcing the reader to step into the narrative (as its "one true character," according to Wong's reading of Morelli in chapter 97) but promising him a transcendant experience of pure, unmediated being. Thus, in chapter 79, Morelli writes of a "text that would not clutch the reader, but which would oblige him to become an accomplice ("lector cómplice"). . . ."[13] As against the conventional, or "female" reader ("lector hembra"), the "lector cómplice" "would be able to become a co-participant and co-sufferer of the experience through which the novel is passing, *at the same moment and in the same form. . . .*"[14] And such a novel, Morelli pompously declares, implies "a rejection of literature" itself; its mission is "to take from literature that part which is a living bridge from man to man . . . ."[15]

It is clearly this "lector cómplice"—this reader that, in theory, comes before, or leaps instantaneously beyond all representational mediacy—that must read *Hopscotch* for it to succeed as a novel, or indeed, as a work of art *tout court*. The evident fact that such a reader does not, indeed, cannot exist, given the representational mediacy of all verbal processes—even those that postulate a leap beyond representation—is what often makes reading *Hopscotch*, in practice, so ennervating to the reader. Indeed, as Concha, in what remains the most thoughtful of the Marxist critiques of *Hopscotch*, observes: "nowhere is this theory [of the "lector cómplice"] less valid than in the actual text of [Cortázar's] novel itself."[16] This, however, is not the fundamental point at issue here. Rather, it is to take note of a historical and cultural shift: whereas, ca. 1963, one could still perhaps *desire* to *be* such a reader and therefore take on *Hopscotch*'s aesthetic failures as one's own readerly shortcomings, over the last generation or so this desire has effectively withered away. One no longer wants to read the "last book" —to, as Oliveira demands, "destroy literature". One wants to read, if it can be put this way, *another* book—not the book that was to bring modernism, finally, to its teleological climax of self-negation, but a book—or, indeed, multiple *books*—that high modernism could not have allowed for or imagined. Sometime after *Hopscotch*'s appearance it gradually began to dawn on readers such as myself that modernism had developed a suspicious habit of producing a new "last book" at regular intervals. And as one of the latest of these "last books," *Hopscotch*'s grace period seems fated to have been relatively short. It is now the "lector hembra"—and not the "new novel"—that seems entitled to be demanding "accomplices."

To make matters more complex, however, the alternative or "expend-able" *Hopscotch*, with Morelli as its effective hero, seems almost to anticipate this development. Morelli, after all, unlike Oliveira, must face his actual, flesh and blood readers in the members of the Serpent Club. And for all their strenuously orthodox, almost monastic pledge to become Morelli's reader-accomplices, Oliveira, Gregorovious, Wong, Etienne—not to mention the camp-following La Maga and Babs—show rather telling signs of impatience with this task. Or so, at least, is suggested by a selective re-reading of the chapters (124, 141, 60, 109, 95 and 99) in which the club not only trades citations but engages in outright *disputatio*. In chapter 109, for example, the narrator—unidentified, but who, one senses, speaks for the club as a collective subject—describes Morelli's plan for a narrative analogous to a set of photographic stills, rather than to a film. It is to be left to the "lector cómplice" to set the pictures into motion, thereby "participating, almost, in the destiny of the characters."[17] "The book would have to be something like those sketches proposed by Gestalt psychology, and therefore certain lines would induce the observer to trace imaginatively the ones that would complete the picture."[18] There is a pause, however— marked graphically by an extra space between paragraphs—which is then followed by this evidently less than gratified observation: "Reading this book (for Morelli has, evidently, written this would be narrative) one had the impression for a while that Morelli had hoped that the accumulation of fragments would quickly crystallize into a total reality."[19] "Had hoped"— but, clearly enough, had hoped in vain. And, in any case, such a crystallization, even if it were possible, would only be the image of a "world that was taking on coherence." Thus "there was no cause for confidence," the narrative voice continues, "because coherence meant basically assimilation in space and time, an ordering to the taste of the female reader."[20]

Thus the "lector cómplice"—although he does exactly what is required—will somehow always end up as "lector hembra." And even Morelli himself, as the directly discoursing subject of the "Morelliana," lapses occasionally into similar moments of melancholic self-irony. In chapter 112, for example, Morelli soliloquizes on the "deliberate poverty" of his narratives.[21] Perhaps, after all, it is "preferable to renounce all writing" since there is "no hope of dialogue with the reader."[22] And chapter 94 begins with a dictum that, for all its evident grotesque humor as fictionalized self-deprecation, comes uncomfortably close to describing the fate of *Hopscotch* itself: "A piece of prose can turn rotten like a side of beef."[23]

Not only, that is, does Morelli's reception by his disciples prefigure the "postmodern" reading of *Hopscotch*; the very sequence of affect in which the supreme instant of "prophetic syncretism" is promised, only, in the next moment, to be sheepishly dismissed as whimsical nonsense, assumes concrete, dramatic configuration in the character of Morelli himself. In this way, one might argue, Morelli takes on the rough outlines of what might, or indeed, what *ought* to have been the true, *comic* hero of *Hopscotch*. (The novel aimed at by Morelli, remember, is the *roman comique*.) *This* hero, as against Oliveira, in whom this same quest for a transcendent experience of pure, unmediated being becomes something we, as readers, are urged to take with complete seriousness. But, whereas Morelli's comic enactment of this quest, although banal, achieves a certain degree of artistic integrity, in Oliveira's story it becomes both merely pretentious and unbearably tedious. Held up against Morelli, Oliveira is exposed as the *mock tragic* hero of *Hopscotch*—or at least of the *Hopscotch* that, above all others, Cortázar seems to have meant us to read.

II. Authenticating circumstances

> ". . . the ethical torture of knowing one is tied to a race or to a people . . . "[24]

However, I would like to turn away, now, from *Hopscotch* and pose the question of a "postmodern" Cortázar on a more general, literary-historical plane. For if my intuition is right and Cortázar is less and less read these days, this cannot be solely the fault of one novel. Let me begin, again, by stating things bluntly: the same, generally prevalent standard of literary taste—or "canonicity"—that awards *Hopscotch* honorific status as a "boom" inaugurating text has also gradually affixed to Cortázar the stigma of his seeming *inauthenticity*. Doubts persist as to whether, in fact, Cortázar can be considered a genuinely "Latin American" writer—whether classifying him as "European" or perhaps simply as "cosmopolitan" might not be a better fit. In its crudest form, the case for Cortázar's "inauthenticity" rests on literary geography: Cortázar's decision to live in Paris rather than Buenos Aires. Despite his frequent visits to Latin America (revolutionary Cuba and Nicaragua included), Cortázar's "voluntary exile" is somehow felt to foreground his writing in a way that, for example, the cosmopolitan location of a García Márquez or a Vargas Llosa (both of whom have lived for long periods in Europe) does not. Yet even if this "residency requirement" is waived, questions remain about Cortázar's Latin American "identity" as they do not in the case of practically any other major figure of twentieth-century Latin American literature, Borges included. Why is this?

Part of the answer clearly lies in a more global shift within what we might call the ideology of reading—a shift towards what, *grosso modo* has come to be termed the postmodern and even, in Latin American contexts, the "postcolonial," and which has condemned not only Cortázar but entire generations of authors to relative neglect. As concerns Latin American literature in particular, this shift has coincided with a progressive loss of enthusiasm for the "boom" and in corresponding gains for more heterodox genres, most notably the "testimonial" narrative. Underlying this shift, especially as it pertains to readers in the metropolitan North, is a complex political and cultural realignment: while an earlier ideology of reading, swayed by an upsurge in de-colonizing and anti-imperialist struggles in the 1960s and early 1970s, welcomed the boom in a spirit of what I have elsewhere termed "canonical decolonization", the more recent trend, reflecting a general panorama of imperialist "reflux", has been to question whether this initial utopianism may not have concealed a certain overdetermining drive to re-colonize Latin America (and the third world generally) through a subtle "voicing-over" of the "subaltern." Enter, then, the testimonial, not so much as a "postmodern" genre in its own right (although some have argued for this) but as a kind of cultural marker for Latin America—i.e. as a new "ideology of reading"—within the overall postmodern scene.[25] In fact, this same readerly tendency to escalate the demand for the authentic seems to have operated within the "boom" itself, as the earlier hunt for—so to speak—the Latin American *Ulysses* (with *Hopscotch* as the main contender) shifted its sights onto the texts of "magical realism" (enter *One Hundred Years of Solitude*). Now, of course, even a Rulfo or a Guimarães Rosa may arouse suspicions insofar as they still appear to be speaking *for* the subaltern, while in the case of a Rigoberta Menchú or a Guaman Poma de Ayala true subalternity or alterity is somehow sensed as certified. But in any case the point is that Cortázar has, by this time, long since dropped out of the picture.

Thinking more locally, the key intellectual and literary event to consider here is probably the famous journalistic "debate" between Cortázar and

Arguedas, as rehearsed in the pages of the Cuban literary journal *Casa de las Américas* in 1969. Cortázar, of course, had begun to draw fire from various quarters of the Latin American left soon after publication of *Hopscotch*, often entering the fray himself in defense of his own "revolutionary" credentials. The interchange with Oscar Collazos, later published as *Literatura en la revolución o revolución en la literatura*[26] is perhaps the most frequently cited of these. But my guess is that over the years the bitter dispute with Arguedas—punctuated, of course, by the latter's suicide—has done the most to inaugurate, as concerns Cortázar, the new "ideology of reading" of which I have spoken. A full recapitulation would be impossible here, but the essential facts are these: Cortázar had, in 1967, published a long "open letter" to Roberto Fernández Retamar in *Casa de las Américas* (it later appeared in the second volume of *Último Round* as "Acerca de la situación del intelectual latinoamericano") in which he sought to justify his decision to remain in Europe as necessary for anyone who aspired to the condition of a universal or "planetary" intellectual:

> On the margins of local circumstances, removed from the inevitable dialectical give and take that grows out of the political, economic and social problems of a country and that demands the immediate commitment of every conscious intellectual, one's sense of the human process becomes, so to speak, more planetary, operating through aggregations and syntheses, and if it loses the concentrated force of an immediate context, it gains, on the other hand, a lucidity that is sometimes unbearable but always clarifying.[27]

This prompted an angry response from Arguedas, which first appeared in 1968 in a species of prologue to *El zorro de arriba y el zorro de abajo* known as the "Primer Diario" ("First Journal"). Arguedas complains of

> this Cortázar who goads us with his "geniality", with his solemn convictions that the national essence is better understood from the upper spheres of the supra-national. As if I, raised among the people of don Felipe Maywa and thrust, for some years of my childhood, into the very *oqllo* [breast] of the Indians, only to return to the "supra-Indian" sphere from which I had descended among the quechuas, were to propose myself as a better, more essential interpreter of the spirit of don Felipe than don Felipe himself. What a lack of respect and due consideration! [28]

Arguedas contrasts Cortázar with García Márquez and Guimarães Rosa, who, purportedly like Arguedas himself, had "descended" to the "the very root ["cuajo"] of their people."[29] Cortázar becomes, for Arguedas, the typical "professional writer", as against Arguedas *et al.* (Rulfo is added to the list at his point), who embody, as a positive virtue of course, the writer as "provincial."[30]

Writing in *Life en Español* in April of 1969, Cortázar then retorts by asking Arguedas to consider the case of Vargas Llosa, who, says Cortázar, had "disclosed a Peruvian reality in no way inferior" to that depicted in Arguedas, but had done so from Europe. "As always," Cortázar continues, "the error lies in generalizing a problem whose solutions are exclusively particular: what matters is that . . . 'exiles' cease to be 'exiles' as concerns those who read them, that their books keep, exalt and perfect the most profound contact with their native soil and people."[31] To this, finally, Arguedas replies (in a letter originally published in *Marcha*) that, be this as it may, exile for Cortázar was still not the same as exile for, say, a Vallejo, since in Cortázar's case exile was not only willed but implied a patronizing contempt for "those of us who work *in situ*."[32]

Again, Cortázar is historically the loser in this debate, in that it makes painfully obvious what we would now label his "Eurocentrism." As in the case of feminism, Cortázar here again shows a curious incapacity, despite his "planetary" perch in Paris, to see which way the political-intellectual edge was cutting. Arguedas, on the other hand, clearly anticipates here (as in the text of *El zorro* itself) what was to become a new, postcolonial, "ideology of reading" epitomized in the metropolitan reception of testimonial narrative. And yet, as one re-reads this exchange *post festum*, a number of "postmodern" ironies become apparent. One is that, on philosophical grounds, Cortázar seems the clear winner of the debate here: for even if we assume that a genuine criterion for a Latin American literary "authenticity" exists, this can hardly be reduced to a question of whether the writer writes *in situ*. Even Rigoberta Menchú, after all, gives her testimony in Paris. "What matters is that . . . 'exiles' cease to be "exiles" as concerns those who read them . . . ." Precisely so. And yet, with these very words, Cortázar furnishes the argument for a repudiation of his *own* literary practice—an argument, moreover, to which Arguedas himself remains insensible, oblivious, as he seems to be, to the problem of the reader. For is it not precisely "as concerns those who read" him that Cortázar cannot elude his image as a self-willed and opportunistic "exile"? Writing in "Acerca de la situación del intelectual latinoamericano," Cortázar openly espouses the ideal of a universal standpoint or "mental ubiquity" from which it would, in theory, be possible to "proceed in the gradual discovery of the radical truths of Latin America without losing, for that reason, a global vision of history and of man."[33] "From my country," he writes, "there departed a writer for whom reality, as Mallarmé imagined, ought to culminate in a book; in Paris there was born a writer for whom books ought to culminate in reality."[34] One can only admire such sentiments. But the problem—and perhaps it is here that the Cortazarian tragedy *is* finally enacted—is that *Cortázar*'s books do not, in the final analysis, discover those "radical truths," do not "culminate in reality."

The further irony of this debate over authenticity has to do with what, in the end, its two sides have in common. For, as becomes apparent to anyone who re-reads it now, *both* Cortázar and Arguedas take as given a kind of conceptual or allegorical map in which "Europe" automatically has assigned to it the category of the "universal," while "Latin America" occupies the site of the "particular". Cortázar, it is true, envisions an ideal location from which the "universal" would encompass all possible co-ordinates; and perhaps an analogous urge to synthesis is latent in the Arguedian principle of transculturation. But both initially concur in locating authenticity on the side of the "particular." The only question is *how best to situate oneself in relation to this particular*—whether as "provincial" or as "planetary" intellectual. Thus if Cortázar's thinking remains en-trapped in "Eurocentrism" then Arguedas's, by merely reversing the initial polarity of values, offers no real means of escape here either. Arguedas' defense of the "provincial" restricts itself to the logic of what Samir Amin has termed "inverted Eurocentrism": in repudiating "Europe" one leaves unchallenged its prior conceptual mapping as the "universal." [35]

In this regard it is instructive to recall another of the more polemical left-wing critiques elicited by Cortázar in the late 1960s. I am thinking of David Viñas's *De Sarmiento a Cortázar*. Viñas here locates Cortázar within a tradition of Argentine intellectuals, for whom the inevitable "trip to Europe" is both rationalized and experienced by the subject as a flight from a violent and aggressive "body" (Viñas's precise word is "escisión" or a "schism") and a quest for "espíritu." Cortázar, however, represents a novel complication of this—as Viñas terms it—"master metaphor" ("metáfora mayor")—a "new way of being a writer."[36] that would seem to go beyond that of the mere "escritor profesional". Having once realized the spiritual quest, Cortázar nevertheless senses the continual absence of the "body," of "materia," as a threat to the maintenance of his new, purified writerly self. It becomes necessary to bring this body—which, as Peronism, prompts the original act of flight from violation—into some new relationship of proximity to the writing subject. Cortázar finds this new, spiritually safe and "universalized" body, argues Viñas, in revolutionary Cuba. And yet

> this latching on to Cuba is already sensed as an effort of generosity (under-stood as a recognition of the "others") and as a way of resolving, somewhere else, local impossibilities. For Cortázar, [Cuba becomes] the "purification" of what here [i.e. in Argentina] occurred as something confused and intolerable. Cuba—in essence—was an American situation refined . . . through its Europeanization.[37]

Cuba, that is, can satisfy Cortázar's need for a Latin American "body" —his "universalizing" need for an authenticating "particular" —primarily because of the body—Argentina—that it is not. Viñas does not, it should be stressed, disdain Cortázar's publically pro-Cuban stance as somehow "insincere" because of this. In fact, he discerns, with remarkable insight and critical integrity, a curious parallelism between Cortázar's abstract-universalist "Cuba" and the philosophy of *foquismo* itself: Cortázar is likened to Regis Debray[38] but also—in answer to Cortázar's allusion to "the future Ernesto Guevaras of Latin American literature"—to Che himself:

> Here we have an exemplary case of texts inseparable from their body; a body that at no time lags behind the theory of the revolution being advanced. Or at least, not until Bolivia, because, if anything is to be posed for frank criticism now it is the space that opens up for the first and only time between the final Guevara and a people—as the prolongation of his body—that, alloying itself to him, might have sustained him. It's not easy to write this; but, for now, the niceties are for others: through this space there appears among other things an image of failure and schism ("escisión") a reversion to an individualized omnipotence as all that was finally left of a man who desired himself a socialist but who, in that conjuncture, found himself separated from the body of the masses. [39]

What Cortázar finds so attractive in the *foco*, then—to follow Viñas—is principally the manner in which it seems to replicate, *qua* politics, the vanguard writer's own heroic isolation: his "revolución en la literatura." And so it is that we are left with a Cortázar who, despite adopting all the political opinions demanded of him by his critics on the Latin American left, still cannot quite seem to transmute personal solidarity into literary authenticity.

Yet this is not quite the end of the story, I think. For if the new "ideology of reading" prefigured in Arguedas' defense of the "escritor provincial" has condemned Cortázar to increasing marginality, it nevertheless seems to me that we can find in Cortázar certain vantage points from which to see through, if not beyond, this ideology itself. I have in mind here one of Cortázar's later short stories, "Apocalypse at Solentiname."[40] As the reader will recall, the story recounts, in a quasi-autobiographical mode, a trip taken by Cortázar to Solentiname, the Nicaraguan island community of radical Christians founded by Ernesto Cardenal. While there, the narrator, impressed by their vivid colors and visionary energy, takes a number of photographs of paintings by peasant residents of Solentiname. Later, on his return to Paris, he has the film developed and sits down for a private slide-show, only to discover that the images of the paintings have been mysteriously replaced by photographed scenes of torture and political repression, among them the execution of Roque Dalton. Terrified, the narrator arranges to have his companion, Claudine, see the slides as well; she, however, sees only the paintings. He decides to say nothing to her.

Given its open and clearly somewhat vexed allusions to the authenticity question—"why don't you live in your country?",[41] the narrator is asked on arrival in Costa Rica—it is hard not to read "Apocalypse at Solentiname" as a gesture of self-criticism and rectification. The hero behaves like the stereotypical progressive "cultural" tourist, filled with enthusiasm for popular causes in Latin America, but ultimately driven by the affluent cosmopolite's will to *collect* such causes in the form of its cultural artifacts that, especially when made by peasants, effectively become the *fetishized* tokens of a hypothetical and abstract political commitment. In fact, the hero of "Apocalypse at Solentiname" does not even deign to buy any of the paintings, preferring the cheaper and more efficient method of making photographic copies. (The character of Cardenal laughingly accuses him of being an "art thief" and "image smuggler."[42]) But divine—or supernatural—retribution is not long in coming, as the comfortable apartment back in Paris, in which the collection is to be housed and enjoyed, turns out to be insecure against the "return of the repressed." The "cultural" coach has turned back into the "political" pumpkin.

However, it seems to me possible to go further here and read "Apocalypse at Solentiname" as a parable intended to dramatize not only the foibles of progressive cultural tourism but also the latent ideological distortions of the "provincial" writer-as-committed ethnographer celebrated by Arguedas. Is this writer—Cortázar seems to be asking—any less implicated, finally, in the practice of cultural fetishism than the character of Cortázar himself in "Apocalypse at Solentiname"?

The word "fetish" is necessarily a provocative one, but I think it is the exact concept required to bring into full view the "ideology of reading" under critical examination here. For, to state things abstractly, what but a fetish form of the object can be the result when the desire for its authenticity is overdetermined by the more powerful and "provincial" aversion for the universal or "planetary"? Should not the goal of a "provincial" literature, as Arguedas initially conceives of it in his repudiation of Cortázar, be the "authentic," not as against the universal, but as against the *abstract*: the "authentic," that is, as the *concrete*? But the concrete, as we learn from Marx, "is the concrete because it is the concentration of many determinations, hence of unity in the diverse."[43] The concrete, that is, only becomes fully concrete as the concrete *universal*. In flight from universals, however, the "provincial" desire for authenticity must satisfy itself with a mere abstract particular—with a fragment falsely magnified into a totality, i.e. with a reification, a fetish.

To speak of this abstract particular as "culture" may be true enough in its way. And certainly Arguedas's "provincial" writer (and reader) is as sincere in his or her quest for the cultural truth of Latin America as anyone could wish. But the point is that the fetishizing interest in "culture" is itself a symptom of entrapment within the reified categories of what might be termed the ethnographic reduction: "culture" as the rationalized object of the ethnographer does not progress *beyond* but merely substitutes itself *for* the disdained categories of an abstract, universal reason. The "provincial" writer may, to be sure, reject the ethnographer's claim to objectivity or neutrality, but the world he or she depicts through fiction falls within the same narrow, reified conceptual limits. That Arguedas, especially in *Todas las sangres* and *El zorro*, struggled to break through this reified frame is evident. But one must be skeptical of his success here. By seeking to make indigenous culture the active, form-giving principle of his poetics, Arguedas nevertheless could not, it seems to me, cease to frame this culture itself as ethnographic.[44] Thus the ethnographic fetish is opposed, but only within the framework of a thinking generated by the fetish itself.

Much less, of course, does "Apocalypse at Solentiname" free itself of such fetishism, for all of Cortázar's allegorizing cleverness in pointing to its existence. "Apocalypse at Solentiname" is essentially a variation on the standard, fantastic plot device that Cortázar resorted to over and over again, and which has its popular-cultural equivalent in any "Twilight Zone" episode. The difference is simply that Cortázar has here used it to thematize his own "authenticity" problem in relation to the question of fetishism. At the "setting" prompt he pulls down the "Latin America" menu before making his selection. We meet "authentic" Latin Americans such as Ernesto Cardenal, Roque Dalton and Sergio Ramirez in "authentic" Latin American locales such as Costa Rica, Los Chiles and Solentiname. So in what sense is this any less "authentically" Latin American a piece of fiction than *El zorro* or, say, or Rulfo's "La Cuesta de las Comadres" (see chapter 10)—or even a contemporary testimonial narrative? For, to give Cortázar his due here, the fact that we still tend spontaneously to read the latter sorts of texts as authentic while remaining doubtful of Cortázar suggests, to my thinking, not any fundamental difference *qua* literary content, but rather how completely we, as readers, have internalized the ethnographic reduction, how adept we have become at recognizing and attempting to suppress any discursive or poetic reminders of our postmodern cultural fetishism. Again, the fact that "Apocalypse at Solentiname" is able to thematize this "ideology of reading" does not mean that Cortázar succeeds in breaking with it—merely that he has caught a glimpse of how fungible a substance "authenticity" has become, and exploits this knowledge to ironic and purely formal effect.

To gain some insight into what a radical, progressive break with cultural fetishism entails in objectively aesthetic terms would, to my mind, mean leaving behind *both* the "planetary" and modernist Cortázar *and* his "provincial", postmodern opposites and looking to other Latin American narratives entirely. I have in mind here a species of "suppressed lineage" of modern realism that would, in particular, include the great Latin American feature films made over the last three decades, from *Blood of the Condor* and

The Last Supper to *The Official Story*. And with respect to the novel itself, I am thinking—not without trepidation and a heightened sense of ethical and political irony, I must confess—of Vargas Llosa. In a work such as *The Storyteller*, it seems to me, the latter realizes in practice an authentic— because both richly concrete and *non*-provincial—portrayal of certain "radical truths of Latin America"—truths that Arguedas, although for far better political motives, reduced in practice to ethnography, and that Cortázar, with his heart similarly well placed, could only contemplate as theoretical abstractions. An enigma, to be sure. But that is the subject for the penultimate chapter in this volume.

Alejo Carpentier:
Modernism as Epic

One of the more striking paradoxes of current critical discussions of Latin American literature and culture is how, even as the question of post-modernism arouses widespread and sometimes vehement argument, that of modernism itself remains only slightly less open-ended and controversial. No doubt this reflects something about the postcolonial condition itself, the tendency for its intellectual life to "start from scratch with each generation" given a "lack of conviction, both in the constantly changing theories and in their relationship to the movement of society as a whole."[1] One suspects, of course, that such a "lack of conviction" may often be well founded. But the evident uncertainty as to just what Latin American modernism was or is— an uncertainty palpable in the absence of a precise Spanish or Portuguese equivalent for the English term itself: *modernismo* seems too narrowly generational a marker for either the Brazilian or the Spanish-American contexts, while *vanguardismo* risks being overly sectarian—is surely also reflective of something intrinsic to the literary and cultural objects themselves. It is easy enough, of course, to check off the many formal re-semblances between, say, Faulkner and García Márquez, or *Ulysses* and *Hopscotch*, but these never quite seem to add up to an unproblematic aesthetic or cultural identity. The list may go on *ad infinitum*, but without eliminating the sense that an underlying and irreducible difference may at any time reveal the pointlessness of the formal exercise itself. The ten-dency, at this point, may be to explain all this as a consequence of the inherent Eurocentrism or cultural imperialism of the aesthetic or literary category *per se*, along with a corollary postulate that the irreducible difference of the would-be but never-quite modernist texts be understood as merely the sign of their radically non-European, "Latin American" essence. Critiques of Eurocentric literary theory and scholarship, such as those put forward by Edward Said, have recently thrust these kinds of considerations into the mainstream of academic discourse. But the general denunciation of Eurocentrism, while largely justified, strikes me as having little to no explanatory power when it is a question of probing more deeply

into the specific difference of the heterogeneously modernist works themselves. Beyond both the sheer fact of difference and the fact that this
difference points on a very general level to the social and historical
condition of colonialism and imperialism, what must be disclosed here is
how, *concretely*, this difference is to be linked with—using Schwarz's terms
again—"the movement of society as a whole."

What I would like to do in what follows is to attempt briefly such a
disclosure in the case of a particular text: Alejo Carpentier's *Explosion in a
Cathedral* (the unfortunate English title given to his novel *El siglo de las luces*,
"The Century of Lights").[2] My reasons for choosing this novel are partly
circumstantial—the fact that it is still fairly widely read and taught in
courses on Caribbean and Latin American literature.[3] But they also pertain
to what seems to be a peculiar sort of problem that, perhaps along with
certain other of Carpentier's works, *El siglo de las luces* poses for any effort
to read it as either "modernist" or not. This is, in a word, the problem of
history. *El siglo de las luces* is, pretty clearly, a narrative about history, a
narrative that consciously sets out to tell the story of a particular set of real
events in a particular setting. These are the various political repercussions
of the French Revolution as they affect the area of the Caribbean—specifically, Cuba, Haiti, Guadeloupe, French Guiana and Surinam. One can even
be quite precise as to the time period involved: the twenty years that
intervene between the outbreak of the Revolution in France itself, resulting
directly or indirectly in both the abolition of slavery in the "revolutionary"
French territories of the region as well as in its subsequent reinstatement
(Haiti excluded) after the Napoleonic decree of 30th Floreal, Year 10, and
the spontaneous mass uprising against Napoleon's troops in Madrid in
1809, during which Esteban and Sofía, two of the novel's principal
characters, are presumed to meet their deaths. The novel's central figure,
Victor Hugues, is, by Carpentier's own report, based closely on a factual
personage of that same name.

Thus if one had to classify this novel using the standard array of poetic
and generic designations, then the terms "epic" and "historical novel"
might not seem out of place. Do we not appear to have, in *El siglo de las
luces*, what Lukács once referred to as the determining essence of the epic,
i.e. the "extensive totality of life"?[4] And yet, there is something oddly
deficient and imprecise about such a classification. For the imaginative re-
experience of history that one typically expects to find in classically epic
narratives such as *The Iliad* or *War and Peace* seems to have been altered in
El siglo de las luces: what one "experiences" in reading it is less the pheno-
menal form of history as such—at least as we are accustomed to recognize
it—than its random epiphenomena, in the form of exotic period costumes,
snatches of once popular song lyrics, Masonic rituals, forgotten literary-
historical references, bizarre architectural details, etc. Consider, as only one
of many possible instances of this, the episode (see chapters XLVI and

XLVII) in which veterans of Napoleon's Egyptian campaign are brought into Cayenne for use in hunting down escaped slaves, and the subsequent epidemic of the "Egyptian disease" in the city:

> The Egyptian Disease had appeared in Cayenne. The Hospital of Saint-Paul-de-Chartres no longer had room for all the sick. Prayers were sent up to St. Roch, St. Prudentius, and St. Carlo Borromeo, who were always remembered in time of pestilence. People cursed the soldiers who had brought this new plague, picked up in God-knows-what cave full of mummies, in God-knows-what world of sphinxes and embalmers. Death was in the town. He leapt from house to house and the disconcerting suddenness of his appearance gave rise to a proliferation of terrified rumours and legends. People said that the soldiers from Egypt, furious at being made to leave France, had wanted to exterminate the colony so that they could take it over; and that they were concocting unguents, liquids, and greases mixed with all manner of filth, with which they marked the fronts of the houses they wished to contaminate. Marks of any sort were suspect. Anyone who leaned his hand on the wall during the day, and left behind the ephemeral outline of a sweaty palm, was stoned by passers-by. Because his fingers were too black and greasy, an Indian was beaten to death, early one morning, by people watching over a corpse.[5]

Anyone familiar with Carpentier's painstaking habits of research will have no difficulty believing in the historical veracity of what is recounted here. And Carpentier's ability to evoke for the reader the sensual, almost visceral reality of the plague itself is not to be disputed. And yet, this episode, like so many in the novel, has no essential connection to the epical or dramatic unfolding of the narrative itself. Although Hugues himself is stricken, and, falsely believing his death to be imminent, reveals to Sofía his desire to be buried in his old Jacobin, pre-Napoleonic insignia, the incident in no way bears on what is already the inevitable parting of ways and political falling out between the two lovers. The plague in Cayenne *is* history, but it is not *as* history that it claims the narrative interest of the reader. History, rather, has become a kind of vehicle for the production of a set of aesthetic effects— here the mild shock or *frisson* induced by the amplification of violent and macabre details as well as by the juxtapostion of "exotic" settings. These effects seem more wedded to the present than to the past. Moreover, these effects themselves appear analogous, if not homologous to those produced in a canonically modernist or avant-garde work of art: the principles of *montage* are clearly enough at work in passages such as the one cited above. Thus all that separates the above passage from, say, a surrealist prose-poem is, from this perspective, the fact that Carpentier has foraged his material out of the *arcana* of history itself rather than out of a private sphere of dreams or intoxications.[6]

Readers of Carpentier will by now, of course, have been prompted to recall Carpentier's well-known espousal of the "real maravilloso" in the preface to the first, 1949 edition of *El reino de este mundo* (*The Kingdom of this World*) as well as discussions of the "neo-baroque" in later essays.[7] Here, in fact, Carpentier, in publically breaking his ties to Surrealism, had already anticipated the question of how his own aesthetic was to be judged *vis-à-vis* that of the European avant-garde. This he did with the theory of a literary work of art that was *both* realist *and* modernist and yet somehow, at the same time, neither of the two—a work in which the "maravilloso" is no longer a literary contrivance but can simply be permitted to "issue freely out of a reality followed strictly in all its details."[8] Simply by writing about "América" in its real, but radical alterity, we were told, it had become possible to transcend what, in the European metropolis, still seemed an ineluctable duality. There is even a suggestion of old-fashioned "New World" utopianism here insofar as the privatized, neurotic and decadent culture of metropolitan Surrealism is offered a chance at redemption simply by turning its gaze across the Atlantic where "all becomes 'maravilloso' in a history impossible to situate in Europe."[9]

Literary history leaves little doubt as to the efficacy of the Carpentierian "real maravilloso" in instituting a new vocabulary within critical and aesthetic discourse—and one whose success can be measured in how often one still hears talk of "magical realism" across the whole spectrum of mainstream literary culture. But as theory, the "real maravilloso" does not really carry us very far towards solving the specific aesthetic problem that arises in a narrative such as *El reino de este mundo* or *El siglo de las luces*: namely, how, given the co-presence of epical (realist) and modernist aspects within the same narrative text, both to specify the relation between them and to explain, in sociohistorical or genetic terms, their specific form of relationship. For, to reiterate, the problem here is not merely a terminological one, nor is it a matter of simply staking a claim to difference as such. It is, rather, to formulate a critical perspective from which to evaluate concrete literary works, yet one that will, at the same time, reflect within its scope the specific social truths of Latin America, or of postcolonial society generally. Carpentier's various theoretical excurses certainly move in this direction. But, in the last analysis, the aesthetics of the "real maravilloso", the "neo-baroque", etc. revert to a cultural, even an ethnographic rather than to a fully social or historical order of difference[10]. The privatized, bourgeois desire for (in Benjamin's convenient phrase) "profane illumination"[11] may, indeed, as Carpentier proclaimed, become the collective and public desire embodied, say, in Afro-Cuban religious ritual. (The "profane" reverting, here, to the sacred.) But that still leaves the question of just where Carpentier as author of the "magical realist" text—or we ourselves, as non-communicant or agnostic readers, for that matter—fit into the scheme, if not precisely as would-be ethnographers, gazing out onto the ecstatic spectacle from what is still our securely private spheres of consciousness. All of this is merely to say that, if we are to take seriously the implicit theory of a distinctively Latin Amercan *realism* voiced in Carpentier's aesthetic manifestos, then this theory must be rigorously evaluated in terms of literary practice itself and not merely displaced onto another sphere.

How to proceed, then? At the personal risk of provoking a charge of Eurocentrism, the inescapable reference here must be, I think, to Lukács's *The Historical Novel*—a theoretical work that could not, in some respects, be less attuned to the "postcolonial," but one that is indispensable if we are to enter more deeply into the question of the epical/modernist dynamic in *El siglo de las luces*.

Written in Moscow in 1936–7 and first published in Russian, *The Historical Novel* is probably sufficiently well known and of a piece with the larger corpus of Lukács's literary criticism and aesthetic theory after *History and Class Consciousness* to obviate an extensive recapitulation. However, a brief review of certain of its decisive theoretical contributions will prove useful to what follows. Lukács begins with a consideration of the historical novel in its classical phase, epitomized in the work of Walter Scott. Basing himself in the works of eighteenth century English social realism (Fielding, Sterne, Defoe, etc.), Scott revolutionizes this tradition by—in the manner of the ancient epic—portraying the objective reality of society as both quintessentially and uniquely the product of history. Scott, to repeat Lukács's phrase, produces an artistic reflection of history not as mere past but as the "concrete prehistory of the present."[12] This achievement is then refined by a series of writers who carry the historical novel through to the end of the classical period, above all Balzac, Stendhal, Cooper, Pushkin, Manzoni and Tolstoy.

Lukács specifies the historical precondition for Scott's classic rendering of the form to be what he refers to as the "historical spirit" or new "mass experience of history"—the product of the English and especially the French Revolutions and the following period of Napoleonic wars. It is during this period—the classical instance of "bourgeois revolution" —that, argues Lukács, everyday life is for the first time confronted with the direct reality of world history. Lukács cites as an example the experience of mass conscript armies and geographically unlimited warfare. "If experiences such as these," he writes,

> are linked with the knowledge that similar upheavals are taking place all over the world, this must enormously strengthen the feeling, first that there is such a thing as history, that it is an uninterrupted process of changes, and finally that it has a direct effect upon the life of every individual.[13]

It is only because history has become a "fact of life" for the people *en masse* that writers such as Scott and Balzac, themselves intimately linked to

popular life, are able to reflect this new mass historicism in a medium of
epic representation.

The terminal point of this development is, of course, the failed
revolutions of 1848, especially the June Days in Paris, when the European
bourgeoisie and proletariat first clash openly over questions of fundamental
economic interests and political power. The general reader of Lukács is
doubtless familiar with the literary transformations attributed to this onset
of bourgeois counter-revolution and "apologetics": the increasing isolation
and estrangement of the leading bourgeois intellectuals and writers from
the social and historical arena of class struggle; growing tendencies toward
ideologies of subjective idealism, aestheticism and outright reaction—all of
this culminating in the decline of epic realism and the rise of a literature of
increasingly impoverished social content expressing itself first as naturalism
and ultimately as modernism itself. As concerns the historical novel, the
effect of counter-revolution is best seen in the artistic deformations of
a post-1848 narrative such as Flaubert's *Salammbô*. These deformations
Lukács includes within the key concept of "modernization":

> Since history, to an ever increasing extent, is no longer conceived as the
> prehistory of the present, or, if it is, then in a superficial, unilinear, evolu-
> tionary way, the endeavours of the earlier [pre-1848] period to grasp the
> stages of the historical process in their real individuality, as they really were
> objectively, lose their living interest. Where it is not the "uniqueness" of
> earlier events that is presented, history is *modernized*. This means that the
> historian proceeds from the belief that the fundamental structure of the past
> is economically and ideologically the same as that of the present.[14]

Flaubert's elaborately researched efforts to resurrect ancient Carthage are
themselves premised, according to Lukács, on an implicit failure to grasp
the present as historically derived, and thus can only appear as a lifeless
"monument," bearing no comprehensible relation to life as immediately
and commonly experienced.

Reading *El siglo de las luces* into the critical-theoretical system of *The
Historical Novel* there seems at first no way to evade the conclusion that
it, too, succumbs to "modernization." Many of Lukács's strictures against
Salammbô can be invoked against Carpentier: the overwhelming of the
narrative by the sheer descriptive weight and extension of objects; the
tendency to reduce historical accuracy to a matter of "costumes and decor-
ations"; the seeming absence from Carpentier's exotic historical backdrop of
a "discernible connection with any concrete form of popular life that we may
experience";[15] the approach to history "from the standpoint of an idea"[16]—
here the "real maravilloso" itself—; a disproportionate emphasis on scenes
of brutality and depravity, etc. Indeed, the exploitation of obscure historical
data for purposes of quasi-Surrealist "shock" effect, remarked on earlier in

reference to the plague episode in *El siglo de las luces*, seems as clear cut an instance of "modernization" as one could require.

But a difficulty arises here. For despite showing all the literary symptoms of "modernization" in Lukács's sense, *El siglo de las luces* is clearly also the narrative vehicle for a conception of history quite unlike that associated by Lukács with narratives such as *Salammbô*. This historical conception we might summarize, borrowing again from Roberto Schwarz's work, as that of "misplaced idea." In his essay of that same name, Schwarz analyzes with wonderful insight the peculiar cultural and ideological effects generated in nineteenth-century Brazil by the "preposterous" attempts to join the ideology of classical European liberalism to a society resting on slave labor. In contrast to capitalist Western Europe, where liberal notions of equality, freedom, etc., operate as "[necessary] illusions well grounded in appearances," in colonial and neo-colonial Brazil the overt social fact of slavery renders them ideologies that "do not describe reality, not even falsely," that "do not move according to a law of their own."[17] Liberal ideas are "misplaced" in Brazil; they become, to employ another of Schwarz's conceptual innovations, "ideologies of the second degree"—the objects of a "conscious desire to participate in a reality that appearances did not sustain."[18] Thus an "ideological comedy is set up, different from the European."[19]

It requires little effort of interpretation to discover in *El siglo de las luces* a re-enactment of this same "ideological comedy." Here, moreover, it is the Revolution, the very greatest of liberal historical icons, that, in being "misplaced" into the Caribbean, enters into the realm of "ideology to the second degree." Indeed, Carpentier's novel at times reads almost like something out of Schwarz's essay. See, for example, Esteban's bitter reflections when, after living the Revolution first hand, he returns to Havana exhausted and disillusioned, only to find his cousins Sofía and Carlos enrolled in an "androgynous" Masonic lodge, spouting Rousseau and generally enthused with Revolutionary doctrine:

> The *ideas* which he had left behind had now caught up with him, in an environment where everything seemed organised to neutralise them. The people who were pitying the lot of the slaves to-day had brought fresh negroes to work on their haciendas yesterday. The men who talked about the corruption of the colony's government had themselves prospered in the shade of that corruption, which had favoured their profiteering. The men who were beginning to talk about possible independence had been only too delighted to receive some title of nobility from the Royal Hand. The same state of mind that had led so many artistocrats in Europe to build their own scaffolds was becoming general among the rich here. Forty years too late, people were reading books in favour of revolution which that revolution itself, impelled into unforeseen channels, had made inappropriate.[20]

El siglo de las luces, that is, far from conforming to a view of the past as "economically and ideologically the same as the present," at least on an overtly ideological plane, directly poses the question of historical difference and "uniqueness" here, not only as concerns past and present but likewise metropolis and periphery, colonizer and colonized, etc. It holds up the official, utopianized version of the Revolution-as-history to the mirror that will reveal to it its unsuspectedly dystopian features—an image of the "preposterous" brilliantly evoked in *El siglo de las luces* by the spectacle of Billaud-Varenne, the sternest of Jacobin ideologues and the erstwhile scourge of the privileged classes of France, making the best of exile in French Guiana by becoming a slave-owning plantocrat.

But how then explain, from the Lukácsian standpoint, the evident disparity or rift between modernization as an aesthetic and modernization as an ideology, as a "view of history"? Are we simply to conclude that *The Historical Novel* here demonstrates its theoretical incapacity to explain a literary phenomenon exceeding its "Eurocentric" scope?

Perhaps so—but I think that would be too peremptory a conclusion. Rather, what I believe is suggested by the seeming dissonance of *El siglo de las luces* with respect to the Lukácsian theory and critique of modernism is the need to rethink, not just modernism as it is "transculturated" within the postcolonial context, but to rethink the changed relationship between its aesthetic and ideological moments within the structure of the literary work itself. What Lukács depicts in his readings of the "modernized" historical novels of Flaubert, of Conrad Ferdinand Meyer, etc., is a process in which a given change in the ideological consciousness of history is, so to speak, spontaneously crystallized in a new aesthetic or literary form. But note how there is assumed in this very process of crystallization an initial relationship of unity or adequacy between the "experience of history" in its raw, everyday, mass dimension and the aesthetic forms through which it is given narrative representation. Suppose, however, that this relationship of adequacy were absent at the outset, and that "modernization" in its aesthetic form functioned as a kind of given here, to which the effort was then made to join or adapt an "experience of history" that in fact could *not* be adequately expressed or conveyed by the given formal means. Suppose, that is, that modernism itself as a discrete "aesthetic", were to inhabit the narrative work as itself a species of "ideology to the second degree," whose relation to the "experience of history" was such as to produce the continual impression of dissonance or the "preposterous."

I suggest that it is only by thinking of Carpentier's "modernism" in this way that we can square it with the specific poetic or readerly effect of a novel such as *El siglo de las luces*. This in an effect in which the explicitly formal dimension of the narrative, *despite* what is evidently a kind of prior will to self-estrangement, a drive to enthrall its readers with the "neo-baroque" profusion of sensuous detail as "for itself" (thus prompting—

ideally—the Carpentierian version of "profane illumination"), never quite succeeds in diverting us from the more "conventional" dimension of the plot as such. For all that Carpentier strives to allegorize them, or to submerge them in a bath of exotic *mises-en-scène* and antiquarian lore, it is the destinies of the main characters—Esteban, Sofía and Victor Hugues himself—that drive the narrative forward and that ultimately succeed, as nothing else really does, in sustaining the prolonged, epic interest of the reader. Moreover, I propose that it is here—at the level of what, to employ an Aristotelian term, we might call the novel's objective "unity of action"— that *El siglo de las luces* offers a "discernible connection" to a "mass experience of history." For the reader who takes a genuine concern in what happens to the novel's protagonists will do so not in obedience to the principles of the "real maravilloso" but precisely because he or she senses that in these outcomes there is reflected a truth of fundamental relevance to the present reality of the postcolonial world: namely, that, to cite Fanon in *The Wretched of the Earth* (a work first published only a year after *El siglo de las luces*):

> the bourgeois phase in the history of underdeveloped countries is a completely useless phase. When this caste has vanished, devoured by its own contradictions, it will be seen that nothing new has happened since independence was proclaimed, and that everything must be started again from scratch. [21]

Esteban and Sofía come to acknowledge this truth, while Victor Hugues must struggle continuously to conceal it from himself; but all three experience it as the objective, historical threshold that will deny them passage and determine their variously tragic endings. To the extent that we, as Carpentier's readers, intuitively grasp the rightness, the poetic truth of *El siglo de las luces* in its *peripeteia*, it is because we detect in them, whether consciously or not, the "prehistory" of the imperialized present in settings such as the Caribbean and Latin America.

But again, the key point in all of this is that such an epical principle unfolds "against the grain" of the "modernized" aesthetic theory upon which the narrative is self-consciously erected—an aesthetic with which, to be more still more exact, the "epic" *El siglo de las luces* co-exists in a state of latent ideological tension. Unlike the process theorized by Lukács, however, in which such a tension necessarily results in the decay of epical realism and the concomitant growth of modernism, in *El siglo de las luces* we appear to have—*in statu nascendi*, at any rate—the inverse process. For here it is modernism that, dialectically speaking, suffers a negation, while the superseding moment, or *Aufhebung*, falls to an emergent epical realism of the postcolonial "margins." Lukács, recall, identifies modernization in narratives such as *Salammbô* as strictly the literary outgrowth of a crisis in

bourgeois realism and historical consciousness heralding the end of bourgeois ascendancy in the European metropolis. Modernization can thus be
fully and correctly understood only in its inner, albeit negative connection
to the classical, metropolitan tradition out of which it develops. But if that
is so, then the detection of modernizing deformations in *El siglo de las luces*
must become problematic for the simple reason that it does not fully
partake of this inner connection. The deformations seem palpable enough—
but with respect to what, precisely, are they "deformations"? Thus although
it may be true that the petty bourgeois intellectual type represented by
Carpentier finds itself, like its metropolitan counterpart, estranged and
isolated from class struggle in its immediate, daily forms, one must also
consider to what extent this is in fact the primordial condition of the
colonial and postcolonial intellectual—an intellectual who must, to again
borrow from Fanon, "begin at the end."[22] The question of Carpentier's
relationship to the Cuban Revolution poses itself here, of course; but
whether ideological or political values specific to the Cuban experience are
or are not detectable in *El siglo de las luces* seems to me essentially irrelevant
for our present purposes. The larger fact remains that Carpentier's
historical condition, however he himself consciously understood it, is not
exclusively or even primarily that of postrevolutionary bourgeois decadence, but rather that in which the bourgeoisie in its classic role as
historical agent is lacking—split between an ultramarine, metropolitan
agglomeration of abstract commercial and financial interests with little or
no direct participation in national cultural life in the Caribbean and a local
"lumpenbourgeoisie" that has never enjoyed anything like the broadly
hegemonic position of its pre-1848 European counterpart. The very
concept of "bourgeois revolution"—so central to the conceptual system of
The Historical Novel—takes on a radically changed meaning in the
Caribbean and Latin American context.

This is not an exact inversion of the classical realist/modernist dialectic
familiar to cosmopolitanism, of course, since what has in effect become the
"old" still presents itself here in the guise of the "new". It is for this reason
that Schwarz's notion of "ideology to the second degree" comes so perfectly
to hand here—supplying what has been, it almost seems, the conceptual
missing link in so much of postcolonial literary and cultural criticism
heretofore.[23] For with it Schwarz has seemingly worked out a way to think
the complex and, so to speak, doubly inverted relation of colonizer to
colonized—a relation in which even the idea of revolution itself can serve to
conceal the very essence of reaction—as fully social and historical, thus
avoiding the inevitable reversion to some more or less nuanced form of
cultural nationalism or "essentialism."

From this perspective it is illuminating to reconsider one of the more
influential readings of *El siglo de las luces* that has come out of the US
academy. I refer to Roberto González Echevarría's chapter devoted to the

novel in his important book-length study of Carpentier, *The Pilgrim at Home*. Here González Echevarría too encounters the problem of whether to read *El siglo de las luces* as realist epic or as "modernization." In conceding that the novel's "attention to social, historical and political details," together with its publication during the early days of the Cuban Revolution, has led critics to "underscore its historical and realistic values," González Echevarría nevertheless pronounces such readings an "illusion."[24] Masked by this epical appearance is a "radical experiment with history and narrative."[25] Unlike the utopian or teleological narratives of dialectical historicisms, in which progress does not fall away but rather assumes contradictory forms, in *El siglo de las luces*

> there is no counterpoint between ideal project and historical execution but constant re-enactment of the gap between project and execution, as well as an affirmation of their indissoluble link. By making the future also past, history becomes the dynamic textual counterpoint between means and ends. In other words, the future that the history narrated in the text implies is, of necessity, nothing but the text—which forecloses any projections beyond its own specificity but allows for linear free play within itself. Contradictions are not bypassed and resolved in the novel, but merely begun again and again within the text's own dialectical free play. [26]

One's first impulse here is to wonder whether González Echevarría, in his eagerness to claim *El siglo de las luces* for an erstwhile Yale School-deconstructionist canon, has not perhaps declared such "traditional" literary categories as plot to be "illusions" simply so as not to have to account for them in his analytical presentation of the novel. But surely "contradictions," if not "bypassed," *are* "resolved" in the novel: the contradiction between Victor Hugues's Jacobin-egalitarian opposition to slavery and his mercantile-capitalist sense of political expedience is unmistakably resolved in favor of the latter. Slavery is re-instituted in the once "revolutionary" French possessions in the Caribbean. Here, at any rate, there is no sign of "dialectical free play."

If by his affirmation of endless "counterpoint" González Echevarría simply means that no unproblematically "progressive" outcome is allowed for in *El siglo de las luces*, then one can perhaps agree. But then, his reading of the novel is going much further than this: history, we are told, not only ceases to progress, but, in Carpentier's conception of it, reveals itself, in the last analysis, to be nothing but the movement of "textuality" as such. *Because* history cannot progress therefore it *must* be "textuality." In fairness to this line of reasoning, it must be allowed that *The Pilgrim at Home* does undertake to solve a real problem in Carpentier's text, one that cannot be conjured by simply reading that text as if its modernist/realist duality were non-existent or by renaming such a duality the "real maravilloso." That

González Echevarría proposes a *false* solution—at least as I read the novel—results not so much from a simple misreading or an excess of deconstructionist zeal, but from a failure to recognize in this duality, this "gap between project and execution," a reflection of a duality *intrinsic to post-colonial social being* and to a postcolonial "experience of history" as "mis-placed" that pre-exists any and all textualization. Lacking the crucial concept of "ideology to the second degree," *The Pilgrim at Home* in effect has no choice but to invert this objective relationship of history and text, falling back onto the classically ideological practice of "standing things on their heads." Would we be wrong to conclude that, beneath this ideological turn of interpretation, lie those very same peculiarities of metropolitan social being that have generated—and in many ways go on generating—the ideology of modernism itself?

Preselective Affinities: Surrealism (and Marxism) in Latin America

Intellectual and aesthetic historiography record only a relatively brief interlude during which Marxism and Surrealism could regard each other as political allies. Assuming its Parisian epicenter, we might date this period roughly from 1925, the year in which the Surrealists joined with the French Communist Party in opposing French imperialist repression of the Riff rebellion in Morocco, to 1935. In his written address of that year to the International Association of Writers for the Defense of Culture, Breton, now excluded from all PCF organizations, had defended Surrealism's Marxist (or, at any rate, Communist) credentials for one last time, not only against the Zhdanovite socialist realism newly adopted by the Third International, but against a wave of sympathy for realism of a broader, more classical mold.[1] This latter trend is best embodied in Lukács' polemical essays of the time and reflects the new political realities that would launch the Popular Front Against Fascism. The most critically optimistic assessment of its possibilities—Walter Benjamin's essay "Surrealism: Last Snapshot of the European Intelligentsia" written in 1929—argues for a Marxist/Surrealist alliance founded on an organization of "pessimism" that "expel[s] moral metaphor from politics and . . . discover[s] in political action a sphere reserved one hundred percent for images."[2] But in view of how little this left politics of images was to bear on subsequent historical events—or how readily fascism usurped and mastered such a politics—it is hard to read Benjamin's essay now except in a pessimistic, not to say an elegiac, spirit. By the time of Adorno's "Looking Back on Surrealism" (1956) the Marxian elegy for Surrealism has become a veritable eulogy, i.e. last words of praise for something irrevocably dead and buried. Adorno concedes that after the "European catastrophe . . . Surrealist shocks [had] lost their force," but now finds even its seeming obsolescence redeemed in the face of a more dangerous and shock-proof "denying . . . of denial" purportedly endemic to the post-catastrophic world.[3]

But a less philologically sectarian and less European-centered view of things tells a rather different story of Marxism's cohabitation with

Surrealism. While seeking to ally itself with the European Communist movement in the 1920s and 1930s, Surrealism, along with other, kindred outgrowths of the post-World War I avant-garde, had made certain *socially* radical, if not quite political, inroads across the Atlantic. True, in the United States, Surrealism's reception by literary and artistic culture never greatly exceeded the sphere of high-brow gossip in which its Parisian and, more importantly, its Freudian accents tended to drown out any Marxist echoes. But throughout *Latin* America a less sanitized Surrealism evoked an almost instantaneous surge of fascination and sympathy, alike in radical and more quietist circles. This is clearest in the case of vanguardist Latin American poetry of the 1920s, '30s and '40s, most particularly that of Jorge Luis Borges, César Vallejo, Octavio Paz and Pablo Neruda. Indeed, it is safe to say that the Neruda of the two volumes of *Residencia en la tierra* (1933/1935) has long since emerged as the most widely read poet of Surrealism anywhere, far outstripping the international popularity of a Breton, an Aragon or an Eluard.[4] And although the poems of *Residencia en la tierra* precede Neruda's embrace of Communism, no one more readily typifies the Surrealist as Marxist.

But the Latin American affinity for Surrealism becomes more remarkable still when one considers the latter's somewhat less direct role in initiating the tradition of prose fiction known as the "real maravilloso" (the "miraculously real") or, more colloquially, "magical realism."[5] There are differing theories of how to reconstruct this particular aesthetic genealogy: one (see the preceding chapter in this volume) traces it through the Cuban writer Alejo Carpentier's novel *El reino de este mundo*, whose now famous preface to its first (1949) edition amounts to a Latin American Surrealist counter-manifesto. Another favors the novels of the Guatemalan Miguel Angel Asturias (see, for example, *El señor Presidente* [1946] and *Hombres de maíz* [1949]), who, like Carpentier, inhaled the Surrealist vapors at their source. But one way or the other, the ultimate outgrowth of "magical realism" has been the conversion, if not of the jargon of Surrealism, then of its rhetorical (one might almost say, marketing) strategy of prescribed dosages of "shock" into what is practically an item of household consumption. The name of Gabriel García Márquez used to be the obligatory reference here, but even the global event of *One Hundred Years of Solitude* (*Cien años de soledad* [1967]) now pales before the international success of an Isabel Allende or of a film such as *Como agua para chocolate* (1992). Indeed, in its reincarnation as "magical realism," Surrealism ironically finds its way back to the European and North American metropolis—as witness, for example, the recently successful Dutch film *Antonia's Line* (1995), which transposes the standard Isabel Allende plot formula, complete with "magical realism's" stock-in-trade of profane "miracles," into, of all places, post-World War II Holland! The small corps of purists who rail against the vulgarization and disarming of a once "revolutionary" aesthetic are no doubt justified, but without, so to speak, farming itself out to the colonies, Surrealism would have deserved Adorno's post-war epitaph, having dwindled down to little more than what its one-time icons—say, one of Breton's manifestos, or a Magritte painting—have since become: over-academicized, intellectual- and art-historical curios, reproduced for sale in museum gift-shops.

What explains the Latin American affinity for Surrealism? The circum-stantial factors are all well known: the Latin American literati's traditional francophilia; the presence of future Latin American literary legends such as Asturias and Carpentier at the earliest Surrealist congregations; the mediating link provided by Spanish Surrealism, etc. But they only beg the deeper, social and historical question of this evidently strong affinity itself—one in which Marxism, a somewhat older import that had begun to take firm root in Latin America only in the 1920s and '30s, shared in as well.

To answer we need to consider more closely Surrealism's fundamental aesthetic principle, namely, montage. Its theory is simply formulated: merely by removing the objects of daily existence from their familiar context and then juxtaposing them again, only in the "wrong" sequence or constellation, an effect of estrangement or shock is produced. In Breton's version of it—heavily indebted to his reading of Freud's *Interpretation of Dreams*—the montage permits a conscious simulation of the dream state, so that its shock effect serves not only to "defamiliarize" the everyday (a common objective of virtually all schools of vanguard aesthetics) but to penetrate the barriers of repression that have sealed it off from the unconscious. "The poet of the future," says Breton,

> will surmount the depressing notion of the irreparable divorce of action and dream. [. . .] He will maintain at any price *in each other's presence the two terms of the human relation* . . .: the objective awareness of realities and their internal development. . . . This action can pass for magical in that it consists of an *unconscious, immediate action of the internal on the external*.[6]

That is, montage does not seek to reproduce the *content* of a dream-narra-tive, as might, e.g., a fantasy or a fairy-tale—for by being reproduced in such a way, the dream-narrative merely takes on the form in which the conscious, everyday world of existence finds it easiest to assimilate. Rather, montage replicates what it takes to be the *formal* principle of the dream narrative, seizing on the conscious, everyday object world—"the objective awareness of realities"— as its content. Breton speaks as though this could result spontaneously from the drives of the unconscious itself, but failing that, the conscious object must, it is clear, be methodically and *consciously forced* into an "unconscious" form. Measured against the simple, pre-psychoanalytical principle of defamiliarization (as advocated, for example, by Russian Formalism), Surrealist montage thus demonstrates what should be its enormously more powerful (because more strategic) method for undermining a routinized, "bourgeois" existence "from within." Everyone, after all, has an unconscious.

But all of this, of course, *in theory*. In practice, the Surrealist montage cannot fail to meet with obstacles in its will to overturn, where least expected, the repressed and familiarized—obstacles that have now come to seem rather obvious. For even the most violent juxtaposition, once it is registered and its initial shock dissipates, has nothing to save it from its *own* rapid familiarization. We see this, as mentioned above, in the ignominious fate that has lain in wait for all the scandalous images and word-plays of avant-gardes past: relegation to the museum, the research library and the slide collection, not to say to the advertising campaign and the book-jacket. The most daring and exciting possibility of montage is also its most vulnerable: for the shock that releases the unconscious energies of a liberating destruction has to work the first time, once and for all.[7] It has no second chance, and, in fact, its very first repetition not only signifies its failure but helps to innoculate the repressive, "civilized" order against all further assaults. Thus the shock effects of montage evolve into the fast-cut editing and "special" effects that now drive the Hollywood production process in its desperate need to amortize itself at the "box office"—"effects" essentially no less the beholden objects of market speculation than are their mechanical means of production . . . or than athletic shoes or pork bellies for that matter. Benjamin's "politics of images" appears to have ensconced itself securely within the cultural parameters of capitalist reproduction.

But suppose the familiarized or routinized object world were structured in such a way that the shock effects of montage were themselves the spontaneous, even, in a sense, the routine experiences of everyday life and thus did not have to be consciously induced, but only pointed out or rendered self-aware. Suppose that, rather than taking the form of a self-encasing modernity that had rationalized daily existence down to its last detail and thus had managed to protect itself on all sides from the "repressed" or negated forces continuously pushed beyond its margins, history itself were structured like a Surrealist montage?

Consider, from this perspective, the well-known opening episode of García Márquez's *Cien años de soledad* in which Colonel Aureliano Buendía, "many years later, as he faced the firing squad," remembers his boyhood in Macondo when Melquíades' band of gypsies first introduced the "modern" conveniences of ice, magnets and magnifying glasses into the then remote settlement. The novel relates how José Arcadio Buendía, Aureliano's father and Macondo's patriarch, traded a mule and two goats for two magnetized ingots, with which he intended, against Melquíades's admonitions, to prospect for gold. After months of dragging the magnets across the entire region:

The only thing he succeeded in doing was to unearth a suit of fifteenth century armor which had all of its pieces soldered together with rust and inside of which there was the hollow resonance of an enormous stone-filled gourd. When José Arcadio Buendía and the four men of his expedition managed to take the armor apart, they found inside a calcified skeleton with a copper locket containing a woman's hair around its neck.[8]

Ice, magnets, magnifying glasses: these are just the sorts of mundane, modern, but now overfamiliar objects Surrealism appropriates as the materials for its montage. But in García Márquez's narrative their de-familiarization does not result from their juxtaposition to others drawn from a noncontiguous sector of daily existence, but from their placement in a historical present that counts as a *past* in relation to them. Adorno, it is true, notes a temporal factor in the workings of Surrealist montage as well, attributing the affinity of Surrealism for psychoanalysis not to the "symbo-lism of the unconscious" but to "the attempt to uncover childhood experiences by means of explosions." "The subjective aspect . . . lies in the action of the montage, which attempts . . . . to produce perceptions as they must have been then."[9] But the modernity of these objects, given their placement in what is already the child-remembered, fantasy space of the novel, no longer needs to be stripped away so as to disclose the dream-like immediacy they once were believed to—and, in the unconscious, pre-sumably still—possess; rather, it is just this modernity that now makes them the possible agents of shock or de-familiarization. For in the Latin American reality depicted through the microcosm of Macondo, history itself resists the rationalization of existence and openly exposes the colliding planes of the rational and the irrational. Thus the anecdote of the magnets and the suit of armor—something that might have come straight out of Lautréamont or a Surrealist prose-poem—need not in fact sacrifice for a moment its simultaneous quality of historical plausibility, even factuality. The montage-like joining of magnet to suit of armor does not generate the shock of a dream that the real must "repress" so much as the shock of the real itself, of the real as *history*. What is dug up from its forgotten burial place is not something restricted to a subjective, psychic realm but the historical truth of the past—a past that itself comes to occupy the place, in the Freudianism of the Surrealists, of the unconscious.

In the case of *Cien años de soledad* the effect of such a shock is softened by its comic, even its parodic quality. José Arcadio Buendía plays the part of (in Aristotelian poetics) the *alazon*, or self-deceiving hero, while we, as "modern" readers who know only too well that magnets do not attract gold, are able to greet the hero's shocking find with a mitigating sense of condescension. In a novel such as Carpentier's aforementioned *El reino de este mundo*, however, the identical historicizing redeployment of montage dispenses with irony. The story, as told through the eyes of the slave Ti

Noël, of the slave revolts leading up to the Haitian Revolution, *El reino de este mundo* is also the first Latin American fictional narrative to attempt a "realist" narrativization of Surrealist aesthetics.[10] In episodes such as the one in which the rebel mastermind and *vodun* shaman Mackandal uses his African tribalist's knowledge of plants and fungi to carry out the mass poisoning of the white slavocrats of Saint Dominigue, the resulting shock effect is far more menacing than in *Cien años de soledad*, closer, still, in its spirit, to Breton's manifestos.[11] Yet this is no less the shock of the real, at least if we are to credit Carpentier's claim in the first preface to the novel that he has followed the historical record of events in Haiti with complete fidelity. In *El reino de este mundo* we are made to see how a Haitian slave revolt sets out quite literally, in the words of Benjamin's adoptive Surrealist's motto, to "win the energies of intoxication for the revolution."[12]

Irony apart, however, the significant thing in both narratives is that montage ceases to act merely as a momentary, therapeutic catalyst, working (or not) "once and for all." The (putatively) therapeutical properties of montage are here exploited for the purpose of re-experiencing a Latin American modernity in full view of the "repressed lineage" of its own, shock-filled past. Indeed, from a more abstractly formal and poetic standpoint, montage itself becomes the generative principle of a *narrative* rather than merely the formula for an aleatory "automatic writing" in which only the momentary, phenomenological effect matters. The shock elicited by a first, tropical experience of ice, or by the mining of a dead *conquistador* in the virgin South American jungle results from the collision of past and present, not merely of free-associated images; and the ensuing alteration of consciousness is at the same time an involuntary act of remembering . . . or of glimpsing the future. The episode in which the gypsy Melquíades brings his "modern inventions" to Macondo is, in effect, the first event in a chain that stretches into the narrative of *Cien años de soledad* as a whole. Ice and magnets are followed by trains, armies and the United Fruit Company, each with traumatic effects equal to or greater than those brought on by the preceding juxtaposition. The buried suit of armor does not, in this instance, result in any further narrative development, but its formal potential for doing so is to be inferred here. Think, for example, of García Márquez's *Love and Other Demons* (*El amor y otros demonios*) in which the discovery of the skeleton of a young woman whose copper-colored hair has not ceased to grow since her burial several centuries before sets the plot of the entire novella in motion.

Montage, that is, seems here to furnish what Benjamin was the first to term a "dialectical image," not just of the possible unity (as desired by Surrealism) of the modern subject crippled by the rationalizing laws of "civilization," but of the possible, trans-subjective unity of historical time itself. Benjamin comes close to formulating this possibility in his writings on nineteenth-century Paris: "In the dream in which, before the eyes of each epoch, that which is to follow appears in images, the latter appears wedded to elements from prehistory, that is, of a classless society."[13] This formula, however, still presumes that the epoch dreaming of its future with images from the past experiences its own present-ness or modernity as itself a *unity*. Benjamin's Paris—still, by and large, the Paris of Surrealism—raids the past for a dialectical vision of utopia, but it never doubts its own *self*-contemporaneity. In the case of Latin America, however—and arguably of any social formation that traces its historical origins back to an act of colonization—this unity or self-contemporaneity of the present cannot be so readily presumed. As the opening episode and general narrative structure of the "magical realist" *Cien años de soledad* suggest, the past cannot simply be made a source of images for a present-tense dream if both past and present continue to inhabit the same space. It is as if in modern Paris one were to encounter not only a nineteenth-century arcade but also the vanished social types for whom it had been built, or even the illiterate peasants who had come to marvel at its ultra-modernity. The very duality of past and present is experienced as if something spatial, already present at the very source of historical movement.

It was, in fact, just this spatialization of history that constituted something like the "political unconscious" of Latin America's traditional liberal elites. For Domingo Faustino Sarmiento, whose 1845 portrait of Argentina, *Civilización y barbarie, o vida de Juan Quiroga Facundo* (nominally the biography of a notorious gaucho warlord) was to codify the historical imagination of the Latin American intelligentsia for generations to come, the past had a *location*: it was the *pampa*, the wilderness of "barbaric" tribal nomads and half-breed gauchos that lay just beyond the city-limits of Buenos Aires, if not—as during the years of the dictatorship of Juan Manuel de Rosas, who had sent Sarmiento into exile—within the city itself. Consequently, if Argentina was to implant "civilization" in its own midst, this would mean not only replicating the modernity of the European metropolis (in principle, a straightforward question of importation) but restructuring the very space in which this modernity was to take root. Sarmiento, for example, complained that, despite the abundant navigable streams that drained Argentina's wild interior and that might have linked it to the port city of Buenos Aires, the gauchos treated a river merely as something to be traversed on their nomadic route from one remote outpost to another.[14] The gaucho's unwillingness to exchange his horse for a berth on a steamboat, to route himself through the metropolis, was tantamount, for Sarmiento, to a prior refusal to enter history—or at least a history based on the modern, liberal ideal of "progress." It meant a perverse will to live in the past—but a past which, in its spatial presence, endangered the historico-philosophically sanctioned present that lay downstream. In subsequent decades, of course, the gaucho's freedom to cross rivers would be violently curtailed, and the entry into "modernity" obtained by direct coercion. But this then would only have the effect, not of conquering a uniform, indivisible "civilized" space for History, but rather of introducing the same historical duality into the space of the city itself.

Against such a backdrop it should now become clearer, at any rate, how the effect of the "dialectical image" produced through montage, while in no sense an antidote to the spatialization of history, can nevertheless become a formal means for imagining or projecting the space of historical experience as a *unity*. Even if the effect of "magical realism" is invariably ironic, when not simply and openly mystificatory (more on this below), it has at least abandoned the older, liberal-elite insistence on spatializing— and thus, in effect, naturalizing—those "backward" social elements that could not find a role in the Eurocentric narrative of "progress" and "civilization." It is by following the seemingly aimless route of Sarmiento's river-crossing gaucho nomads that Melquíades's "modernizing" gypsies eventually reach Macondo. The result is not the heroic synthesis of which Sarmiento had already begun to give up hope, but neither is it the natural-izing, profoundly reactionary historicism that subsequently flowed from this elite despair.

And it is here, in my view, that we discover the seemingly mysterious source of Latin America's "preselective affinity" for Surrealism and mont-age. The latter encounter in Latin America a pre-existing need (itself partly unconscious) to think local reality as *both* a product of history *and* as containing within itself an immanent promise or hope of genuine emancipation. Ironically, Surrealism "catches on" so readily not because (as, say, in Paris or Berlin) it promises to shatter the oppressive, reified unity of a modern, neurotic daily existence, but precisely because, in its juxta-position of the most disparate elements, it supplies a "dialectical image" of the possible *unity* of an existence *already* in a condition of disparity. For in the Latin American or generally "postcolonial" setting, disparity is before all else—*pace* Bhabha—the mark of an oppressive, bourgeois/neo-colonial order, not of its subversion. The shock afforded by "magical realist" montage is thus not limited to the shock of the "real" as something exceed-ing the merely dreamed or imagined, much as the mouthpieces of "magical realism," from Carpentier on, were to repeat such a claim. It is the shock of recognizing that this "real" is the result of a unitary, total historical process.

It is this fact, too, that best explains the strong historical attraction exerted by Surrealism and an aesthetics of montage on Latin American Marxism. When, beginning in the late nineteenth century, Marxism first found its way into Latin America, along with other currents of generally socialist, anarchist and trade unionist doctrine, it did little, one must recall, to unsettle the "spatialized" historicism of the dominant intellectual and theoretical culture. What has been termed the Marxism of the "mode of production narrative," according to which socialism would have to be preceded by a fully developed industrial capitalism, tended in fact to

confirm what the new urban and mercantile elites were already promul-
gating themselves. Not until the first major outbreaks of strikes and open
class warfare in semi-industrialized cities such as Buenos Aires did Marxism
emerge as a threat to these elites, but even then its local exponents had not
effected any substantive break with Sarmiento's modernizing disdain for
the "backward," rural world of "barbarie." It is the Peruvian Marxist José
Carlos Mariátegui who, in the 1920s, was effectively the first to give serious
thought to the idea of a more direct road to socialism in Latin America,
routed, in the case of Peru, through the communalist traditions of a
dispossessed, racially oppressed indigenous peasantry.[15] Mariátegui, of
course, had read Lenin, and could point to the worker/peasant alliances of
early Soviet society as a possible model, but it is significant that, in
Mariátegui's case, there seemed to be no inconsistency between a Leninist
Marxism and the then newly arriving doctrines of avant-garde aesthetics,
Surrealism among them. The Peruvian poet César Vallejo, whose importance Mariátegui had been among the first to recognize, exemplifies this
affinity in the most profound way. As the originator of a poetic style in
which the most electrifying possibilities of montage are brought into
intensely intimate, synthetic relation to a hatred of capitalist, neo-colonial
existence, Vallejo saw no contradiction in claiming adherence to doctrines
of both the avant-garde and of socialist realism. The disputes and ideological tensions that eventually broke the Surrealist/Communist alliance in
pre-World War II Europe seem somehow irrelevant to the poetics that
suffuse a collection such as *Poemas humanos* (1939), Vallejo's final,
posthumously published volume. Here, as in the case of the radicalized
aesthetics of authors from Neruda to Asturias, Surrealism's relationship to
Marxism is less that of an analogue than of a kind of supplement—as if
montage were providing a "dialectical image" not only of an emancipatory
break in its objective, historical dimension but of the mental category of
revolution itself, within an intellectual mind-set still accustomed to
associating revolution with a history centered in the colonizer's metropolis.

But even a "dialectical image" is, in the end, no proof against an anti-
dialectical conception of the real—as concrete *totality*—thus pictured or
imagined. A history which must *supplement* its own presumed "laws" with a
promise of emancipation still views this emancipation itself as an ultimately
irrational occurrence, for the notion that history could administer to itself
the "shock" that would propel it out of its own impasse and into a utopian
future is, itself, profoundly ahistorical. Like the theological and subsequently secularized naturalisms that have traditionally furnished colonial
and neo-colonial elites the world over with alibis for maintaining the most
oppressed and marginalized sectors of humanity in social and economic
reserve, if not in quarantine, Surrealist or psychotherapeutically inspired
politics still presuppose social duality as a pre-historical, naturally evolved
condition, rather than the specific historical form of development of

(neo-)colonized social formations. Only the ethical and aesthetic polarities are reversed: it is in the "backward" that hopes are now placed, as we await the moment of eruption, or, in more therapeutic terms, the "return of the repressed." The wait, of course, goes on indefinitely, and perhaps that is its strongest ideological attraction.

This final lapse of a historical dialectic of liberation manifests itself in *Cien años de soledad* in its cyclical, rather than progressive and cumulative narrative teleology. The montage-like device of continuously forcing past and present, traditional and modern, into jarring collisions comes to rest, as the reader will recall, in the extinction of the Buendía line and the annihilation of Macondo itself, at the very moment that Melquíades' cryptic manuscript, which had prophesied this end, is finally decoded. This is a departure, it is true, from the spatialized temporality of naturalism, in which the foregrounding historical duality simply remains in place, no matter whether in a final "victory" for "civilization" (e.g. the seemingly providential triumph of the modernizing hero Santos Luzardo in Rómulo Gallegos's *Doña Bárbara* [1929]) or in its defeat (e.g. the final lapsing back into brutishness and disease of the poor peasant community that frames the action in Manuel Zeno Gandía's *La charca* [1894]). But remove the overlay of allegorizing and "sociological" diagnosis and it becomes apparent that Macondo's fate fits essentially the same "historical" template. The resort to montage has made it possible to imagine Latin America as historically integral with itself, but only on an isolated, phenomenological plane. Up to this point the *structure of social action* itself remains static, even if now viewed from an ironizing, aestheticizing perspective.

The following chapter takes up the question of the eventual and radical epicalizing of this structure. But in conclusion here one notes, in the relative ease with which the "magical realist" formula is appropriated by late capitalist culture industry, what may be the limiting condition of Surrealism itself, from its very beginnings: in pinning all hopes on a "profane illumination" it prepares for its own inevitable deterioration into little more than a mock religion, a supplier of "miracles" for a reified existence that can no longer be shocked by anything short of its own overthrow.

══10══

Rulfo and the Transcultural:
A Revised View

The fiction of Juan Rulfo has enjoyed canonical stature for what is now more than a generation, not only in Mexico and Latin American but in the North American and European literary and academic world as well. For some literary figures such stature has become grounds for suspicion and—even worse—for neglect; but this seems not to be the case with Rulfo. This may in part be due to the fact that Rulfo's fiction, like that of Borges, shows no obvious debt to intellectual or cultural fashion prevalent at the time of its writing and thus migrates more easily into the new "counter-canons" linked to theoretical trends such as postmodernism or cultural studies.[1] Many other Latin American oeuvres associated with the "boom"—those of Cortázar and Fuentes, for example, whose "experimental" and *nouveau roman* pretensions are now precisely what make them seem so dated (see chapter 7)—have had much greater difficulty in making such transitions. And Rulfo's legendary silences and avoidance of publicity have obviously done him no harm here.

But Rulfo continues to engross even those readers who—like many of my students, for example—are merely obliged to read him. And I think this is because, in ways that remain to be fully understood, his best fictions continue to produce, in its nearly pure state and with a seemingly perfect economy of artistic means, a literary or narrative effect that finds a deep and persistent confirmation in contemporary historical experience, especially but not exclusively in Mexico and Latin America. I shall return shortly to this "effect" in greater detail.

I speak here as a reader and critic who has himself voiced strong suspicions of Rulfo for precisely the "counter-canonical" motives alluded to above. In *Modernism and Hegemony*, a study published in 1990, I raised certain questions about a still common predisposition to interpret the salient literary features of Rulfian fiction as a product of its "transcultural" genesis.[2] The concept of "transculturation," coined by the Cuban anthropologist Fernando Ortiz in response to Malinowski's concept of "neo-culturation" and turned, brilliantly, to literary critical purposes by Ángel Rama, challenges the assumption that the clash of cultures experienced in the process of colonization leads, necessarily, to the assimilation of one by the other.[3] This holds true whether, as in the case of the fall of the ancient Roman empire to tribal invaders, the more "primitive" is formally subordinated to the more highly "civilized" culture of the conquered political entity, or whether, as in the case of most modern imperialist colonization of tribal and other pre-capitalist societies in Asia, Africa and Latin America, it is the cultures of the latter that appear to give way. Ortiz pointed to the strong and clearly living, self-reproducing presence of African cultural practices at practically all levels of Cuban society as grounds for concluding that politically or historically opposed cultures do nevertheless combine to produce new, syncretic or "transcultural" forms. In *Transculturación narrativa en América Latina* Rama argued in similar terms that the "neo-regionalist" fiction of, for instance, an Arguedas, needed to be read as the literary equivalent of such syncretic cultural forms—as fictions in which the modern, "civilizing" discourse of, to use Rama's later terminology, the "*ciudad letrada*" (the "literate city" and its "cultured speech" or "*lengua culta*") itself became the object of a cultural trans-coding undertaken by the discoursing subject of a "lengua popular."[4] And although Rama did not explicitly apply this thesis to Rulfo, it requires little imagination to link the sharp difference between Rulfo and the earlier, still essentially naturalist narrative of, say, a Mariano Azuela, to the stronger, more poetically formative presence in *El llano en llamas* and *Pedro Páramo* of "*lengua popular*." Recall Rulfo's much cited claim in his interview with Luis Harss to "*escribir como se habla*," to "write as you speak."[5]

The objection I voiced in *Modernism and Hegemony* to this mode of interpretation was that, while convincing as a description of certain of the formal aspects of Rulfian narrative, it could furnish no grounds for concluding that *El llano en llamas* and *Pedro Páramo* were themselves the narrative embodiment, the authentic "voice" of the regional culture whose language they had adopted. In fact, it might be just as convincingly be argued that such a "transcultural" principle of narration served precisely to disguise, in a kind of populist masquerade, a deeper, reactionary and pathologizing representation of rural, peasant culture, placing Rulfo securely within the naturalizing ideology that stretches from Sarmiento down to the positivist ideologues of the *porfiriato*. At best, the "transcultural" reading of Rulfo left this question in a condition of undecidability. Two terms—country and city, the oral and the written—were clearly being mediated. But which was mediating the other?

But it now strikes me that, whether invoked in defense of Rulfo or in a more critical spirit, the concept of transculturation effectively leaves untouched and unilluminated those literary or narrative qualities—what Alfonso Reyes once simply termed his "style"—that make Rulfo's fiction so starkly emphatic and so apparently irresistible to most readers. The revised thesis I wish briefly to argue here, bluntly stated, is that Rulfo's style owes, in the end, little or nothing to questions of cultural experience and nearly everthing to those of historical experience. These are fictions about history before they are about culture, about time before they are about space.

But to understand why this is so we need to return again briefly to the theory of transculturation, at least in relation to the underlying problem to which it proposes (in my view) an abstract, mystificatory and thus false solution. This is the problem of the extreme social duality characterizing most Latin American (and indeed, "postcolonial") national formations. But such duality subsists not only in the empirical fact of the deep divisions separating rich and poor, city and country, elite and popular culture, etc., in societies such as Brazil or Mexico but in a historico-ontological condition that fundamentally alters the social ground of national and regional experience itself. We recall here again how, in essays such as "Misplaced Ideas" and "Nationalism by Elimination," Roberto Schwarz has argued that the seeming paradox of the Brazilian cultural and intellectual elite's historical compulsion to discover its own national-cultural essence without, however, ceasing to import its ideas and fashions from the imperial metropolis can itself only be explained as a result of that elite's near-total social and cultural alienation from the "Brazilian" masses. With its very social existence resting on forms of exploitation so extreme that the possibility of a shared or reciprocal national-cultural existence tends to zero—forms of exploitation that are the objective result of colonial and neo-colonial dependency—this class must experience its own national-cultural identity as a sort of desire incapable either of fulfillment or of extinction.

The essential point here, as argued earlier in the conclusion to chapter 6, is to grasp the cultural duality that separates rich and poor, city and country, etc. as a problem that cannot be solved on its own cultural terms. Its solution must be social, historical—and ultimately political. Thus, while transculturation may enable a more precise, empirical description of cultural life on its most immediate level in Latin America, it cannot give even the slightest indication of how to resolve the social dualities that are and continue to be the historically inevitable result of colonization and a persistently enforced neo-colonial relation to the global economic order. The very historical forces that have produced the deep cultural divisions reflected—more objectively than before, no doubt—in transcultural theory continuously reproduce these same divisions even as the spontaneous tendency to transculturation blunts their edges.

Now, if the historically determined forms of extreme social inequality that afflict national societies in Latin America can give rise to an experience of cultural duality, they might clearly generate much the same effect in the national or collective experience of historical time itself—especially in relation to the idea of modernity. It has now in fact become something of an intellectual commonplace to remark on the distinctly Latin American and perhaps generally "postcolonial" sense of being both modern and traditional, both "ahead of" and yet "behind the times" at once, as if not one but two or multiple histories were being lived out in one and the same space. In "postcolonial" circles one now habitually encounters the "theory" that this multiple or heterogeneous temporality might even supply an unsuspected basis or location from which to elude the more sinister aspects of modernization themselves. But this rests in fact on the same intrinsic fallacy as does transcultural theory in that it fails to grasp the social appearance of multiple temporalities as itself a concrete, determinate form of the overall, unified historical development of a colonial and neo-colonial capitalism.

Putting aside the more abstract debate for now, however, we might at least agree on a description of this social experience of a split or dualistic modernity as, more simply, the experience of the present as non-self-contemporary. And it is precisely this historical experience of the non-self-contemporary that, I now think, lies at the root of Rulfo's fictional style and that elicits a constant intensity of literary effect in *El llano en llamas* and *Pedro Páramo*. Rulfian narrative does not depict or evoke this experience directly, however, but by means of a very simple, but ingenious twist: instead of a historical present that cannot shake off the past, we are told the story of its under-, or flip-side: of a past that, paradoxically, has no awareness of, no connection to the present from which it is re-experienced, a past that, in this precise sense, becomes its own present.

Consider, for example, the harrowing and uncanny chain of episodes in *Pedro Páramo*, from the beginning of the novel to the moment Dorotea re-awakens Juan Preciado, now dead and buried, in their shared grave. (The parallel narrative of Pedro Páramo himself has of course already had its sporadic beginnings, but it is only now that, with Susana San Juan's grave within earshot of Juan Preciado, the full story can be told.) In the course of this narrative prelude, Juan Preciado discovers, as all readers of *Pedro Páramo* will vividly recall, not just that he speaks only with the dead, but that he himself—at precisely which moment seems infinitely debatable—has become one of them. What makes this particular instance of reversal or Aristotelian peripeteia especially unusual, however, is that the moment of recognition (anagnorisis) that accompanies it occurs not once but repeatedly: first when Eduviges Dyada tells Juan Preciado she has learned from his dead mother of his impending arrival; again when Damiana Cisneros informs him that Eduviges died years ago; yet again when Damiana herself vanishes as Juan Preciado suspects her as well of being an apparition, etc. The endless interpretive disputes as to whether the incestuous couple (Donis and his unnamed "sister") that shelters Juan Preciado before his re-awakening in a grave are Comala's only living inhabitants are in the end immaterial to the achieved, overall effect of this narrative device. This is the continuous barring or pre-emption of what the peripeteia in its classic form is designed, from a temporal perspective, to reproduce: namely, a sense of destiny or fate as the transparent linkage of past and present, as, for example, in Oedipus' final discovery, after causing the death of his parents, of the truth of his own birth. In *Pedro Páramo* this sense of destiny, this formal, underlying unity of present and past takes the seemingly monstrous form of a reversal-cum-recognition that forces its heroic subject to lose sight of his own location or point of departure in the present. The hero's fate is not only dark; it likewise fails to complete and therefore to redeem the past, to purge the present of past crimes and irrationalities. In Comala the dead literally bury the dead, and yet in doing so they deny this as a right or a capacity of the living. Juan Preciado comes to Comala, not, in Oedipal fashion, to discover the mystery of his birth and then to meet his downfall, but rather to discover that having been born is in itself no proof of living in the present.

Many of the shorter and, in some ways, more formally perfected narratives of *El llano en llamas* render this same effect less aggressively, but no less unequivocally. To return, for example, to "La Cuesta de las Comadres," the focus of my earlier remarks on Rulfo in *Modernism and Hegemony*, we can note the same, so to speak, negative principle of peripeteia in the narrator's abrupt confession that it is he who has killed Remigio Torrico. Recall that Remigio, together with his brother Odilón, had operated as the local *cacique* in the small village named in the title until after the land reform or "*reparto*," when the villagers, still unable to break the hold of the Torricos, began abandoning the place. With no one left on whom to prey, the Torricos take to brigandage, forcing the unnamed narrator of "La Cuesta de las Comadres" to act as their henchman. Thus when the narrator, as the last remaining inhabitant of the village, confesses to having killed Remigio (after he is first accused by him of murdering Odilón) there is a strong predisposition on the reader's part to treat this murder as a destined, poetically justified end. But this reading would in turn require, in accordance with the same poetic law, that the narrator too now leave the village, crossing over the same, mysterious horizon beyond which should lie—as we somehow instinctively know—the modern, the city, the fullness of history as the contemporary. Because he stays, however—ending his tale only with a vivid and gruesome description of his careful disposal of Remigio's corpse—this expectant sense of a destiny about to be fulfilled is drastically altered. The horizon of the modern, of the present as self-contemporary, remains un-crossed, allowing the past in all its seeming irrationality and "barbarie" to prolong itself infinitely and irredeemably. Although not in so literal a fashion as with Juan Preciado, the hero of "La Cuesta de las Comadres" too is fated neither to live nor to die, but rather to be buried alive.

This is, in itself, a terribly grim perspective on the world. But it works brilliantly as a device for giving concrete narrative and poetic form to an experience of the modern as non-self-contemporary—an experience that has innumerable means for ideological self-obfuscation at its disposal. It would be the gravest injustice to Rulfo to accuse him here of simply giving vent to a nostalgia for a lost past, in the style, say, of Jorge Isaac's *María* or of *Gone with the Wind*. Such forms of nostalgia are themselves premised on an absolute assurance of the modern as present in relation to this "lost" past. The loss of the past is complete and irrecoverable because the present appears to have already closed off all the avenues that lead back to it. For political and social motives that may in the end be questioned, Rulfo refuses to believe in this ideologized present, and it is this negativity that gives his writing its profound artistic truth.

One must of course be careful not to exaggerate the scope of Rulfo's narrative ingenuity in this respect. His fictions can, finally, do no more than produce the aesthetic effect of the non-self-contemporary as a kind of pervasive mood or atmosphere. That is why the shorter narratives of *El llano en llamas* often show greater formal integrity than *Pedro Páramo*, a "novel" lacking any real, overall unity of action. The Rulfian practice of "negative peripeteia" can, after all, only work as a kind of atmospheric catalyst. It cannot take the narrative that leads up to it any further than itself, and for this reason its novelistic or epic deployment can only take the form of a repetition. Still, the constant evocation of this unique historical atmosphere is sufficient to retain for Rulfo's fictions their own readerly contemporaneity. Rulfo's ghosts and fantasms are, *pace* magical realism, not real, but the spectral modernity from against whose backdrop they are conjured most certainly is. As the social and political crisis of this modernity assumes catastrophic proportions in Mexico and across the globe, Rulfo's forays into a past both immediate and yet infinitely remote enact a form of historical desire that, if anything, has gained in intensity. His mastery as an ethnographic medium, together with an admittedly unequalled ear and eye for regional idiolects and customs, would not arouse the slightest interest were it not for Rulfo's instinctive grasp of popular culture as a negative principle in relation to modernity's false invocations of destiny. However intimate its narrative positioning, it is not merely a cultural landscape that Rulfo shows us. It is "culture" in its uncanny, temporal aspect as a past that has forgotten the present, a past that goes on speaking.

Mario Vargas Llosa:
The Realist as Neo-Liberal

I.

Suppose a world-renowned novelist were to fall asleep at his writing desk and have the following nightmare: he is a candidate for the presidency of his country, favored to win in an election in which, at the last minute, the electorate turns out to be made of up of his own characters. They vote, without exception, against him. He loses the election and leaves the country angry and disgraced. Sobered by the experience, he decides—awake now, or asleep?—to write a book about it.

The dream is too canny, too much the sketch for a Cortazarian fable to be possible. But we have the book: Mario Vargas Llosa's perversely titled *A Fish in the Water*, in which he interlaces his own account of his loss to Alberto Fujimori in the Peruvian presidential elections of 1990 with a partial autobiography covering 1936–1958, the period from his birth to the first of his many literary "exiles" in Europe.[1]

Awake or asleep? In the sixteenth chapter *of A Fish in the Water* ("The Great Change") Vargas Llosa relates the story of a mass distribution of cheap Christmas toys to poor children in a number of provincial cities, organized by *Acción Solidaria*, the charitable, largely uxorial wing of the candidate's political party, *Movimiento Libertad*. Under the efficient guidance of Vargas Llosa's wife Patricia, the distribution in Ayacucho goes off without a hitch, despite the threat of violence from Shining Path guerrillas. In Puerto Maldonado, however, things go amiss. Despite careful instructions to the local *Movimiento Libertad* organizers that the distribution is to be among children of party loyalists only—"since we didn't have enough gifts for the millions of poor children in Peru"[2]—thousands of alerted mothers and children line up for presents. "The sight," writes Vargas Llosa, "was heartbreaking."

> Children and mothers had been there, roasting in the burning-hot sun of Amazonia, since very early that morning, four, five, six hours, to receive—if they managed to—a plastic sand bucket, a little wooden doll, a bit of chocolate,

or a package of caramels. I was upset, hearing the mothers of Libertad trying
to explain to that horde of children and barefoot mothers dressed in rags
that the toys had been given out, that they would have to go away empty
handed. The image of those sad or angry faces did not leave me for a single
second, as I spoke at the rally and visited the local headquarters of Libertad,
and as I held a discussion that night with our leaders, in the Hotel de
Turistas, with the sounds of the jungle as a background . . . .[3]

The scene, which has clearly captured Vargas Llosa's imagination despite its
implicit mockery of neo-liberal dogmas, is repeated in Cuzco and then in
Andahuaylas, where, Vargas Llosa ruefully concedes, "I don't believe that
that Christmas won us a single voter. . . ."[4]

The "political" chapters of *A Fish in the Water* are filled with similar
anecdotes, related with the author's superb narrative skill and with what,
considering the book is meant, *ultima instantia*, to serve as an apology for
his political beliefs, seems an altogether *un*canny measure of honesty. In
the eighth chapter we read of Vargas Llosa's early enthusiasm and support
for Hernando de Soto, co-author of *The Other Path* (*El otro sendero*, first
published in Peru in 1986), which argued for Peru's burgeoning "informal"
sector of street vendors and black marketeers (but not cocaine producers
and exporters?) as the basis for a new capitalist growth cycle and eventual
prosperity.[5] But having written the prologue to *El otro sendero* and praised
its author in the *New York Times*—out of a conviction that "Hernando de
Soto would be a good president of Perú"[6]—Vargas Llosa's encounters with
the man himself make him more doubtful. De Soto, "a slightly pompous
and ridiculous figure . . . his Spanish studded with Anglicisms and
Gallicisms" speaks at the inaugural assembly of *Movimiento Libertad*, held
on the Plaza San Martín in Lima in August of 1987.[7] That same evening,
however, according to *A Fish in the Water*, De Soto meets secretly with
then president and arch-enemy of *Movimiento Libertad*, Alan García, later
appearing with the head *Aprista* in public and even going so far as to
denounce *Movimiento Libertad* in secret to acquaintances in the US State
Department. *El otro sendero* continues, in his view, to be "a good book" but
its author is reluctantly conceded to be a Machiavellian opportunist of the
worst possible sort.[8] "Those of us who aided and abetted him—and, in a
manner of speaking, invented him—must admit frankly, without mincing
words: we had not contributed to the cause of freedom or that of Peru, but,
rather, whetted the appetites of a homegrown Rastignac."[9]

For Vargas Llosa, who cites Balzac's famous dictum regarding the
novel—"c'est l'histoire privée des nations"—in the epigraph to his novel
Conversation in the Cathedral, the allusion to Balzac, too, seems slightly
uncanny. It is almost as if, to avoid the extreme political embarrassment
caused by the real De Soto, it had become necessary to retreat momentarily
back onto that level of representation in which "inventing" him might

indeed "serve the cause of Peru." De Soto as Rastignac . . . and Vargas Llosa, we might infer, as his "homegrown" Balzac.

In fact, not only do the characters who inhabit Vargas Llosa's real-life political farce begin to appear more novelesque than anything else, but his novels themselves make *political* appearances. When the author takes his campaign to Iquitos, capital of the Amazonian province of Loreto and setting for his comic novel about the militarization of prostitution, *Captain Pantoja and the Special Services (Pantaleón y las visitadoras)*[10] the APRA-controlled local government rouses the populace against him, "the pornographic slanderer who is endeavouring to sully the soil of Loreto."[11] In the Andean city of Puno, one of Vargas Llosa's female lieutenants is heckled with shouts alluding to another of the author's fictions: "Get out of here, Aunt Julia!"[12] And in a later chapter[13] *A Fish in the Water* relates how, in an effort to tag its author as a "pervert," the García government arranges to have *In Praise of the Stepmother (Elogio a la madrasta)*[14] read, chapter by chapter, on a state-controlled radio station.[15] Cited as examples of the outrages to which APRA was willing to resort in order to scuttle his electoral victory, Vargas Llosa seems somehow gratified by these actions, even confirmed in his status, for better or ill, as Peru's best-known living author.[16]

Thus those very things that most gall and embarrass the candidate seem, if anything, to exalt and even strangely inspire the novelist. "Punto Final" or "Period," the book's concluding "political" chapter, details, often more wistfully than angrily, the supremely farcical denouement of Vargas Llosa's political adventure in which his backers stake all on a campaign to present their professedly agnostic candidate as a defender of the Catholic church against the Protestant evangelical sects that had aligned themselves with Fujimori. With a sense of dramatic irony worthy of the greatest works of political satire,[17] Vargas Llosa relates here the story of a secret visit paid him by Lima's archbishop, on the advice of wife Patricia, to convince the candidate not to withdraw from the second round face-off race against Fujimori.[18] In an interview that Vargas Llosa himself describes as "confused in my memory with the most unusual episodes of the good novels that I have read"[19] the candidate draws the blinds of his upstairs study, reads the Bible with Monsignor Vargas Alzamora, and is ultimately persuaded by the prelate's arguments that the preservation of national unity is threatened by heretical sects allied with his Asiatic, perhaps not truly "Peruvian" opponent. The situation might provoke a *coup d'état*, ending Peru's still recent return to "democracy."

Climaxing all, however, is the account of the candidate's final campaign visit to Piura, scene of Vargas Llosa's youth and setting for much of his novel *The Green House (La casa verde)*.[20] Piura is the city with which, perhaps along with his birthplace, Arequipa, Vargas Llosa "took for granted . . . a sort of reciprocity" that would at least guarantee him an electoral victory there.

My grimmest memory of those days is that of my arrival, one torrid morning, in a little settlement betwen Ignacio Escudero and Cruceta, in the valley of Chira. Armed with sticks and stones and all sorts of weapons to bruise and batter, an infuriated horde of men and women came to meet me, their faces distorted by hatred, who appeared to have emerged from the depths of time, a prehistory in which human beings and animals were indistinguishable, since for both life was a blind struggle for survival. Half naked, with very long hair and fingernails never touched by a pair of scissors, surrounded by emaciated children with huge swollen bellies, bellowing and shouting to keep their courage up, they hurled themselves on the caravan of vehicles as though fighting to save their lives or seeking to immolate themselves, with a rashness and a savagery that said everything about the almost inconceivable levels of deterioration to which life for millions of Peruvians had sunk. What were they attacking? What were they defending themselves from? What phantoms were behind those threatening clubs and knives? In the wretched village there was no water, no light, no work, no medical post, and the little school hadn't been open for years because it had no teacher. What harm could I have done them, when they no longer had anything to lose . . . .?[21]

Here, in what is tacitly Vargas Llosa's final concession of political defeat, novelist and ideologue do seem about to converge. The memoir's tone here becomes noticeably false and defensive, and the terrible pathos of the scene prompts only an angry, reflexive retreat into neo-liberal dogma: "they were the best possible proof that Peru could not continue to exist any longer in the populist delirium." [22] (Ergo, the "prehistoric" immiseration of these unfortunate people dates back only to the Velasco government?) Like that of the poor and more docile mothers and children in Puerto Maldonado, the image of the violent "horde" in Piura evokes some measure of sympathy, but is now more reminiscent of a scene out of Sarmiento's *Facundo*, or of Echeverría's "The Slaughterhouse" ("El Matadero") than of *The Green House* or *The War of the End of the World* (*La guerra del fin del mundo*).[23] Similarly stripped of all nuance and just as transparently hypocritical is the postscript or "Colofón" of the memoir. Here Vargas Llosa indignantly refuses to see the crowning irony of his political fiasco in the fact that Fujimori, once in power, promptly implements Vargas Llosa's neo-liberal platform, even including former Movimiento Libertad advisers in his administration. And, true to Sarmentine form, Vargas Llosa's final bitter outcry in the "Colofón" is uttered against Fujimori the "caudillo."[24]

There is of course nothing comic about the neo-liberal "theory" and policies that in the name of an abstract "individual freedom" have justified the "laissez-faire" looting of Latin America by international finance capital and the subsequently intensified immiseration of millions of *real*, unfree individuals.[25] When, preaching Popper and Von Hayek now instead of Sartre and Camus, Vargas Llosa calmly assures his readers that "countries today can *choose* to be prosperous" by "open[ing] out to the world and organiz[ing] [the] economy on a competitive basis"[26] but that, unfortunately, Peru and Latin America "chose to go backward" two decades ago,[27] one laughs more in horrified amazement than in amusement. So monumental, and yet seemingly ingenuous a bad faith is both unforgivable but also difficult to regard as intellectually serious. Vargas Llosa devotes an entire chapter of *A Fish in the Water* to bashing Peru's "cheap" (because "populist") intellectuals, but only a veritable bargain basement intellectual, who has bought his neo-liberalism even more cheaply than his existentialism, could openly declare sinister nonsense of this sort. No wonder De Soto warned the State Department against Vargas Llosa, and, as *A Fish in the Water* duly, but very discreetly notes, the CIA was secretly worried about a Vargas Llosa presidency.[28] There is something pathological in addition to the ideological at work here, an *inanity* of the ideological that gives ironic new meaning to Roberto Schwarz's characterization of the "second degree ideology" of Brazil's nineteenth-century slave-owning "liberals" as not "describ[ing] reality, not even falsely."[29]

But when Vargas Llosa's neo-liberal inanities are considered in more strictly *formal* relation to the narrative accompaniment that is evidently meant by the author to humanize them, to show them to be well-intentioned and sincere if perhaps also naive, the effect is almost *to fictionalize the ideology itself*, to make it seem the utterly appropriate accompaniment to the liminally comic novel that *A Fish in the Water* seems always on the point of becoming. The reality that is ideologically "un-described" by Vargas Llosa's neo-liberalism returns in the form of a mass of anecdotes, each incidental in itself, but collectively of sufficient momentum to throw the unrepentant ideologue's memoir off ideological center. As reader, one must either attend to the true as sheer experiential, narrative concretion or to the true as abstract, doctrinal self-evidence, and Vargas Llosa, despite a clumsy and mean-spirited attempt to close this gap at the memoir's conclusion, remains just *enough* the realist—the "escribidor de historias"[30]—to have opened it in the first place. It seems impossible to believe that the narrator who tells us the story of De Soto, neo-liberal ideologue and "homegrown Rastignac" could do so thinking his own neo-liberal inanities to be any less a legitimate target for satire. How could we take such a writer seriously, unless he were *so much the fool*— the "tonto vivo"—that reality itself could be read in his own blithe willingness to leave it entirely out of account? Is it perhaps possible that Vargas Llosa has made *himself* the unwitting hero of an unintended, still inchoate comic novel about the absurdities, say, of travelling to Puerto Maldonado or Piura to tell people that they have "chosen" their poverty? For the neo-liberal, "second degree" ideologue whom we cannot believe but who tells us stories we cannot help but believe could not himself be anything but a fiction—the Pantaleón Pantoja of neo-liberalism himself!

II

For anyone with a critical interest in Vargas Llosa, *A Fish in the Water*
becomes a necessary point of reference, if for no other reason because of
the extreme risk it takes as it attempts to harness the skills of the story
teller *directly* to the ideologue's *apologia pro vita sua*. The resulting impression of bad faith affects even the autobiographical strand of the memoir.
Here Vargas Llosa undertakes the presumably less dangerous task of
recounting the circumstantial and personal origins of fictions from "The
Chiefs" ("Los jefes")[31] to *In Praise of the Stepmother*. Personal anecdote has
the burden of telling us why the novelist came, say, to write about military
schools or debacles on the Amazonian frontier, not why he set out to make,
on its behalf, the existential "choice" (to be "prosperous") his country had
somehow failed to make on its own. But to anyone who has read, and been
swayed, by the fictions themselves, the memoirist's meta-literary *mise-en-
scène* comes, too, to seem "off," even "second degree." In the eleventh
chapter of *A Fish in the Water* (sixth of the juvenile literary memoir) Vargas
Llosa recounts his brief collaboration in the mid 1950s with *Cahuide*, the
clandestine organization of Peru's Soviet-aligned Communist Party, heavily
repressed and decimated under the Odría dictatorship. In fairness to the
author it must be said that what one reads is not the tale of fanaticism and
betrayal expected of Vargas Llosa the born-again Cold War editorialist and
admirer of Popper, Koestler and *The God that Failed*. Vargas Llosa claims to
have broken with Communism (significantly, *before* the events of 1956)
because, in his words, he becomes "fed up" and "bored." It is not total-
itarian "evil" that shocks the budding novelist into apostasy but the
"puerility" of the Communist "catechism of stereotypes" and "because
there was in my nature, in my individualism, in my growing vocation as a
writer, and in my intractable temperament a visceral inability to embody
the patient, tireless docile revolutionary. . . ."[32]

But compare this—as Vargas Llosa must know that some of his readers
will—to the fictionalized account of *Cahuide* in *Conversation in the Cathedral*
(*Conversación en la Catedral*).[33] Here the novel's loosely autobiographical
hero, Santiago Zavala, breaks with the Party only after the participation of
his San Marcos student cell in a transit workers' strike and his resulting
arrest and release, thanks to a deal struck between his wealthy, capitalist
father and Cayo Bermúdez, Odría's shadowy secret police chief. Although
"Zavalita" expresses some of his "creator's" (Sartrean) doubts about Communist orthodoxy, and cannot quite distinguish between his own political
idealism and his infatuation with Aida, fellow cell member and San Marcos
student (Lea Barba in *A Fish in the Water*'s "real life" account) he does not
find it so easy as Vargas Llosa (ca. 1990) to write off the experience as
youthful folly. Echoing the novel's well-known refrain—"*¿en qué momento se
jodió el Perú?*" "When did Peru get fucked up?"—Zavalita wonders whether

his sudden abandonment of the revolutionary ideals embodied in *Cahuide* (and his failure to declare his love for Aida) are not the precise moment when he himself "se jodió," the moment of his own personal failure. In one of the novel's multiple, interwoven "conversations," Santiago speculates to fellow journalist and bohemian Carlitos on what might have become of his life if, like Aida, he had made a total commitment to revolutionary militancy.

> "It wasn't horror over dogma, it was the reflex of a two-bit anarchist child who doesn't like to take orders," Carlitos said. "Underneath it all you were afraid of breaking with people who eat and dress and smell well."
>
> "But I hated those people, I still hate them," Santiago said. "That's the only thing I'm sure of, Carlitos."
>
> "Then it was the spirit of contradiction, the chip on your shoulder," Carlitos said. "You should have stuck to literature and forgotten about revolution, Zavalita."
>
> "I knew that if everybody set himself to being intelligent and having his doubts, Peru would go on being fucked up forever," Santiago said. "I knew there was a need for dogmatic people, Carlitos."[34]

There is little point in debating which of the two texts—*Conversation in the Cathedral* or *A Fish in the Water*—provides the truer *personal* account of the matter. But the fictionalist's "truth of lies" [35] notwithstanding, the superior historical and moral *truth* of the novel, its finely shaded perception of the real displacements separating doctrinal fidelity, personal sacrifice, individualism, and abiding, legitimate class hatred is inescapable. "There was a need for dogmatic people." Even here the potential for intertextual comedy arises (Vargas Llosa for president?) but this one line, without a hint of apology, tells us more about "Peru," about late-capitalist and "postcolonial" social pathologies than the whole of *A Fish in the Water*. How could an intelligence capable of this kind of dialectical intuition, "fictionalized" or no, later descend to the banality of the libertarian "individualist"? The effect of such extreme, almost aphasic displacement is to make not only the neo-liberal credo of *A Fish in the Water* but even the literary autobiography itself appear gratuitously, "inanely" ideological.

The paradox of this disjuncture between socio-historical, "national" experience as *narrative* object and as would-be secular object of an abstract, *political* rationality is, in fact, what makes not only *A Fish in the Water* but Vargas Llosa's *opus* as a whole a seminal case study for Latin Americanism and perhaps "postcolonialism" itself. The partly analogous case of Borges —the anti-Peronist "conservative" and literary "revolutionary"—comes immediately to mind here, but Vargas Llosa, whose activism and sheer bluntness have made him into one of the most scandalizing, if not reviled figures of recent Latin American intellectual history, renders the paradox impossible to avoid. There is of course no absence of criticism that has contrived to find corroboration for Vargas Llosa's rightward political evolution directly on the plane of his aesthetics.[36] But the danger of a *critical* bad faith, fueled by the still potent, romantic myth of the Latin American writer as *spontaneous* revolutionary (Martí, Neruda, Arguedas, García Márquez, *et al.*) runs high here.[37] The enormous scope and ambition of his fictional output, to which the ever tactful Borges did not aspire, are what, ironically, seem to have fed a corresponding narrowness and evasiveness of approach to Vargas Llosa.[38] But the author of *A Fish in the Water* could write tomorrow in *El País* or *The New York Times* that he now believes that Machu Picchu was built by ancient astronauts, and it would not be enough to dislodge works such as *Conversation in the Cathedral* or *The War of the End of the World* from their place as, arguably, the most signal realizations to date of a modern, Latin American realism. Many may dispute this claim, but it will do here to recall that the universally esteemed critic Ángel Rama, Vargas Llosa's political antagonist from the time of the Padilla affair in the early 1970s, described *The War of the End of the World* in one of his last writings as Latin America's *War and Peace*, and its author as "our greatest living classic."[39]

Borges could playfully allude to the possibility that he too was just a fictionalized "other," the merely formal medium and not the founding subject of his own (seeming) literary/political contradictions. Vargas Llosa, on the other hand, believing himself (with a vengeance!) to *be* this founding subject, actually *produces* the fictionalized, "other" self only imagined in Borges's fable.[40] As a kind of philosophical joke, Borges pre-emptively reduces reality to a privileged fiction—a fact that in nowise subtracts from the often excentric, displaced, but ineluctable realism of many of the fictions themselves—and finds a kind of refuge for himself therein. Vargas Llosa arrives, unconsciously, at the same result thanks to a forced march *through* a reality whose sheer ideological recalcitrance spontaneously fictionalizes all those who, as a show of political faith, already think to possess its key. The point is that in neither case is the paradoxical, seemingly contradictory tendency for fiction and reality to suddenly invert their respective positions an accident, much less a result of outright romantic invention. To make sense of this inversion, this "truth" that makes "liars" of those who proclaim the "truth of lies" as the province of fiction alone, it must be grasped *as rooted in the social, historical*—in this sense "material"—*object itself*. To solve, if possible, the paradox of Vargas Llosa would be to gain a proper and genuine insight into the social bases, not just of a "postcolonial" form of literary realism, but of the possible affinity of this form for the most extreme ideological aberrations and regressions.

III

How, then to unravel the paradox of Vargas Llosa, of the realist as neo-liberal, especially given what seems a general reluctance of his critics, chief among them, as we shall see, the author himself, to concede that it *is one* in

the first place? Even Rama, who detects an irony here, underplays the real
depth and import of the problematic. In his prologue to *The War of the End
of the World* Rama notes that Vargas Llosa's "thought . . . such as it appears
in his essays . . . breaks down within his literary practice proper and works
to the detriment of an exceptional novel."[41] As an example of this, Rama
points to the character of the Baron of Cañabrava, Vargas Llosa's
purported mouthpiece in *The War of the End of the World*, destined to seal his
social and political demise as the leading *fazendeiro* of Brazil's Bahia
province by violently and passionately seducing the mulatto maidservant of
his mentally ailing wife, while the latter impassively, perhaps approvingly,
looks on. Rama accuses Vargas Llosa of having compromised, at the last
moment, the social realism of the novel by refusing to hold the erotic
"fanaticism" of the Baron to the same implicit standard of criticism to
which the religious and political fanaticisms of the Counselor, Moreira
Cesar and Galileo Gall have been subject. It seems to me that Rama's
reading of the novel is, in this instance, quite wrong: Vargas Llosa cannot
be fairly accused of endorsing his *alter ego*'s descent from temperate man of
culture with conservative views into an embittered, cynical rapist out of a
blindness for erotic and physical, as opposed to political, extremisms.
Plotting such an end for the Baron is, to the contrary, both a frank
admission of his "unfitness to rule" and a refusal to exempt the erotic from
the larger social crisis that in fact turns it into something violent and
pathological. It is, if anything, a stroke of remarkable artistic integrity and
brilliance, showing yet again how persistently Vargas Llosa the realist story
teller eludes Vargas Llosa the counter-revolutionary ideologue. (The only
characters in the novel who might be said to enjoy Vargas Llosa's implicit
sympathy are the survivors of the destruction of Canudos: the improbable
pair of lovers made up of the unnamed "near-sighted journalist"—Euclides
da Cunha's dramatic stand-in in *The War of the End of the World*—and the
Mother Courage-like Jurema.)

That Vargas Llosa is capable of prostituting his narrative skills to dogmatic
imperatives is beyond dispute. Consider, for example, the sensationalized,
horrors-of-the-Shining-Path tableaux interspersed throughout *Death in the
Andes* (*Lituma en los Andes*),[42] comparable, in their way, to the most lurid
vulgarities of Zhdanovite socialist realism. But these are lapses in what is
otherwise an *opus* remarkable, even uncanny, precisely for the way it outflanks
its own author ideologically. His fictional *alter egos*, from Zavalita to the Baron
down to the Peruvian *bourgeois gentilhomme* and erotomaniacal-"individualist"
buffoon, don Rigoberto (see *The Notebooks of Don Rigoberto*) are not the place
to look for Vargas Llosa's politico-aesthetic umbilicus.[43] Only in *A Fish in the
Water*, where his non-fictional ego is itself on full, carefully staged display,
does a kind of autobiographical bad faith rise to the surface, again suggesting
how, in retrospect, Captain Pantoja of the "special services" should likewise be
counted among the author's fictional *Doppelgänger*.

But to the improbable Marxist literary critic in search of an answer here, the spectral appearance of Balzac in *A Fish in the Water* ought to be a reminder of an earlier, classical attempt to unravel an analogous paradox. Balzac was, after all, a great favorite of Marx, who ranked him, despite his restorationist views, as second only to Shakespeare in modern European literature.[44] Engels expounded on this view in his well-known letter to Margaret Harkness (April, 1888) where he clarifies his disapproval of the *Tendenzroman* (the "point blank socialist novel [written] . . . to glorify the social and political views" of its author).[45] What follows bears citing more fully:

> The more the opinions of the author remain hidden, the better for the work of art . . . [R]ealism . . . may crop out even in spite of the author's opinions. Let me refer to an example. Balzac whom I consider a far greater master of realism than all the Zola's *passés*, *présents et a venir*, in *La Comédie humaine* gives us a most wonderfully realistic history of French "society," describing, chronicle-fashion, almost year by year from 1816 to 1848 the progressive inroads of the rising bourgeoisie upon the society of nobles . . . . [. . .] . . . I have learned more [from *La Comédie humaine*] than from all the professed historians, economists and statisticians of the period together. Well, Balzac was politically a Legitimist; his great work is a constant elegy on the irretrievable decay of good society, his sympathies are all with the class doomed to extinction. But for all that his satire is never keener, his irony never bitterer, than when he sets in motion the very men and women with whom he sympathizes most deeply—the nobles. And the only men of whom he always speaks with undisguised admiration are his bitterest political antagonists, the republican heroes of the Cloître Saint Mery, the men who at that time (1830–36) were indeed the representatives of the popular masses. That Balzac thus was compelled to go against his own class sympathies and political prejudices, that he *saw* the necessity of the downfall of his favourite nobles, and described them as people deserving no better fate; and that he *saw* the real men of the future where, for the time being, they alone were to be found—that I consider one of the greatest triumphs of realism . . . .[46]

The analogy to Vargas Llosa is already tempting here, and it is difficult not to suspect that, in *A Fish in the Water* at least, the author is subliminally aware of it himself. (The De Soto episode again comes to mind.) Despite its final lapse back into neo-liberal sectarianism, Vargas Llosa's political memoir succeeds *as narrative* because, at base, it mimes precisely this Balzacian compulsion. Like *Conversation in the Cathedral*, *A Fish in the Water* is a story worthy of its intertext with *La Comédie humaine*, but it is one that, unlike the less ideologically burdened fiction, fully exhibits the "opinions" that ought to have "remain[ed] hidden"—the more pointedly, it almost seems, to expose their inanity.

But drawing out the historical and "postcolonial" possibilities of the analogy begs the question that Engels leaves unanswered here—what could *explain* this realist compulsion to "go against [one's] own class sympathies and prejudices"? Engels, who earlier in his letter to Harkness stipulates realism as "besides truth in detail, the truth in reproduction of typical characters in typical circumstances,"[47] in fact mildly rebukes Harkness for failing to accord the "militant proletariat," ca. 1887, such fictional typicality, attributing to it instead the condition of a "passive mass, unable to help itself." "The rebellious reaction of the working class against the oppressive medium which surrounds them, their attempts—convulsive, half conscious or conscious—at recovering their status as human beings, belong to history and therefore must lay claim to a place in the domain of realism."[48] Balzac would thus seem to be the "realist" in an exceptional sense only, his Legitimist hatred for the bourgeoisie the temporary warrant for a realism that, after 1848, must see "the real men of the future" in the working class itself and tell *their* story.

Lukács, who made careful use of Marx and Engels' affection for *La Comédie humaine* in his protracted, ever tactful campaign against Zhdanovism, elaborates at much greater length on what we might term the "Balzac dialectic." In *Studies in European Realism*,[49] this dialectic grows considerably more complex as Lukács compares Balzac to his fellow (and rival) French realist, Stendhal, whose "worldview," in Lukács' words "is much clearer and more progressive than that of Balzac."[50] But Stendhal remains modestly optimistic that bourgeois society can forge an authentic culture and civilization out of its initially degraded and anarchic condition. Balzac, "influenced both by romantic, mystic Catholicism and a feudalist Socialism," sees no basis for optimism whatever. Lukács:

> It is a curious result of this *strange dialectic of history and of the unequal growth of ideologies* that Balzac—with his confused and often quite reactionary world-view—mirrored the period between 1789 and 1848 much more completely and profoundly than his much more clear-thinking and progressive rival. True, Balzac criticized capitalism from the right, from the feudal, romantic viewpoint, and his clairvoyant hatred of the nascent capitalist world order has its source in that viewpoint. But nevertheless this hatred itself becomes the source of such eternal types of capitalist society as Nucingen and Crevel.[51]

That is, Lukács, taking Engels' reading of Balzac as realist a step further, hints at a historically necessary connection, reflecting a "strange dialectic of history," between Balzac's social pessimism and excentricities and a more profound, uncompromising realism. Pessimism regarding what the "nascent capitalist world order" has in store, and the sense that, contra even the faint optimism of Stendhal, this outcome is now all but inevitable, is, simply put, the more *realistic* standpoint. The "Marxist-Leninist" Lukács of *Studies*

in European Realism, of course, adheres, outwardly but firmly, to Engels'
opinion: all of this changes so soon (1848? 1871? 1917?) as the "real men
of the future" enter the "domain of realism," and Lukács' defense of the
realisms of Gorky, Sholokhov and (the early) Solzhenitsyn (genuinely
"socialist") and of a Romain Rolland or a Thomas Mann ("critical" and
anti-fascist) makes a strenuous case for a realism of social optimism. But for
all this, the "strange dialectic" of Balzac, in Lukács' conception of it, very
quietly corrects Engels by pointing to the "methodological supremacy of
the totality"[52] as primary over that of class standpoint *per se* in accounting
for the possibility of a realism *in relation to* the social conditions and
historical limits of capital. Does not Balzac's "pessimism" ground his more
powerfully *realist* poetics because its "hatred for the nascent capitalist world
order", unlike even Stendhal's, is premised on an anticipatory glimpse into
this world as the soon-to-be-systematized, self-reproducing society of the
commodity fetish? Are there not in this "strange dialectic" (as yet) no "men
of the future" precisely because the future, sensed implicitly *as a whole*,
points, for Balzac, at no emergent revolutionary social subject but rather at
a reified "society" that, miming its commodity units, is formally subject and
object at once? From this standpoint, the Balzacian "compulsion" to "go
against [one's] own class sympathies" seems less a paradox than an eventual consequence of hatred for an emergent *form* of society to all objective
appearances indifferent, in itself, to the mutual sympathies or antipathies
of its class units. Balzac's "feudal socialism" and generally "inane" utopian-
isms now begin to look less like the desperately sought but premature
surrogates for a still unborn proletarian hero than the marks of a sheer,
last-ditch ideological will to negativity in the face of a reifying totality—a
commodity producing "modernity"—poised to subsume within itself all
"rational" and "progressive" impulses of opposition.

   In sum, then: the seeming enigma of a Balzacian, "reactionary" and
"pessimistic" realism arises from what may itself be a prematurely "optimistic" historical meta-narrative of a fully formed capitalist modernity
immediately confronted by its "own gravediggers." What if the "nascent"
modernity sensed, and abhorred, in *La Comedie humaine* were, in fact, the
proper subject of a meta-narrative of less immediately heroic proportions
—if it pointed towards a "future" whose immanently narrative possibilities
were simply too abstract to reckon, even tending to zero? This would not
make Balzac's feudal socialism any less "reactionary," but it ought to induce
us to rethink what we assume to be the implicit, formal relationship
between ideology or "worldview" as the representation of a social object
and that same object's poetic (i.e. fictionalized and narrative) structuration.
We rather naturally suppose that political "sympathy" for a given class- or
social-type will directly influence if not dictate the way a story "about" them
is told. But if the social object, the totality or "ensemble of social relations"
itself is such as to make the story teller doubt whether the actions of his

class personae can lead to anything but one, abstract outcome—say, the triumph of money over all—then the question of his "sympathies", too, grows correspondingly more abstract. (Still another instance of "ideology to the second degree"?) What matters is only, perhaps, that they add up to a "pessimism," not whether this pessimism is linked with romantic or quirky attachments to this or that parochial utopia or mirage, and *that* such pessimism is, in accord with its "strange dialectic," as *total* and radical as the object—"modernity"—it reflects.

Here, of course, is raised the highly charged question of whether the "classically" Marxist understanding of nineteenth-century European modernity was not *itself* built around an ambiguity mirrored in the more local, Balzacian paradox. Engels's letter to Harkness and, in the last analysis, Lukács' elaboration on it as well, see in the purported emergence of a revolutionary proletariat an imminent, historical end to a capitalist modernity that, from the standpoint of the Marxist critique of political economy, was only just emerging as a historical and theoretical object. The "strange," abstract social subjectivity of the commodity form had, it seemed, already produced or was even then producing its concrete, subjective negation on a direct plane of "revolutionary" historical events. It is in relation to *this* well-timed dialectic that Balzac's "unevenly" politico-literary one seems "strange." Suffice it here to say that, however deep and far-ranging its theoretical consequences are judged to be, the view of the same "nascent" modernity from a late-capitalist vantage point throws the whole idea of a well-timed, class/commodity social dialectic into crisis. Like it or not, Adornian resonances now become unmistakably audible even in so staunchly "Bolshevik" a Marxist aesthetics as that of *Studies in European Realism*. And, in any case, "classical," nineteenth-century Marxism was, in its truest instances, unpersuaded of its own "classical" stature and willing to examine any and all "strange" dialectics of modernity face-on—think here only of the *Eighteenth Brumaire*.

Or think, for that matter, of what for Lukács essentially typifies the development of "western European realism" after the revolutionary defeats of 1848. *Studies in European Realism* summarizes this development as follows:

> First . . . the real, dramatic and epic movement of social happening disappears and isolated characters of purely private interest, characters sketched in with only a few lines, stand still, surrounded by a dead scenery described with admirable skill.
>
> Secondly, the real relationships of human beings to each other, the social motives which, unknown even to themselves, govern their actions, thoughts and emotions, grow increasingly shallow; and the author either stresses this shallowness of life with angry or sentimental irony, or else substitutes dead, rigid, lyrically inflated symbols for the missing human and social relationships.

Thirdly . . . : details meticulously observed and depicted with consummate skill are substituted for the portrayal of the essential features of social reality and the description of changes effected in the human personality by social influences.[53]

Lukács contrasts the writers whom he sees as the first to embody these trends—Maupassant and, even more poignantly, Flaubert—to Tolstoy, in whom a realism of Balzacian ironies repeats itself, but with this difference: Tolstoy's "class sympathies" belong neither to the "nascent" Russian bourgeoisie nor the aristocracy but to the peasantry. Following Lenin, Lukács reads in Tolstoy's Christian/pastoral socialism a mystified but effective endorsement and anticipation of Russia's coming democratic revolution, and its culmination in October, 1917. Thus the "Balzac dialectic" is to redeem its "strangeness," after all, in a kind of trans-europeanizing (perhaps even "postcolonial") movement towards the margins of hegemonic modernity.

But however one is now obliged to re-think Lukács' great essay on Tolstoy in light of its Leninized teleology, his diagnosis of "western European realism after 1848" rings just as true (even truer, perhaps) without the heroic, "men of the future" meta-narrative. What is described here as a *literary* pathology—the disappearance of the "epic movement of social happenings"; "isolated characters . . . surrounded by dead scenery"; "real relationships of human beings" substituted by "dead, rigid . . . symbols"—reads more plausibly as a *social* pathology, as a description of the anti-heroic modernity of a commodity fetish that has arguably trumped every modern social revolution, failed or triumphant. (Although, it may be, with increasingly faltering degrees of success as history converges on our own present.) In this light it is not Tolstoy but Flaubert—for Lukács a kind of tragic figure who both resists the siren-song of reification but ends up by reproducing it in the form of a "modern" literary "technique"—who caps off the "Balzac dialectic" by reversing its polarity: the ideological "progressive" compelled to go against his own social sympathies on the level of narrative form as such.

IV

Vargas Llosa, then, as a "homegrown Balzac"? Perhaps. But if so, we would now have to add this considerble complication: a Balzac who thinks he is Flaubert. I refer here not only to the fact that, under the likely influence of Sartre's great biography, *The Family Idiot*,[54] Vargas Llosa authors a significant study of Flaubert (*The Perpetual Orgy*)[55] but more generally to a self-consciously Flaubertian will-to-technique that pervades, at different levels, virtually all the author's productions. Other, modernist master-technicians —Faulkner, Dos Passos—clearly are the joint holders, along with Flaubert, of

Vargas Llosa's foreign debt as stylist. But it is the author of *Madame Bovary*
who, according to what is alleged in *The Perpetual Orgy*, discovered the
practical secrets of "modern" narrative technique (free indirect style, etc.)
quite unintentionally in the course of writing what was still a pre-modern,
"realist" novel conceived according to a more conjuncturally entailed idea of
documentary-narrative form.[56] Vargas Llosa, that is, exactly inverts Lukács'
tragic portrait: Flaubert's Balzacian "pessimism" is overcome in a formalism
that, far from signifying the novelist's reified, fragmentary relation to the
social whole, heroically affirms the autonomy of the artist, his apparently
pre-destined empowerment as an individual armed only with "style." [57] To
be both fair and precise one has to acknowledge here that Vargas Llosa—as
literary critic and theorist no less than as politician and editorialist—shows
not the slightest sign of comprehending the Marxian aesthetic (or any
other) that might view modernism critically, or at least with some degree of
ironic regret or suspicion. Vargas Llosa's theoretical and critical adherence
to modernism is in fact totally prosaic and conventional—so much so that,
as we shall see, it too comes to seem "misplaced" in a contemporary Latin
American context. The hero as individual, Flaubertian stylist is, for Vargas
Llosa, a kind of literary entrepreneur, and, along with its Sartrean and
Camusian ethical counterparts, the immediate ancestor of the caricatured
"individual" of *Movimiento Libertad*'s quirky neo-liberalism. The lesson of
Madame Bovary thus becomes entirely utopian: modernity creates, in
response to its greyness and routine, the demiurgic artist-entrepreneurs who
respond in turn by creating "realities" of their own. If Vargas Llosa shows a
Balzacian "pessimism" about anything, it is about the social obstacles placed
by his own countrymen's "backwardness" in the path of a modernity
envisioned exclusively as a new Promethean realm for novelist-heroes and
liberal philosopher-kings such as himself. Vargas Llosa's Flaubert becomes
as much the ancestor of Ayn Rand as of Faulkner or Joyce, making for a
strange "homegrown" Balzac indeed: one "compelled" (if the analogy still
holds at all) to go against class sympathies that would place Vargas Llosa
alongside Hernando de Soto as a rogue in good company with Rastignac or
Nucingen and Crevel.

But let us look more closely at Vargas Llosa's own *praxis* as Flaubertian-
narrative "stylist," taking as our initial point of reference here the famed
scene from Part II, chapter 8 of *Madame Bovary*. In it the private, incipiently adulterous dialogue of Emma Bovary and Rodolphe Boulanger is
cross-cut, montage fashion, by fragments of the bombastic speeches being
delivered beneath their window in the empty town hall by local dignitaries
gathered for the Yonville agricultural fair:

> "We, now, why did we meet? What turn of fate decreed it? Was it not that,
> like two rivers gradually converging across the intervening distance, our own
> natures propelled us towards one another?"

He took her hand, and she did not withdraw it.

"General Prize!" cried the Chairman.

"Just now, for instance, when I came to call on you . . . "

"Monsieur Bizet of Quincampoix."

". . . how could I know that I would escort you here?"

"Seventy francs!"

"And so I stayed with you, because I couldn't tear myself away, though I've tried a hundred times."

"Manure!"

"And so I'd stay tonight and tomorrow and every day for the rest of my life."

"To Monsieur Caron of Argueil, a Gold Medal!"

[. . .]

Rodolphe squeezed her hand. He felt it warm and vibrant in his, like a captive turtle-dove trying to take wing . . . .[58]

This "technique" of fragmenting and interweaving two (or more) separate dialogues, credited to Flaubert, is borrowed and adapted by Vargas Llosa as early as his novella *The Cubs* and becomes one of his stylistic trademarks.[59] In his earliest critical writings on the novel[60] Vargas Llosa refers to it with a term borrowed from the Surrealist manifestos of Breton as the technique of "communicant vessels" or "*vasos comunicantes*."[61] In *The Green House*, and, to an even greater extent in *Conversation in the Cathedral*, it is this principle that structures the entire body of the narrative. What one reads is, to outward appearances, a long series of fragments, plucked out of non-contiguous times and spaces, whose apparently intended effect on the reader is to pre-empt repeatedly any reversion "back" ("lector hembra" style: see chapter 7) to over-familiarized spatio-temporal unities. In my own classroom lectures on Vargas Llosa, however, I have substituted for "*vasos comunicantes*" the more comprehensive poetic term "metalepsis", or "frame-breaking"— encompassing both pro- and analepsis as the narrative equivalents of the flash-forward and flash-back.[62]

Consider now, in its Flaubertian context, the following instance of narrative metalepsis, drawn from Part II, chapter 7 of *Conversation in the Cathedral*. As in all the chapters in this section of the novel, the narration is broken down into a series of smaller narrative episodes or "*vasos comunicantes*," related successively and internally (in Vargas Llosa's modified version of "indirect free style") through the characters of the Muse's maidservant Amalia, the Odría security chief Cayo Bermúdez and Zavalita. In the "Don Cayo" strand of "vasos," his character relates the story of a trip to the provincial city of Cajamarca. Here he is to address a select group of well-to-do *cajamarquinos*, led by the Odriísta senator Heredia, on preparations for an offical visit by the president himself. As he enters the club where the meeting is to take place, and later as the meeting is underway,

Don Cayo's quasi-interiorized narrative of the event switches off at several points into a private sexual fantasy involving the senator's wife. Imagining her in her husband's ranch house, the fantasy briefly inserts her into a lesbian sex scene like the one that Bermúdez's mistress Hortensia (the Muse) and her lover (and fellow courtesan) Queta perform regularly for the scopophilic don Cayo in his house in Lima.

> He began to go up the stairs when he saw the the tall figure appear on the landing, Senator Heredia's gray head, and he smiled: maybe Mrs. Heredia was here.
>
> [. . .]
>
> The deputies came over, they introduced him to the others: names, surnames, hands, how do you do, good evening, he thought Mrs. Heredia, Hortensia, Queta, Maclovia? he heard at your orders, delighted . . .
>
> [. . .]
>
> "If you want we can get started right away, Don Cayo," Senator Heredia said.
>
> "Yes, senator," she and Queta, yes, "whenever you want."
>
> [. . .]
>
> Well, here they were all together to talk informally about the President's visit to Cajamarca, the senator said, that city which everyone present loved so much and he thought: she could be her maid. Yes, she was her maid, a triple reason for rejoicing by the people of the city of Cajamarca the senator was saying, not here but in the ranch house she probably had in Cajamarca . . . .
>
> [. . .]
>
> Cajamarca was a hospitable and a thankful place. Don Cayo, Odría would receive a welcome worthy of his accomplishments at the head of the nation's high destiny. He didn't get up; the glimmer of a smile, he thanked the distinguished Senator Heredia, the parliamentary delegation from Cajamarca for their selfless efforts to make the visit a success, in the back of the room behind some fluttering sheer curtains the two shadows dropped down beside each other in heat on a feather mattress that received them noiselessly, the members of the Reception Committee for having had the goodness to come to Lima to exchange ideas . . . .
>
> [. . .]
>
> The rally would be an unprecedented success, Don Cayo, the senator interrupted him, and there were confirmatory murmurs and nodding of heads, and behind the curtains it was all muffled sounds, rubbing and soft panting, an agitation of sheets and hands and mouths and skin that sought each other out and came together. [63]

Have we, here, in fact, analogous instances of metalepsis? One notes, of course, an obvious formal difference: in *Madame Bovary* the metaleptic break (or the "communication" that, in theory, spans it) juxtaposes a private dialogue—even if Emma is a silent partner to it—with a public, rhetorical display, while in *Conversation in the Cathedral* the "frame-breaks" are located within a single character's quasi-interior monologue. The narrative "techniques" of Joyce and Faulkner have, obviously, intervened here. But if we correct for this variation simply by analyzing both micro-narratives as the immediate juxtaposition of public and private spheres of experience, it appears that both metalepses work to congruent effects. Rodolphe's entreaties to Emma position her within a private dimension that is almost simultaneously traversed by its public "frame" as the voices of the provincial public officials Lieuvain and Derozeray drift in through the window. Don Cayo's private (fantasized) and public dimensions of experience likewise cut across each other metaleptically, i.e. without any prior, meta-narrational framing or preparation. The lurid scenes of his fantasy position him in relation to a public sphere of behavior and speech just as Rodolphe's words position Emma.

But are the resulting, meta-narrative, readerly effects in fact the same here? In his own successive theorizations of this "technique," summed up most recently in *Cartas a un novelista*, Vargas Llosa emphasizes the synthetic virtues of metalepsis. "We can speak of '*vasos comunicantes*' when the unity exceeds the sum of parts integrated within an episode, such as occurs in that of the 'Agricultural Show' [in *Madame Bovary*]."[64] It is important to note here that by emphasizing what is purportedly a higher plane of narrative synthesis, rather than the shock experience of rupture or frag-mentation *per se*, Vargas Llosa has already departed significantly from the still effectively surrealist-inspired formulations of this same, basic formal principle, beginning with Carpentier's theory of the "real maravilloso." (See chapter 8.) (Although, to complicate things further, note also that Vargas Llosa in fact attributes this unifying, synthetic practice of metalepsis to García Márquez in *Historia de un deicidio*.).

But, in a manner typical of his critical thinking, Vargas Llosa formulates this notion as an outright technical abstraction, presumably available anytime and anywhere to apprentice novelists. The truly interesting ques-tion is left unposed: is the metaleptic whole—greater than the sum of its parts—the same whole, say, in nineteenth-century France and twentieth-century Peru?

I think not, and that a careful analysis of the difference here will in fact lead us back to the Vargas Llosian paradox with which we began, but in sight this time of its solution.

Back to *Madame Bovary*: as Lukács observes of the agricultural fair episode in his essay "Narrate or Describe?," the public event that marks off but simultaneously ironizes the private scene between Emma and Rodolphe is, in principle, interchangeable with any other banal, middle-class exercise in public ritual. It is, in Lukács' words, only a "setting" and in this falls short of Flaubert's "purpose": "the comprehensive exposition of the social milieu."

The ironic juxtaposition does not exhaust the significance of the description. The "setting" has an independent existence as an element in the representation of the environment. The characters, however, are nothing but observers of this setting. To the reader they seem undifferentiated, additional elements of the environment Flaubert is describing. They become dabs of colour in a painting which rises above a lifeless level only insofar as it is elevated to an ironic symbol of philistinism. The painting assumes an importance which does not arise out of the subjective importance of the events, but from the artifice in the formal stylization. [65]

Flaubert, that is, in Lukács's critical analysis, operates on what is already a reified image of the public sphere, on a public/private antinomy that in fact no longer adds up to an epic, or social whole.

Vargas Llosa, as naive ideologue of this very same reification, would no doubt rise to the defense of *Madame Bovary* out of a more or less standard modernist faith in the subversive or transformative effects of a purely formal manipulation of mimetic fragments. But whether or not we would agree with him here, his *own* version of *Madame Bovary* in *Conversation in the Cathedral* presents us with something both un-Flaubertian and unilluminated by the theory of "*vasos comunicantes*." For even just a moderately careful reading of the Cajamarca scene shows, in fact, that the public "setting" that prompts and is then metaleptically ruptured by the sexual fantasy is no mere "description" but is intrinsically and epically linked to Don Cayo's "private," subjective dimension as a character. The fantasy built around the senator's wife perfectly captures the complex relationship between the white, traditional Peruvian elite and the darker-skinned, *cholo* functionary. While, as Odría's right-hand man, he must try to secure their loyalty and financial backing, his bitter resentment of his class and racial "betters"—knowing that only his proximity to the current regime even gains him entrance to the private club where the meeting occurs—is not to be assuaged, and is displaced onto an erotic, fantasy plane. Here he can merely look on, and take his pleasure, as the white, aristocratic señora Heredia (or, in the physically staged version of the fantasy, his white-skinned mistress Hortensia) has sex with the *chola* Queta, "so dark, so coarse, so vulgar, so used to serving."[66] The volatile class tension at the heart of Odría's right-wing populism—and perhaps the historically typical experience of "conservative modernization" in Latin America itself—is "resolved" erotically, but re-hierarchized along a gender axis as the scene unfolds under the watchful, masculine eyes and control of Bermúdez. Cross-class, coerced lesbian sex (though, in the case of Queta and Hortensia, the coercion too is part of the act) may be "shocking" and forbidden in the public setting of the club, but it exactly fleshes out the "political unconscious" of what is much more than a private, libidinal subject: a historically concrete and public—or, at least, more than private—form of political power.

That is, public and private spheres of experience, though *formally* separable in *Conversation in the Cathedral*, inevitably lead back to each other. The public scene prompts its own re-scenification in the erotic fantasy because both are the outgrowths of the same, psychosocial symptom. The abstract frontier separating public and private spheres does not dissolve, and hence the effect of their metaleptic juxtapositioning retains its unsettling, potentially critical force. But the concrete *contents* of experience *per se* refuse, in effect, to divide themselves neatly along this line of demarcation, and resituate the public/private antinomy itself as a kind of fiction within a fiction.

This becomes even more palpable when the micro-narrative under scrutiny is re-integrated into the epical whole that is *Conversation in the Cathedral*: even the outward, "publically" political gesture of fealty to Odría on the part of the oligarchs that Cayo Bermúdez must court conceals a more "privately" political will to conspire against him, which finally gains the upper hand with the carefully orchestrated anti-Odriísta uprising in Arequipa. News of the latter event, itself narrated in detail through the character of Trifulcio in Part III of the novel, and which finally forces Cayo Bermúdez's resignation, ends, not coincidentally, the chapter in which the Cajamarca episode is inserted. Indeed, the underlying, typifying action of the novel as a whole—the flight of Zavalita from the privilege and privacy of his *miraflorino*-bourgeois family into a series of class-inappropriate occupations (literature student, revolutionary, bohemian, police reporter) eventually involving him in a murder investigation that implicates his own, closeted-homosexual, father—might be described as the failure of the hero to separate his public, socially transparent fate from that of the private, psycho drama unfolding behind the screen of family relations. The classic hero's venturing forth, *Bildungsroman*-fashion, presupposes, after all, a public space in which private life is strictly compartmentalized, in which, to speak Lacanian, the law of the Father has been successfully inscribed in public institutions. It is the familiar progression, mapped out in Hegel's *Philosophy of Right*, in which the social itself evolves through a dialectical succession of forms—from family, to civil society, to "political" society and the "concrete freedom" of the State—such that the former stages are recontained and sublimated within the latter. But Zavalita enters a world in which the publicly sanctioned law of the Father turns out, sickeningly, to be the law of *his* father; into a "civil society" that is already "political" precisely insofar as it has failed to supersede the patriarchal form of what should by now have become a securely private realm.

Emma Bovary, who, as a woman of her time, must search for and meet her fate within the fissures of middle-class privacy, also discovers, it is true, the bitter truth that the private offers no escape from a public sphere *already* foreclosed to her. Rodolphe's private words to Emma in the empty (public) town hall vulgarize and expose to view cherished bourgeois ideals that the banalities of the public ritual outside only take to a caricatured extreme. But, though it ends with the semi-public display of her dead body, Emma's flight into a falsely utopianized refuge, progressively more privatized and occult, merely re-inscribes, incessantly, the public/private antinomy. It does not, as in *Conversation in the Cathedral*, open onto an epic plane in which the antinomy itself is seen against the social, historical background that both posits and relativizes it.

V

Metalepsis in *Madame Bovary*, though, as Lukács concedes, brilliant in its ironic effects, persists, in the end, as mere technique. The narrative form of Flaubert's novel, as a complex determination of the reified social form underlying it, remains the same, with or without this technical flourish. In *Conversation in the Cathedral*, though consciously *intended* as technique, metalepsis differs from its metropolitan model in two, fundamental ways: it is an essential feature of the novel as a formal whole; and, as such a narrative form, it is mimetically adequate to an underlying, social form—a form, indeed, in which the total "ensemble of social relations" is captured.

To fully develop these arguments would require a lengthy discussion of how significant variations in social form—in effect, departures from a metropolitan, modern social structure—bear on the theory of the novel itself as a corresponding narrative, or epical form. (See, for a set of speculative theses preliminary to such discussion, the following chapter.) But let us focus for now on one of the theoretical categories that would necessarily have to be re-examined as part of such a discussion, what Aristotelian poetics (to follow Northrop Frye[67]) terms the "unity of action" —or simply that which, as one might think of it, narrative *per se* "narrates." We have already implied that such unity of action, in the case of *Conversation in the Cathedral*, places in turn a seemingly unorthodox set of formal demands on the hero himself. Because Zavalita's story, if it is to be one at all, must introduce him into a world that itself complicates and undermines the very process of individuation (a world that will not reproduce the clean separation of public and private realms that is itself presupposed in "modern" individuation) the fundamental relation of the hero to his own action must therefore be altered as well. That is, to tell the life story of an individual—*in nuce*, the theory of the novel—the suddenly vexed question of his very form as an individual must now also be given narrative shape. Zavalita must be represented as *acting* in relation to a society that is simultaneously his other—hence "modern"—but that also acts *alongside him*, so to speak, in what now suddenly appears to be his merely formal, abstract actions as a private self. This "second" society or world is not the "modernity" that gives rise to the novel in its classic form, yet it is not *other* than it either.[68] Neither pre-modern nor postmodern, we might—with due apologies to a terminologically oversaturated public—call it a "dismodern-ity." Because modern in *form*, such a society is made up of a multiplicity of private individuals who then combine to constitute a *public*, a "civil society." But insofar as those material factors that would be required to successfully reproduce this—reified—social relation of public whole to private parts are lacking or withheld, the social relations of these individuals themselves cease to individuate in the customary, "modern" sense, cease to reproduce the form of the individual on the level of its *contents* as a unified set of *actions*. "Dismodernity," then, in order to assume its adequate mimetic/ narrative form, must discover a formal mechanism that can adequately represent this specific, doubly problematic relationship of the individual character or hero to a unity of action that is not finally assignable to an individual social agent.

It is this formal mechanism, I propose, that Vargas Llosa effectively stumbles upon, and designates as *"vasos comunicantes,"* under the illusion that it is nothing more than a technique to be added to the novelist-demiurge's bag of tricks. In fact, in one sense, it *is* a technique, and one that, particularly in *Conversation in the Cathedral*, the novelist is capable of applying with astonishing artistic skill. But, like Vargas Llosa's theory of the novel, and above all of his own narrative practice, the reduction of metalepsis as a socially immanent narrative form to the level of mere stylistic instrument bespeaks the contemporary realist's modernist false consciousness of form itself—Balzac thinking he is Flaubert. The technical flourish in passages such as the one from *Conversation in the Cathedral* we have examined above would quickly grow tedious and narratively super-fluous (something that Flaubert, obviously, understood as well) were it not for the fact of its subservience to a deeper, less transparent formal innov-ation. ("Metalepsis" has by now perhaps ceased to be the most appropriate term for this formal innovation, but, for the sake of economy, we will continue to use it in this now less narrowly technical sense.) What we read in *Conversation in the Cathedral* as a densely interwoven metaleptic fabric that, to the reader's near-amazement, somehow telescopes, at the story's brilliant and harrowing end, back into its point of departure, is, more accurately, the dramatic unfolding of a single action (beginning to middle to end) that is *both* the hero's *and* somehow that of a more complex, trans-individual agent that hints at something virtually unthinkable from the standpoint of modernity: a society as a whole acting—here most unheroic-ally—upon itself. And yet at no point does this metaleptic, reconstructed form of story-telling betray the slightest trace of allegorization. "Peru," as noted in chapter 1, is made the subject of genuinely epical portrayal precisely *because* the pressure to allegorize is consistently elided. To this, however, we might now add this corollary: allegorization can be resisted (as, in the end, it is not in Carpentier, Rulfo, García Márquez) because it has been *formally superseded*. The "Peru" of *Conversation in the Cathedral*, the Peru that, in the course of the novelized action as a whole, always already "se jodió," escapes allegorical abstraction (*and* a Cortazarian-cosmopolitan erasure) because a narrative form adequate to its "dismodern," hypo-individuating social physiognomy has fallen into place.

In perhaps more simplified terms, this form is what permits the extreme social duality of a "postcolonial" social and historical formation like Peru to be represented as *unified*, as a whole, on the level of the actions of its individual members. Looking at Vargas Llosian metalepsis in this way in fact makes it easier to generalize it as a structural feature of virtually his entire narrative opus. As early as *The Time of the Hero*, while still under the shadow of Sartre, Vargas Llosa has discovered the socially-realist narrative powers of metalepsis. Using a Lima military school—a microcosm of Peru—as the immediate scene of action, the novel nevertheless makes not the slightest concession, ironic or otherwise, to "national allegory." The social disarticulations and pathologies that undergo a kind of melt-down inside the walls of Leoncio Prado are held firmly in differential focus. But, by interweaving and *concatenating* a variety of characters and episodic chains within a single framework of social, or, here, institutional behavior, their common social and historical ground, *invisible* as a surface reality, is captured. Think, for example, of the episode in which, through the indirect third person narrative of the character of the Poet (Alberto), a kind of racist-bacchanalia complete with masturbation contest is recounted.[69] The following, juxtaposed incident follows Alberto back to a teenage party in Miraflores, before his induction into Leoncio Prado. A scene of sanctioned, normal middle-class adolescent courtship is carefully reproduced. But the effect of setting this scene against the just narrated episode at La Perlita (the small vendor's stand just outside the walls of the academy, run by a complicit and much abused *cholo*, where the "abnormal" is enacted) is not merely to relativize the ideologeme of "normal" sexuality by pointing to the violence and perversion at its roots, but to insert both, "normal" and "abnormal" sexuality, into the same dramatic and epical framework, the same—"national"—unity of action.

A further variation on this formal principle is developed in Vargas Llosa's most "experimental" and and technically difficult novel *The Green House*—in effect, the formal sketch for *Conversation in the Cathedral* in which the metaleptic interweaving and telescoping of a set of "individual" stories reaches an almost bewildering extreme. One of these "individuals" is Bonifacia, an Amazonian Indian woman who has been abducted from her tribe by missionary nuns, educated in a convent in Santa María de Nieves, expelled for helping other abducted children to escape, and who ultimately finds herself forced into prostitution in a Piura brothel, the "house" named in the title. The story is told "simultaneously"—or metaleptically—in such a way that her own abduction is not fully recounted or grasped until *after* her expulsion from the convent, her marriage to a Piuran soldier stationed in Amazonia (Sargent Lituma) until *after* her appearance as a prostitute ("la Selvática") in the Green House. As, say, a straight-out Faulknerian exercise in fragmenting narrative technique, this method of story-telling looks fairly derivative. But, in fact, Faulkner may not have the last say here, for the effect of metaleptic narration here is to preserve the foregrounding, historical and social acts of violence and subjugation within the "individual" actions of Bonifacia as character/agent. Her prostitution in Piura does not merely reflect back, allegorically, her childhood abduction—it, in effect, *is* this abduction, or rather, *both* are rendered as the same action, without sacrificing (on the contrary, thereby intensifying) Bonifacia's reality as an individual, as—to think back to Engels here—a "type."

This same narrative method operates, with far less technical flourish, in what is, after *Conversation in the Cathedral*, surely the most important Latin American novel of the last generation, *The War of the End of the World*. Here Vargas Llosa, in critical homage to Euclides da Cunha's *Os sertões*, effectively rewrites, intertextually and metaleptically, the Latin American nineteenth century. Both the pilgrimage to Canudos and the crusade that sets out to destroy it, both the apocalyptic, syncretic Christianity of the Counselor and the imported, predatory positivism of Moreira Cesar are narratively concatenated and cross-woven in such a way as to expose, in true epic manner, their common historical ground. The destruction of Canudos, would-be citadel of anti-modernity, already foretells the collapse of the victorious modernity in whose name it is destroyed.

Even the anti-communist, quasi-*roman-à-clef The Real Life of Alejandro Mayta* cannot manage to foreswear the metaleptic realism that, in the end, politely falsifies Vargas Llosa's doctrinal intent. By framing the story of Mayta's failed 1959 insurrection in Jauja with scenes from a contemporary, "apocalyptic" Peru beset by a Shining Path insurgency that has escalated into full-scale civil and regional war, Vargas Llosa clearly means to trace the ills of Peru in the early 1980s back to the earliest days of *foquismo* and revolutionary adventurism. But the effect is, in a sense, quite the reverse. As one reads the novel one cannot help thinking that it is the *failure* of the efforts of the Quijotesque Mayta, of Vallejos and the *josefinos*, that has produced the contemporary nightmare—or that *its* failure already presages the full blown collapse of modernization. Mayta is neither the buffoon nor the villain of this story, but, *pace* Vargas Llosa, its tragic hero. None of the elaborately contrived, meta-fictional devices that Vargas Llosa employs in *The Real Life of Alejandro Mayta* to, it seems, put the brakes on this ideologically out-of-control narrative are sufficient to hide the fact that Mayta speaks the truth and should have succeeded. He is not the precursor to Abimael Guzmán but what might have once been his rational, humane essence. It is *their* fundamental *duality* that emerges from this story, and hence the underlying unity of "dismodernity" that generates it.

VI

Indeed, if one discounts the minor, more or less throw-away works of the order of *Who Killed Palomino Molero?*, *In Praise of the Stepmother* and *Death in the Andes*, virtually the only text in which metaleptic realism breaks down is *A Fish in the Water*. Here the two communicant *"vasos"* of literary and political "memories" are, in fact, indistinguishable from each other within the frame of the ideologically sanitized and policed autobiography. When, as observed earlier, the story wanders away, unchaperoned, from its dogmatic track, it does so on a "metaleptic" course of its own that owes nothing to the self-caricature of the book's overall architecture.

But why would a metaleptic realism, supposing its theory holds true here, be the work of an individual essentially unfit, ideologically, to occupy its corresponding social and ethical standpoint? Why—unless it all really *is* just an accident—would the aesthetic and literary impulse to forge a new epic realism out of so unlikely an assemblage of parts result on the consciously political plane in a non-narrating subject perhaps unable to intelligently *read* much less theorize its own story-telling? Why, again, a "homegrown" Balzac who thinks he is a "homegrown" Flaubert?

The answer, I propose, can be now be inferred in Lukács's allusion, with reference to Balzac, to the "uneven growth of ideologies." Balzac saw the future, the emerging, "modern" society of the commodity fetish while looking backwards to a mythical,"romantic anti-capitalist" past, but also *because* he was looking backwards. Unlike his more progressive contemporaries, who tried putting the best possible face on what was then an emergent and faceless social abstraction, Balzac stared away in disgust, and, fixated on a more venerable and figurable fetish, saw the Gorgon's head reflected in his shield. Vargas Llosa, who tells us plainly in *A Fish in the Water*[70] of his distaste for the "teluric" and indigenist manifestos of his more socially engaged and nationalistic contemporaries, looks, if not backwards, then *northwards* to the very same, liberal, cosmopolitan modernity that Balzac "saw" by looking away. It is to this mythified and abstract standard, figured for Vargas Llosa in its aesthetic mythologies, in Flaubert and the modernist avant-garde, that Vargas Llosa desires his own society to conform. "Magical realism," though he understands its formula as well as anyone, is not the "technique" he reaches for, because it has already conceded to "dismodernity," already substituted the allegorical nation for the purely individuated, modern one. Unable to see the real, social and political face of "dismodernity" as clearly as his contemporaries, he thereby avoids the ideological predicament that would press him into apologizing and compensating for it on the aesthetic and narrative plane. The "Peru" he sees is reflected back to him in an ideological mirror so distorting, so topsy-turvy, that the nation's real features, already self-occulted and adapted to their own apparent formlessness, suddenly come into focus. "Dismodernity" must, that is, be *held up against the modern ideal* that it must continuously disappoint if its *real* difference is to be made out.

No political credit is due to Vargas Llosa, any more than it is to Balzac, for occupying this peculiar place in literary and intellectual history. Engels' "triumph of realism", in both cases, belongs, ironically, to the "strange dialectic" of a modernity that seems to more easily allow its real features to be beheld and aesthetically figured by those least equipped to understand it theoretically. The modernity that Balzac, in this sense, "sees" in its historical moment of birth, Vargas Llosa sees from just that liminal standpoint at which, as we argued, its form and content begin to fail to reproduce each other. Vargas Llosa can "believe" (inanely) in Peru as the proper site for the modern "individual" of liberal theory and also bear witness to the essential falsehood of this theory in his fiction because he happens to be situated at this particular point in "historical space." Even though it chronologically precedes it, his fiction is essentially the after-thought to his political philosophy—it is the correction, still politically "unconscious," induced by the crumbling of the formal abstraction as its putative contents sweep over and past it, "horde"-like.

What we clearly *can* credit to Vargas Llosa, however, is an artistic integrity that, faced, with the choice between an allegorical fiat or fetishized "technique" and a story that has begun to tell *itself*, almost invariably chooses the latter. This is, after all, the story that will sooner or later sweep away the ideologue himself.

Nation and Novel:
Critical-Theoretical Speculations
and a North/South Postscript

". . . the structural categories of the novel constitutively coincide
with the world as it is today."[1]

I

"Reading" the nation as "narration" has now become a virtual routine of
literary and cultural studies. On a certain, narrowly drawn intellectual-
historical plane, this can be credited largely to the influence of Benedict
Anderson's *Imagined Communities*, first published in 1983. Though since
expanded, re-edited and subjected to extensive commentary and critique
Imagined Communities was able, by formulating a modest but carefully focused
corollary to the theory of the nation, to dramatize, especially for humanists,
an idea whose time had evidently come: that the long-established Romantic
practice of reading, classifying and evaluating literature in relation to a
theoretically pre-existing set of national essences or *Volksgeister* could no
longer be automatically treated as legitimate. Despite what is probably still
a statistical preponderance of literary scholars who prefer to continue
adding new entries to a nineteenth-century philological archive, the crisis
of a late-Romantic, nation-centered literary studies is common knowledge,
even to many university administrators and budgetary officers. "Nations,"
whatever else they are, are the abstract entities postulated by nationalisms—
as modern historians of the nation from Gellner to Hobsbawm had been
telling us for some time.[2] And nationalisms, like any form of ideology, are
only too obviously the stuff of narratives, "master", "meta" and just plain
literary. Pre-Romantic thought no doubt understood this in its way, but the
Romantic idea of nationhood is so deeply lodged within the assumptions of
modern literary study that the very idea of literature itself might be argued
in some sense to be its product. Even the "high theory" of the 1960s and
1970s, in reducing literature to a function of signs or of some other, supra-
national category could not finally dislodge the national "essentialism" of
the literary, but only erect a kind of parallel universe of abstraction, inside

which the keepers of the canons could travel about if they chose to without having to ward off a national aura. The abstract ahistoricity of "theory" would, in principle, have been no obstacle to, for example, a *Cervantista* for whom the "language" of the *Quijote* could double as something "national" *and* as a mere "system of signs." Perhaps no wonder then that it took the appearance of a book by Benedict Anderson, a Chinese-born, Anglo-Irish professor of Government and Asian Studies in the United States to help initiate a critical chain reaction that has now effectively rendered opaque the Romantic and neo-Romantic filters of literary-critical and historical consciousness. The change that has given us "Cultural Studies" in place, say, of "Comparative Literature," is, of course, a much more sweeping affair than the postnationalizing of literature. But there is no better clue to its secular and ideological conditioning than what now seems the perfectly commonsensical idea that "literature"—as a subset of "narrative"—simultaneously "constructs" the "national" culture or tradition that it had formerly been assumed merely to embody and represent.

I have earlier speculated (see chapters 3 and 6) about what this secular and ideological conditioning might be in the case of the new literary postnationalism: not merely the now purportedly obvious factor of an increased globalization and porosity of national borders, but the seeming counter-fact that, as a sheer cultural, narrative manifestation, nationalism lingers on, and even grows in intensity. It persists as a central question for cultural and literary critique precisely *because* the economic and political crisis of national polities, particularly peripheral and poorer ones, violently foregrounds it. If globalization were only what its liberal, finance-capitalist promoters claim it is, presumably we would all be cruising the spacious boulevards of *Weltliteratur* and cyber-culture without a thought for this arcane nineteenth-century institution.

But my focus here is a somewhat different one, having more to do with the "narration" side of the relationship. For surely the relatively new interest in inverting the Romantic predication (Nation→Narration) and placing narration in the subject position (Narration→Nation) would, if it were to be of any further critical value, have to make possible a strict, determinable correlation between the national as a secular reality and definite *formal* properties of narrative. Are there particular narrative genres or subgenres more adequate as the narrative vehicles, or equivalents, of the national?

Under the influence of *Imagined Communities* and, subsequently, of Fredric Jameson's "Third World Literature in the Age of Multinational Capitalism," the various strands of what we might term a political narratology have tended to settle on the novel and a quasi-generic concept of allegory as these vehicles.[3] And, indeed, an empirical examination of the narratives known, empirically, to have shaped modern nationalist movements and consciousness—from Fenimore Cooper to *I promessi sposi* to

Rizal's *Noli Me Tangere*—reveals a set of often markedly allegorizable novels and/or novelized allegories. But can a more intrinsic, formal affinity, even a homology, be discovered in this correlation?

We will discuss below Anderson's now familiar and ingenious attempt to answer this question from a theoretical standpoint. What must be stressed here is the suspicious facility with which the formal problem is reduced to little more than the discovery of a narrative mechanism for the "production" of "national subjects" in this or that text. To return to an example cited earlier (see chapter 1): the character of Sab in Gertrudis Gómez de la Avellaneda's novel of that name—a light-skinned, almost "passing" slave who saves his white mistress from unscrupulous foreign merchants and a fortune-hunting suitor, only to die tragically in still unrequited love for her—is easily read as a symbol, however ambivalent and cross-coded, for a future Cuban nation embodying the principles of both economic independence and racial democracy. Even if this could be proved, however, it would beg the more difficult, more radically structural question of what makes it possible in the first place for the novel- or allegorized hero to pass directly, if s/he does, into the imaginary or phenomenological space of national identity and consciousness? Why would a "nation" want to imagine itself as a heroic figure in a fiction and not merely as a setting or landscape, or as a parenthetical reference to culture or folklore? To answer commonsensically that the "national" novel is all of these things is already to concede the indeterminacy and circularity of the exercise. At a certain point fairly early on one starts reading back into this or that text—which text becomes finally a matter of indifference—what one in fact has *already* learned to imagine the "nation" to be. What if *Sab* only prefigured or "imagined" a Cuba that has itself already been reduced to a standardized, imaginary form? And would we know whether this were the case or not? If the novel did in fact play some historical part in producing this standard we would be making a relatively limited discovery unless we could also show that *Sab* possessed certain *formal* differences that explained its capacity to do this where other narratives, and other kinds or forms of narratives, did or could not. This in turn would be impossible without having elaborated a theory of how the novel itself—if that is really what *Sab* is—is or is not the generalized form of such a difference.

As already suggested (see chapter 1) Jameson was surely right to suggest a correlation between *allegorization* and the specific historical problems of "third world" nationalism. But allegory as *form* is scarcely adequate to the more rigorously theoretical problem here. One can find national allegories wherever one looks, because, in detecting allegorical correspondences, one basically proceeds tautologically: Sab can equal Cuba, or Cuba Sab, only because both sides of the equation are still in themselves essentially empty, theoretically unspecified entities. One can equal the other because, as still indeterminate forms, neither one equals anything. The kind of Easter egg hunt for "national allegories" that Jameson's essay inadvertently helped to inspire has left the nation and narration question still standing pretty much where studies like his and Anderson's left it in the mid-1980s: as a general idea for a secular, or political narratology lacking, with few exceptions, the formal categories or abstractions needed to elaborate it any further. There is a certain irony here, in that, with the general trend away from a narrowly formalist, nominalist theory of genres to theories of transliterary narrative as, in Jameson's words, "the primary instance of mind"[4] one is left with only some vague notion of "national allegory" with which to elaborate a more rigorous political narratology.

II

Anderson's theory of the nation as narration, though supple and, as its reception has shown, readily nuanced, can be stated simply: all "communities larger than the primordial villages of face-to-face contact . . . are imagined [. . .] and to be distinguished . . . by the style in which they are imagined."[5] The "community" that is the modern nation differs from earlier forms of community—the "religious community" and the "dynastic realm"—because, unlike them, it is "imagined" as a "sociological organism moving calendrically through empty, homogeneous time." National space is, likewise, an "empty and homogeneous" one, experienced as the same by all the nation's "citizens." The nation is that "imaginary" time/space, that "confidence of community in anonymity"[6] analogued and reproduced in the two most typical, narrative devices associated with the rise of "print capitalism": the novel and the newspaper.

As illuminating as this formulation is, however—especially as combined with Anderson's encyclopedic knowledge of history and anthropology—its explanatory and critical power seems fundamentally limited. While it adds significantly to what is effectively a phenomenology of the nation, and points out the previously overlooked role of novelistic and journalistic prose in the "social construction" of nation-ness, it rests on a correspondingly phenomenological theory of *narrative* that tells us little to nothing about narrative *form* in relation to "community." In its lucid and elegant presentation of what I shall refer to here as the "symbolic" theory of the nation-narration nexus—

Nr→Cm: nation (in which Nr=narrative; Cm=community)—

the "Nr" side of the relation is reduced to being little more than the passive term of an analogy. Nations are like novels because, whether "real" or "imagined," the experience of time and space is the same in both. The analogy is, of course, perfectly valid and interesting in itself, and it would be unjust to blame the author of *Imagined Communities* for not adding a more formally complex knowledge of narratology to an already ample basis for historico-cultural synthesis. But, as analogy, the symbolic theory provides little support for subsequent differentiation and analysis on the level of either the formal elements *per se* of (novelistic) narrative or of individual texts. If one were to ask, say, how Balzac's *Père Goriot* and Flaubert's *Madame Bovary* differ significantly in relation to the French nation as "imagined community," the symbolic theory advanced in *Imagined Communities* would either have nothing concrete to say beyond the fact that both reproduce the same general phenomenological form—simultaneity in "empty, homogeneous time"—or would be reduced to the customary mock-expedition in search of national-allegorical correspondences. The same explanatory poverty would, and does, result when the symbolic thesis is "applied" to the question of a possible North/South differential in the case of "**Nr→Cm: nation**"—a question foregrounding the present work as a whole and to which we will return briefly at the chapter's conclusion.

This "bad" abstraction reflects, in my view, a less obvious fallacy embedded in the "symbolic" theory. As incurred by *Imagined Communities* and more generally, this is the fallacy of presupposing that, regardless of the specific form of the "community," the two terms of the relation, "imaginary" and real—**Nr—Cm**—maintain the identical, externalized and symbolic relation. "Communities," to cite Anderson again, here without ellipses, "are to be distinguished not by their falsity/genuineness, but by the *style* in which they are imagined."[7] But note that this takes it as a given that narrative, or the "imagined" form of community, is "to be distinguished" *a priori* from "communities" regardless of *their* "style" or specific form. The possibility that the general structural relation **Nr—Cm** might *vary* with the form of "community"—that, moreover, the specifically *symbolic* relation **Nr→Cm** might *itself* be *determined* by that *modern* form of community we refer to as the nation—is excluded *ab initio*. In effect, the "symbolic" theory treats narrative as something already sufficiently abstracted from the social relations of a community as to be transparent to them, as to function, precisely, *as* their *symbolic* medium. Here we have already ceased to think of narrative as *itself* a direct form of social relation, whose structural position within a concrete form of community is, in fact, determined by this communal form itself.

This latter way of conceptualizing **Nr—Cm** I will term the *genetic* theory, and abbreviate it as follows:

$$\text{F: cm} \rightarrow \text{[Nr—Cm]}$$

where "**F: cm**" denotes the concrete form or structuring principle of "community" and the vector "→" its determination of the specific form taken by the narrative/community relation. Such a genetic theory allows for the possibility that certain forms of community—perhaps among them those designated by *Imagined Communities* as the "religious community," etc.— determine a relation **Nr — Cm** that is *not* structurally symbolic in nature, even if it may subsequently appear to take on an immediately symbolic or "imaginary" form. At the very least, it serves to alert us against the tautology threatening to vitiate the theoretical powers of *Imagined Communities:* for novel and nation readily become each other's analogical— and, even worse, allegorical—reflection only because both reflect the specifically modern form of "community" in which their *symbolic* relation is already inscribed. One easily discovers the nation in the novel, and the novel in the nation, because in fact these are only variant, still relatively indeterminate, underdefined and overlapping forms of the *same, genetic* social relation.[8]

In short, *Imagined Communities*, in posing the question of "nation and narration" with an unprecedented theoretical coherence, can nevertheless be argued to have done so incorrectly. This question is not, in fact, what the "style" of the "imagined community" is in the case of the nation—to which the answer is then given: the "print capitalist" narrative forms of the novel and the daily newspaper. Such an answer fairly rapidly exhausts its empirical novelty and settles into a tautological routine in which two phenomenological experiences of, say, "time," are linked to each other analogically, or even causally, and then termed "nation" and "narration" as if this were enough to prove that a deeper-level, genuinely structural discovery had been made. The symbolic theory turns out not really to *be* a theory because all possible relations of the type **Nr — Cm** are reduced, *a priori*, to symbolic ones. The real theoretical question is begged, namely, is there a truly structural, or genetic link between nation and novel, and if so, then *what* underlying, genetic form of, so to speak, *narrative socius* conditions and determines it? In our abbreviated format, then, if, in general

> **F: cm→[Nr — Cm]** and, moreover
> **[Nr — Cm]** is the symbolic relation
> **[Nr: novel→Cm : nation]** then
> **?＝F: cm.**

This format should at least serve to clarify still another fallacy, perhaps the least obvious, plaguing the contemporary interest in "political narratology": the fact that the concept of "nation" itself, for reasons having no doubt to do with its own exceedingly complex and protean genealogy, is both so resistant to definition and yet so ready to hand discursively that the question of its general *form* is easily ignored. Theories of the nation, especially those with the most to gain conceptually, turn so readily into exercises in tautology because a thing about which one is uncertain as to *form* can all the more quickly come to be equal only to itself in the illusory guise of a real predicate. *Imagined Communities* at least makes a genuine attempt to avoid this circularity by positing the more general term "community." But here Anderson's theoretical purchase is essentially exhausted, and community itself is left on a conceptual plane of abstract generality. All we know is that the nation is a *kind* of community, but not the more concrete, historically determinate sense—requiring, evidently enough, a great deal of conceptual mediation—in which the nation is a *form* of community.

III

Before attempting to answer the question of nation and narration as now re-formulated, however, several modest digressions may help to better clarify and concretize the question itself.

The first concerns what is, in the US, the still far too little-known work of Alfred Sohn-Rethel, *Geistige und Körperliche Arbeit* (*Intellectual and Manual Labour*).[9] In this work, impossible to summarize adequately here, Sohn-Rethel proposes a historical-materialist derivation of the "timeless" abstractions of modern scientific rationality by tracing them back to the commodity-form as it first emerges, albeit as a relatively isolated social phenomenon, in the mercantile practices of ancient Athenian society. In the "exchange abstraction" postulating that the time-space in which the act of commodity exchange occurs is, in effect, "empty and homogeneous," Sohn-Rethel claims to have located the historical, or socially genetic root of abstract, scientific thought.

According to Sohn-Rethel, however, it is only when the production and exchange of commodities becomes the basis for all economic activity and social reproduction—in modern capitalist society—that the genetic link between the exchange, or "real" abstraction and the "thought abstractions" of science suggests to immediate social consciousness the appearance of a purely abstract *a priori* (whence, in Sohn-Rethel's materialist account, the epistemology of Kant). The exchange abstraction becomes the ultimate nexus for all the mutual relations of society and hence is only to be perceived in its genealogical essence by a theory—Marxism, in historical fact—able to distinguish and theorize the social form built up around this nexus as itself historical and subject to further historical transformation.

The very concept of such a nexus, though already implicit in *Capital*, takes on new importance in Sohn-Rethel's argument, particularly as he attempts to theorize the consequences for a social theory of scientific rationality of the increasing dysfunctionality of the exchange-based nexus in our own period of "late," monopoly capitalism. Here the historical possibility for a *modern* social form built around a nexus that is not that of commodity exchange—a social "logic of production" in place of a "logic of exchange"—comes into historical and theoretical view.

Sohn-Rethel's term for the general concept of such a nexus—exchange and non-exchange-based—is "social synthesis." This he defines as

> the functions that, in differing historical epochs, mediate the joint existences of human beings so as to produce a viable form of society. As the forms of society develop and change, so do the syntheses that bind together the corresponding division of labor and its mutual dependencies into a viable whole.[10]

Sohn-Rethel's principal concern in *Intellectual and Manual Labour* is with "social synthesis" in its form as "exchange abstraction." But in his discussion both of ancient, feudal and "Oriental" formations he advances the general thesis, carefully, extrapolated from Marx, that such synthesis here lies directly within the *production* rather than the exchange process. Despite the fact that, except in its most primitive, communal forms, pre-capitalist society rests on a process of "one-sided appropriation" (what Samir Amin has termed the "tributary mode of production") the relations of production themselves remain transparently social to the direct producers. This is, in its still historically undeveloped form, the social "logic of production" that Sohn-Rethel claims to be detectable in a potentially fully realized, proto-socialist form in the modern Taylorized, flow-production process as such. This then leads him to designate the period of structural, political-economic transition of "late capitalism" as one of "dual social synthesis."[11]

The specifics of this part of *Intellectual and Manual Labour* do not directly concern us here But the concept of "social synthesis" as Sohn-Rethel formulates and develops it is useful to our own attempt to sketch a "genetic" theory of **Nr—Cm** in two ways: (1) It provides us with a precise, conceptual means for overcoming the abstract generality of the concept of "community," which now can be typologized on a more rigorously structural, rather than merely empirical or phenomenological level: **F: cm** can thus be more narrowly specified as a *synthetic* form of social relation. (2) It further suggests a crucial basis for distinction between a social synthesis that is sufficiently abstract to become socially unconscious (exchange) and a radically different form of social synthesis that, in addition to being based directly in the production process, is socially *conscious*. From this standpoint we may at least speculate that the "symbolic" relation **Nr→Cm** already presupposes an abstract—*de facto*, an exchange-based—social synthesis, while, inversely, a pre- or non-exchange based, non-abstract social synthesis implies the possibility of a relation **Nr—Cm** in which the symbolic "distance" is absent and the two terms are collapsible into each other, becoming in this sense moments or aspects of the *same* social relation: **Nr↔Cm**.

That is, we can now formulate in more conceptually precise, if still speculative terms the "genetic" theory as the theory of narrative as itself a possible form, or essential formal aspect, of (non-exchange-based) social synthesis.

A systematic development of this idea clearly would be the subject for a treatise rather longer that the present work itself. In the more modest, essayistic and speculative spirit of the latter, however, I want to pursue my second promised digression—more accurately a kind of meta-citation—in the hopes of further concretizing and situating the narratological hypothesis indicated above.

My "text" here, not coincidentally, is Walter Benjamin's "The Story Teller." In this exquisitely resonant and suggestive essay, Benjamin reduces narratology to what are perhaps it most elemental and yet most human, social terms: "story telling" (*Erzählung*) as the direct, social exchange of "experience" (*Erfahrung*) and a kind of "post"-*Erzählung* that Benjamin does not name *per se* but which at degree-zero is the non-story of an "experience"-purged "information" and, in its sublimated, perhaps ironic form is that minimalized story telling that "carries" the "incommensurabilitity" of modern experience "to extremes in the representation of human life."[12] This latter Benjamin calls the "novel," and his own meta-citation here is, of course, to a work that will enter into our discussion below, Lukács's 1916 essay, *The Theory of the Novel*.

It seems mildly blasphemous to seek to systematize and further abstract from this "constellated" and itself vaguely storied, elegiac presentation of an elementary theory of narrative. Benjamin's characteristic method of resisting, until the last possible, crystalizing moment, the urge to systematize his findings, as if to allow the historical object itself time to reclaim its "experiential" form, invites other kinds of extenuating, less violent readings. But the theoretical syntheses here are lying practically on the surface: if we start from the general premise of the *directly* social character of "experience"—the fundamental, yet for us counter-intuitive fact that experience is social, is "ours," before it is, and in order for it to be, "mine" —then, making Benjamin's connection between experience and story telling (*Erfahrung* and *Erzählung*) we arrive immediately at the speculative result postulated, in the abstract, above: story-telling as itself a *directly social relation*.

Further than this Benjamin does not venture theoretically, except to observe the outstanding, so to speak, arche-empirical ruins that loom up before us when experience loses, slowly and over an enormous historical time-span, its directly social character, its "commensurability." (It is from here, evidently, that Anderson, in his own, theoretical extrapolation of "The Story Teller," sets out his theory of nation-ness as a kind of pseudo-social "experience" encased in "information.") But what if we add to this theoretical kernel a further postulate: that story-telling is a practice that is not merely coincident with the social relations of *Erfahrung*—the same way, say, as Gothic architecture or the ballad form are coincident with them—but is a practice that, in its general form, is *constitutive* of the general form of these relations themselves. Story telling, that is, as a direct, socially *synthetic* relation. The effect would be to complete, but also, in the same movement, to invert Benjamin's narratology: to postulate "experience" and therefore story telling not merely as having once been directly social, but more fatefully still, to disclose the further necessity that *this* form of society be directly "experienced" *as* social—and therefore be *erzählt* or narrated—in order for it to be constituted and reproduced as Sohn-Rethel's *"lebensfähige Gesellschaft"*—a viable form of society.

IV

But what, then, of our principal question, that of the specific form of "narrative socius" (**F: cm**) that mediates the symbolic relation **Nr: novel→ Cm: nation** ? Have we not now set ourselves the contradictory task of searching for a narrative form operant on a socially synthetic level, but within a society that, out of its sheer abstraction and reification, has already banished the very thing we seek?

But let us turn back, one last time, to *Imagined Communities*. So as to illustrate his theory of the nation as an "imagined community" situated, phenomenologically, in an "empty, homogeneous" time, Anderson provides a number of discreet literary examples: the "old-fashioned," Balzac-like plot formula in which several separate individuals, all mutually inter-related, undertake simultaneous actions known to the narrator/reader but mutually unbeknown to each other; the passage from José Rizal's *Noli Me Tangere* in which Captain Tiago plans a dinner party, and all of Manila, quite independently of Captain Tiago and of each other, learns about it; the reference to the early nineteenth-century Mexican proto-novel *El Periquillo sarniento*, in which a "solitary hero [moves] through a socio-logical landscape of a fixity that fuses the world inside the novel with the world outside"; and finally the analogous "imagined community" constructed by—or constructing—the institution of reading a mass-distributed, daily newspaper: "performed in silent privacy, in the lair of the skull" but in which "each communicant is well aware that the ceremony he performs is being replicated simultaneously by thousands (or millions) of others. . . ."[13]

The theoretical point seems well illustrated, but closer consideration here will reveal a by now familiar pattern of circularity: granting the "empty, homogeneous" and anonymous time/space in which all these "soli-tary heroes" and isolated "communicants" co-exist, *whence* the "solitary heroes", etc. *themselves*? Were *they* already *there* beforehand, in the "mes-sianic" time/space of pre-modernity and pre-nationality, only now to have lost immediate sight and knowledge of each other? Or are they not in their common social form—termed by Marx in the introductory passage of the *Grundrisse* the "isolated individual"[14]—*products themselves* of the *same* social and historical forces that have generated "empty, homogeneous time"? In the case of *El Periquillo sarniento*, Anderson claims to have identified the mapping formula for a primitive, Mexican nation-space in the movements of the hero Periquillo, but in fact the example is both unconvincing—the hero's movements take him over a section of the globe a good bit larger and more multifarious than colonial Mexico—and, more importantly, it once again assumes the very thing that, in a structural linkage, is to be discovered: that which itself produces the general structure of, shall we say, "post"-*Erfahrung* of which novel and nation-ness, "solitary hero" and the space defined by his/her movements, are simply the formal, genetic variations.

But if *Imagined Communities* has failed to pose the question properly, it nevertheless points us the way to its answer: is not that which mediates novel and nation on a genetic plane precisely the "isolated individual" itself as social form?

Had Anderson read "The Story Teller" more carefully, and less in thrall to its empirical self-presentation, he might have been led back to one of its principal theoretical sources, where, in fact, the structural relationship around which *Imagined Communities* circles is—though the nation *per se* does not enter into its problematic—already well formulated. To cite this source: "The contingent world and the problematic individual are realities which *mutually determine* one another." [15] Here and throughout chapter 4 ("The Inner Form of the Novel"), Part I of *The Theory of the Novel*, Lukács elaborates on the essential dialectic of the novel as form, one in which, paradoxically, the abstract, alienated relation of the "solitary hero" to an "empty, homogeneous time" is given a concrete, palpable configuration. No question-begging resort to a phenomenological subject, nor to a too narrowly empirical causality is necessary here. The "contingent world," or "bad infinity" that *Imagined Communities* treats in abstract isolation is disclosed as the structural or dialectical flip-side of the "problematic individual," but in an internal relation of two unremitting abstractions that in fact makes possible their *narrative* concretion:

> The novel overcomes its "bad" infinity by recourse to the biographical form. On the one hand, the scope of the world is limited by the scope of the hero's possible experiences and its mass is organised by the orientation of his development towards finding the meaning of life in self-recognition; on the other hand, the discreetly heterogeneous mass of isolated persons, non-sensuous structures and meaningless events receives a unified articulation by the relating of each separate element to the central character and the problem symbolised by the story of his life. [16]

I want to draw two inferences from these specific aspects of *The Theory of the Novel* here. The first, though Lukács himself clearly saw no reason to formulate it, is that we can discover in this structural-dialectical relation of "problematic individual" to "contingent world" or "bad infinity" a relation that in fact finds its mediation not only in the directly narrative form of the novel, but in the, so to say, phenomenological, "meta-narrative" form of the *nation*. The nation would thus count here as the "scope of the hero's possible experience," or, in a possible working definition, as the outward limits placed on a public time/space such that a private, individual life is possible within it. What *The Theory of the Novel*, if read carefully, allows us to see is the profound, structural interrelation of nation, novel and individual such that the relation of the individual as social form to the novel as narrative form is homologous with its relation to the nation as phenomenological, perhaps even ideological form. The nation, after all, is a "community" formally constituted as a conglomerate of "citizens," i.e. formal, abstract individuals. Ideologically and conceptually, the nation is *itself* a kind of individual—equivalent in principle to others, as say, a republic or a state, but at the same time, as Anderson has also noted, only *itself*.

Returning to our abbreviated formula **F: cm→[Nr: novel→Cm: nation]** we can now define the variable **F: cm** as the abstract individual itself as social form, i.e.

$$\textbf{Cm: individual→[Nr: novel→Cm: nation].}$$

The second, and far more speculative inference here is that what *The Theory of the Novel* terms "biographical form" can be thought of not only in a narrowly and immediately narrative sense but as what I earlier termed a "narrative socius," or a directly reproductive, "synthetic" *social*-narrative form.

The modern, private "isolated" individual is, evidently, an abstraction in itself, a monad experientially "incommensurable" with other monads—but one that by that very fact becomes abstractly interchangeable with them. Yet must not such an individual therefore relate to *itself* in a social sense if the abstract, "modern" social totality is not to grind to a psycho-social halt? Must it not reproduce itself as "ego", as the subject of its own "life" ? The abstract individual would, as we might express it, have to assume *itself* a kind of narrative form, would need to relate to its own "life" and destiny as "its" alone. The "empirically given" individual therefore would itself assume a *directly* "biographical form," would have to "live out" the unwritten, virtual novel that inscribes its "hero" within the abstract social whole. In this somewhat paradoxical sense we can perhaps identify in "biographical form" not only the underlying structural nexus grounding the symbolic relation of novel and nation:

$$\textbf{Cm: "biographical form"→[Nr: novel→Cm: nation]}$$

but—as designated by the doubled sided arrow, "↔"— a socially *synthetic* relation at the level of which novel and nation, community form and narrative form, coincide genetically with each other:

Cm: "biographical form"→**[Nr: novel↔Cm: nation]**

The "nation," at this synthetic, structural level, becomes that mediated form of "bad" infinity necessary to the social self-reproduction of the individual "subject": nation as that which, "politically," mediates between the individual and its "life."

V

But what, finally, of the North/South axis in relation to the above? Rather than continue any longer in the heretofore rather mercilessly abstract mode, I want to suggest how to begin to pose this question, and to conclude, with a brief pair of literary allusions.

In chapter 3 of Henry James's *Washington Square*, after a drawn out introduction of Catherine Sloper, the novel's heroine—and before embarking on the action of the novel itself, which begins at the party at her cousin Mrs. Almond's, where she is to meet for the first time her eventual suitor and betrayer, Morris Townsend—the following account of the heroine's Manhattan neighborhood is provided:

> I do not know whether it is owing to the tenderness of early associations, but this portion of New York appears to many persons the most delectable. It has a kind of established repose which is not of frequent occurrence in other quarters of the long, shrill city; it has a riper, richer, more honorable look than any of the upper ramifications of the great longitudinal thoroughfare— the look of having had something of a social history. It was here, as you might have been informed on good authority, that you had come into a world which appeared to offer a variety of sources of interest; it was here that your grandmother lived, in venerable solitude, and dispensed a hospitality which commended itself alike to infant imagination and the infant palate; it was here that you took your first walks abroad, following the nurserymaid with unequal step, and sniffing up the strange odor of the ailanthus trees which at that time formed the principal umbrage of the Square, and diffused an aroma that you were not yet critical enough to dislike as it deserved; it was here, finally, that your first school, kept by a broad-bosomed, broad-based old lady with a ferule, who was always having tea in a blue cup, with a saucer that didn't match, enlarged the circle of your observations and your sensations. It was here, at any rate, that my heroine spent many years of her life; which is my excuse for this topographical parenthesis.[17]

James, himself a narrative theorist of some considerable historical importance, here provides us with a near-exact phrase—"topographical parenthesis"—for the relationship of novel to nation we have sought to define.
Washington Square—but, by extension or substitution, New York and the
"country" itself—can be reduced to a mere parenthesis in the story of
Catherine Sloper's life because her own "biographical form" is *already* the
mediation of this (metonymically) national time/space. As this meto-
nymical nation "Washington Square" is essential to the unity of individual
actions that equals the life story of Catherine, but its more than
parenthetical reference is not necessary. This in itself bespeaks the
existence of a definite, historically evolved form of narrative socius as
biographical form.

My second allusion is to Machado de Assis' novel *Dom Casmurro*. My
interest lies in the sequence marked off by chapters XXIII to XXXI.[18]
The action is as follows: the hero, Bento (later known as Dom Casmurro)
is in love with his next-door neighbor Capitu. He must persuade his
mother's trusted dependent José Días to convince her not to keep a
promise to God to send Bento to a seminary. Bento arranges to speak to
José while the latter is doing errands by omnibus in downtown Rio. The
two get off the bus and walk through the waterfront Promenade where
Bento convinces José to recommend to his mother that he be sent to São
Paulo instead to study law. Overjoyed, Bento can scarcely wait to go home
and tell Capitu the news—and, in a conventional novelistic diegesis, this
is the action that should immediately follow the walk in the Promenade,
barring some further dramatic complication. Instead, the action is
diverted and slowed down, describing a chance meeting with a beggar at
the entrance to the park, a sighting of the Emperor Pedro II passing by in
his carriage, and an impromptu participation in a procession of the
Sacrament. Here Bento and José happen to see Padua, Capitu's father.
Padua is Bento's family's social inferior (as is Capitu), a fact that José
exploits to oust him from a prominent position in the procession and
replace him with Bento.

I lack the space here to do interpretive justice to this unusual, rather
haunting sequence in *Dom Casmurro*, a pattern of seemingly diverted and
retarded action repeated frequently in Machado's novel. But I will venture
the observation that, despite the recognizably "biographical form" of the
novel, the "topographical parenthesis" seems not to be in effect here. The
surrounding, identifiably "national" space through which the hero moves,
and which provides the setting for his life story, diverts this biographical
narrative in a manner that suggests the possibility of a relationship of
"problematic individual" to "bad infinity" quite different than what is to be
found in *Washington Square*. (Catherine Sloper does not, nor can she be
imagined to run across mid-nineteenth century Manhattan's version of
Pedro II—say, J.P. Morgan?—on her way home from Mrs. Almond's party.)

But in *Dom Casmurro*, biographical form seems, at the same time, to have become itself a form of "*biographical* parenthesis" in relation to a national topology that almost possesses "biographical" features of its own.

Herein lies, no doubt, a "national" tale that *The Theory of the Novel* did not anticipate—and the germ of a political-narratological economy that, as the previous chapter sets forth, produces one of its most enigmatic, troubling and powerful variations in the novels of Mario Vargas Llosa. But it is to Lukács' great essay and the formal, dialectical categories it develops that we must look first if the deeper, *social*-structural laws of a Latin American, perhaps even a "postcolonial," novel are to be discovered.

Notes

Preface

1 See Aijaz Ahmad, *In Theory: Classes, Nations, Literatures*, London, New York: Verso, 1992.
2 *London Review of Books*, vol. 21, issue 10, 13 May, 1999 pp. 3–6.
3 Theodor W. Adorno, "The Essay as Form," in *Notes to Literature*, vol. 2, trans. Sherry Weber Nicholsen, New York: Columbia University Press, 1991, p. 17.
4 Roberto Schwarz, *Misplaced Ideas*, trans. John Gledson, London, New York: Verso, 1992.

Chapter 1

1 Aijaz Ahmad, "The Politics of Literary Postcoloniality," *Race and Class*, vol. 36, no. 3, 1995, pp. 1–20.
2 See Bill Ashcroft, Griffiths, Gareth; and Helen Tiffin, *Key Concepts in Post-colonial Studies*, London: Routledge, 1998 p. 186.
3 Note that when Jameson first published the essay in 1986 the term still needed no apology. Fredric Jameson, "Third World Literature in the Era of Multi-national Capitalism," *Social Text*, no. 15, 1986, pp. 65–88.
4 Michel Beaud, *A History of Capitalism, 1500–1980*, trans. Tom Dickman and Anny Lefebvre, New York: Monthly Review Press, 1983, pp. 117–44.
5 This helps to explain, I think, the uncertain relation of Latin America to postcolonialism. With the historical exceptions of Cuba and Puerto Rico, Latin America's first great national and anti-colonial revolutions (1810–25; cf. Tulio Halperín Donghi, *The Contemporary History of Latin America*, trans. John Charles Chasteen, Durham: Duke University Press, 1993) consciously model themselves on the bourgeois revolution of Western Europe (especially France) and its political precursor and cognate in the (North) American Revolution of 1776. These are not (conscious) breaks with the hegemony and centrality of the European metropolis, but only with the latter's anti-democratic, anti-modern fringe, namely Spain and Portugal. Beginning with the radical-democratic nationalism of José Martí, born of the new historical conditions affecting the development of the Cuban independence struggle and the global transform-ations of modern imperialism itself as heralded, for Latin America, in the events of 1898, this Eurocentrism comes seriously into question for the first time. Thus the radical and revolutionary Latin American nationalisms of the twentieth century, culminating in the Cuban revolution of 1959, are indeed central to the

material-intellectual genealogy we wish to trace here. The relative absence of a self-designating "postcolonial studies" among Latin American intellectuals (except in northern universities) has more to do with the history of jargons (e.g. the Anglo-centered, "Commonwealth Studies" ancestry of postcolonialism) than with genuine intellectual differences. To a Latin American political and cultural criticism stretching from Martí to Vasconcelos, Mariátegui, Guevara, Retamar, Schwarz, Quijano and Sarlo the question of the nation poses itself just as it has for a DuBois, a Fanon or a Said.

6 Up until the outbreak of World War I in 1914, approving and even utopian evocations of "imperialism" —most famously Cecil Rhodes's observation in 1895 that to avoid civil war "you must become imperialists"—were commonplace. As Hobsbawm remarks: "In 1914 plenty of politicians were proud to call themselves imperialists, but in the course of our century they have virtually disappeared from sight." Eric Hobsbawm, *The Age of Empire*, New York: Vintage, 1987, p. 60.

7 V.I. Lenin, "On the Slogan of a United States of Europe," in *Selected Works*, vol. I, Moscow: Progress Publishers, 1970, p. 664.

8 Karl Marx and Frederick Engels, *The Manifesto of the Communist Party*, London: Verso, 1998, p. 49.

9 "The bourgeois nationalism of *any* oppressed nation has a general democratic content that is directed *against* oppression, and it is this content we *unconditionally* support." Lenin, "The Right of Nations to Self-Determination," *Selected Works*, vol. 1, 1970, p. 611. It is true, of course, that Marx and Engels already speak of "oppressed" and "oppressor" nations in the *Manifesto* and in their so-called "Letters on Ireland." See Karl Marx, *The First International and After: Political Writings*, Vol. 3, London: Penguin, 1974, pp. 158–71.

10 J.A. Hobson, *Imperialism: a Study*, London: G. Allen & Unwin Ltd, 1938; Rudolf Hilferding, *Finance Capital*, trans. Morris Watnick and Sam Gordon, London: Routledge and Keagan Paul, 1981; Rosa Luxemburg, *The Accumulation of Capital*, trans. Rudolf Wichmann, New York: Monthly Review Press 1976; Karl Kautsky, *The Agrarian Question*, trans. Peter Burgess, London: Zwan Publications, 1988; Nicolai Bukharin, *Imperialism and World Economy*, New York: International Publishers, 1929.

11 Hobsbawm writes, however, that Lenin's original title for his work referred to imperialism as the "latest" not the "highest" stage of capitalism. "Highest" apparently replaced "latest" after his death. *The Age of Empire,* 1987, p. 12.

12 Lenin lists five "basic features" of imperialism: (1); the creation of "monopolies" and their "decisive role in economic life"; (2) the creation of "finance capital" out of a merger of bank and industrial capital; (3) the increased importance of the export of capital relative to the export of commodities; (4) "the formation of international monopolist capitalist associations which share the world among themselves"; (5) the completion of the "territorial division of the whole world among the biggest capitalist powers." *Selected Works*, vol. I, 1970, p. 737.

13 Samir Amin, *Eurocentrism*, trans. Russell Moore, New York: Monthly Review Press, 1989, pp. 124–51.

14 Lenin, *Selected Works*, vol. I, p. 667.

15 See Marilyn B. Young, *The Vietnam Wars 1945–1990*, New York: Harper Collins, 1991, pp. 11–12.

16 Aijaz Ahmad, *In Theory: Classes, Nations, Literatures*, London: Verso, 1992; Samir Amin, *Empire of Chaos*, trans. W.H. Locke Anderson, New York: Monthly Review Press, 1992.

17 See "Three Worlds Theory; End of a Debate," in *In Theory: Classes, Nations, Literatures*, pp. 287–318.

18 Mao Zedong, *Talks at the Ya'nan Conference on Literature and Art*, trans. Bonnie S. McDougall, Ann Arbor: Center for Chinese Studies, University of Michigan 1980.

19 CLR James, *The Black Jacobins: Toussaint L'Ouverture and the San Domingo Rebellion*, New York: Vintage, 1963.

20 Frantz Fanon, *The Wretched of the Earth*, trans. Constance Farrington, New York: Grove Weidenfeld 1963; *Black Skins, White Masks*, trans. Charles Lam Markmann, New York: Grove Press, 1967.

21 Fanon, "The Pitfalls of National Consciousness," *The Wretched of the Earth*, p. 171.

22 Ibid., p. 176.

23 Ibid., (see "Concerning Violence") p. 40.

24 Ibid., (see "The Pitfalls of National Consciousness") p.204.

25 Ibid., p. 222.

26 Ibid., p. 224.

27 Ibid., p. 227.

28 Ibid., p. 236.

29 See the conclusion to chapter 2 for further discussion of the cultural legacy of national liberation.

30 Jameson, 1986.

31 Ahmad, 1992.

32 Jameson, 1986, p. 69.

33 These and other questions are analyzed at considerable length in chapter 11 of this volume.

34 Nicolás Guillén, *Man-making Words: Selected Poems*, trans. Roberto Márquez and David Arthur McMurrray, Amherst: University of Massachusetts Press, 1972.

35 Aimé Césaire, *Discourse on Colonialism*, trans. Joan Pinkham, New York: Monthly Review Press, 1972, p. 68; my emphasis.

36 Robert Kurz, *Der Kollaps der Modernisierung: Vom Zusammenbruch des Kasernsozialismus zur Krise der Weltökonomie*, Frankfurt am Main: Eichborn Verlag, 1991, pp. 189–228.

37 Robert Kurz, *O retorno do Potemkin: capitalismo de fachada e conflicto distributivo na Alemanha*, trans. Wolfgang Leo Maar, São Paulo: Paz e Terra, 1993.

38 Fanon, 1963, p. 149.

39 Ibid., p. 150.

40 Kurz, 1991.

41 Francis Fukuyama, "The End of History", in *The National Interest*, vol. 16, 1989, pp. 3–18.

42 Edward Said, *Orientalism*, New York: Vintage, 1979.

43 Ibid., pp. 3 and 39.

44 Ibid., p. 326.

45 Gayatri Chakravorty Spivak, "Can the Subaltern Speak?", In Lawrence Grossberg and Cary Nelson, eds, *Marxism and the Interpretation of Culture*, Champaign-Urbana: University of Illinois Press 1988, pp. 271–313.

46 A misconstrual already evident in the practice of stressing the last of its terms—"Can the Subaltern *Speak?*"—when the logic of what it is saying would require that the first—"Can the *Subaltern* Speak?"—receive the emphasis.

47 Spivak, 1988, p. 287; my emphasis.

48 Sumit Sarkar, *Writing Social History*, Delhi: Oxford University Press/Chennai Mumbai, 1997, pp. 82–108.

49 Spivak, 1988, p. 292.

50 Ibid, p. 311.

51 Implications chillingly evoked in Kurz's reference to "Welt-Bürgerkrieg" or "world civil war."

52 Benedict Anderson, *Imagined Communities: Reflections on the Origin and Spread of Nationalism*, London: Verso 1991. For a more extended discussion of *Imagined Communities* see chapter 12 in this volume.

53 Homi K. Bhabha, *The Location of Culture*, London: Routledge, 1994. See chapter 2 for more detailed discussion of this essay.

54 Edward Said, *Culture and Imperialism*, New York: Knopf, 1993.

Chapter 2

1 By way of circumstantial clarification I should note that this essay was first drafted shortly after the appearance of *In Theory* and before the explosion of controversy touched off by the book, especially by its criticisms of Edward Said's *Orientalism*. The reader should therefore avoid interpolating into the text of "DetermiNation" any direct or allusive engagements with Ahmad's many and vociferous detractors. This said, however, I also reaffirm my general agreement with the critical and theoretical core of *In Theory*. Having read the bulk of its hostile reviews, I find nothing in them that would lead me to alter the substance of the present essay. For the most comprehensive record of the "debate" itself see the special issue of *Public Culture* dedicated to *In Theory* (vol. 6, no. 1, Fall 1993), including Ahmad's own long response to critics (pp. 143–91).

2 Aijaz Ahmad, *In Theory: Classes, Nations, Literatures*, London: Verso, 1992, p. 292.

3 Ibid., p. 45.

4 Ibid., see "Languages of Class, Ideologies of Immigration."

5 Ibid, p. 86.

6 Ahmad is not alone in this respect, although, due to the notoriety of *In Theory*, he is unquestionably the most visible. Other works that have taken up positions critical of poststructuralism within postcolonial studies include Arif Dirlik, *The Postcolonial Aura: Third World Criticism in the Age of Global Capitalism*, Boulder, Colo.: Westview Press, 1997; Neil Lazarus, *Resistance in Postcolonial African Fiction*, New Haven: Yale University Press, 1997 and *Nationalism and Cultural Practice in the Postcolonial World*, Cambridge, England, New York: Cambridge University Press, 1999; Timothy Brennan, *At Home in the World: Cosmopolitanism Now*, Cambridge, Mass.: Harvard University Press, 1997; *Cultural Readings of Imperialism: Edward Said and the Gravity of History*, eds. Ansell Pearson, Benita Parry and Judith Squires, New York: St. Martin's Press, 1997.

But while many postcolonial theorists and critics engage poststructuralist theory with some degree of skepticism and caution, the result is not atypically a "critical" acceptance of certain aspects of, say, Foucault, Laclau/Mouffe, Deleuze/Guattari, etc., a rejection of others, but no sustained or rigorous posing of the ideological question as such. Thus we are left, in the end, with a theoretical "hybrid," in which the basic premises of poststructuralist thought are grudgingly retained. In this respect it is striking that, in the course of her long and painstaking rebuke to *In Theory*—a rebuke that also doubles as a defense of Said as well as of other, more orthodox poststructuralist critics of imperialism—Benita Parry (see "A Mishandled Critique," *Social Text*, vol. 35, Summer 1993: pp. 121–33) consistently elides this issue. Parry, for example, accuses Ahmad's critique of Said of having "distorted a narrative of how a field of textual representations naturalized political power and enabled the invasion of geographical and cultural space" (p. 125) That the thrust of Ahmad's critique is in any way to deny the role of "representations" in "naturalizing" political power is spurious. But note that the operant notion here—that of the capacity of "textual representations" to "enable" the "invasion" of not only "cultural" but "*geographical*" space, i.e. that certain "discourses" constitute, in and of themselves, an imperialist act, against which other "discourses" could then, presumably, intervene as counter-actions—is presented as a truth so obvious that *any* criticism, explicit or implicit, is self-evidently a "distortion." *In Theory*, on the other hand, not only questions the tacitly accepted self-evidence of such poststructuralist tenets (for, whether Said is really an orthodox poststructuralist himself or not, the provenance of such "truths" is indisputably poststructuralist) but poses the question of their historical and social conditions of emergence and possibility, i.e. of ideology *strictu sensu*.

7 Néstor García Canclini, *Hybrid Cultures: Strategies for Entering and Leaving Modernity*, trans. Christopher L. Chiappari and Silvia L. Lopez;, Minneapolis: University of Minnesota Press, 1995; Roberto González Echevarría, *Myth and Archive: a Theory of Latin American Narrative*, Cambridge, New York: Cambridge University Press, 1990; Enrique Dussel *The Invention of the Americas: Eclipse of "the Other" and the Myth of Modernity*, trans. Michael D. Barber. New York: Continuum, 1995; Mary Louise Pratt, *Imperial Eyes: Travel Writings and Transculturation*, New York: Routledge, 1992. Rolena Adorno, *Transatlantic Encounters: Europeans and Andeans in the Sixteenth Century*, eds. Kenneth J. Andrien and Rolena Adorno, Berkeley: University of California Press, 1991. Antonio Benitez Rojo, *The Repeating Island: the Caribbean and the Postmodern Perspective*, trans. James Maraniss, Durham: Duke University Press, 1992. Walter D. Mignolo, *The Darker Side of the Renaissance: Literacy, Territoriality, and Colonization*, Ann Arbor: University of Michigan Press, 1995.

8 Ahmad 1992, p. 34.

9 See *Misplaced Ideas: Essays on Brazilian Culture*, trans. and ed. John Gledson, London: Verso, 1992.

10 Ahmad, 1992, p. 36.

11 In *Marxism and the Interpretation of Culture* eds., Lawrence Grossberg and Cary Nelson, Urbana: University of Illinois Press, 1988, pp. 271–313.

12 See "Shades of Althusser, or, the Logic of Theoretical Retreat in Contemporary Radical Criticism" *Socialism and Democracy*, vol. 9, no. 2, Fall 1995.

13 Spivak, 1988, p. 279.

14 "Signs," first appeared in *"Race," Writing, and Difference*, ed. Henry Louis Gates, Jr., Chicago: University of Chicago Press, 1985, pp. 163–84. "DissemiNation," in *Nation and Narration*, ed. Homi K. Bhabha, London: Routledge, 1990, pp. 291–322. Both essays have since been republished as chapters 6 and 8, respectively, of Bhabha's *The Location of Culture*, London: Routledge, 1994.

15 This historical irony has been explored at length in Gauri Viswanathan's *The Masks of Conquest*, New York: Columbia University Press, 1989.

16 Bhabha, "Signs," pp. 168–9.

17 Ibid.

18 Ibid., pp. 177–83.

19 Ibid., p. 173.

20 Ibid.

21 Ibid., p. 175.

22 Ibid., p. 181; my emphasis throughout.

23 See, for example, Anderson, *In the Tracks of Historical Materialism*, London: Verso, 1983; Terry Eagleton, "From *Polis* to Postmodernism," in *The Ideology of the Aesthetic*, Oxford: Basil Blackwell, 1990; Peter Dews, *Logics of Disintegration: Poststructuralist Thought and the Claims of Critical Theory*, London: Verso, 1987; Roy Bhaskar, "What is Critical Realism?" in *Reclaiming Reality*, London: Verso, 1989;

Ellen Meiksins Wood, *The Retreat from Class: a New "True" Socialism*, London: Verso, 1986.

24 I emphasize the word "typically." There are exceptions, in fact, if we include under the rubric of "postcolonial theory" not only the work of Ahmad himself but earlier works by Ranajit Guha and the "subaltern studies" collective, as well as, e.g., the more directly historical and political-economical investigations of a Samir Amin. But here—with the later exception of Guha at least—the post-structuralist nexus is either broken or absent, with the link to Marxism taking its place.

25 See "Marxism and Cultural Politics," unpublished ms.

26 The storm of anger and protest this critique has elicited is now notorious. As Ahmad remarks in his response to critics in *Public Culture* (see note 1), "I seem to have said what must always remain unsaid." (p. 174)

27 Bhabha, "DissemiNation," p. 292.

28 Ibid., p. 297.

29 Ibid., p. 299.

30 Ibid., p. 300.

31 Ibid., p. 294.

32 Ibid., p. 292.

33 Ibid., p. 292.

34 Ibid., p. 300.

35 Ibid., p. 301.

36 The term is Samir Amin's. See *Eurocentrism*, trans. Russell Moore, New York: Monthly Review Press, 1989, especially chapter 4, "The Culturalist Evasion: Provincialism and Fundamentalism," pp. 124–35.

37 Edward Said, *Culture and Imperialism*, New York: Knopf, 1993, p. xxiii.

38 Ibid., p. 7.

39 Ibid.

40 Ibid., p. 12.

41 Ibid., p. 14.

42 Ibid., p. 13.

43 To those who object here that Said incorporates certain aspects of Marxism and class analysis into *Culture and Imperialism*, I think the following remarks of Ahmad, here in sympathetic response to Michael Sprinker's criticisms, are sufficiently apposite: "That Said says a great many things in *Orientalism* that would be perfectly acceptable to a Marxist ought not to be elided into the claim that its methodological premises are the same as the ones that normally regulate Marxist analyses of imperialism's cultural domination, any more than Foucault's incorporating entire passages of Marx into his texts makes him a proponent of the labour theory of value." ("A Response," *op. cit.*, p. 186.)

44 Said, 1993, pp. xxiv–xxv.

45 Ibid., p. 212.

Chapter 3

1 See chapter 1, sections I and IV, and chapter 12 in this volume.

2 On the "Bandung Era" see Aijaz Ahmad, *In Theory: Classes, Nations, Literatures*, New York, London: Verso, 1992.

3 Robert Kurz, *Der Kollaps der Modernisierung: Vom Zusammenbruch des Kasern-sozialismus zur Krise der Weltökonomie* Frankfurt am Main: Eichborn Verlag, 1991.

4 See Teresa Ebert, *Ludic Feminism and After: Postmodernism, Desire and Labor in Late Capitalism*, Ann Arbor: University of Michigan Press, 1996.

5 See, for further discussion of this point, my "Postcolonialism's Unsaid" (review essay, Aijaz Ahmad's *In Theory*) *Minnesota Review* nos. 45 and 46, Fall 1995 and Spring 1996.
6 New York: Random House, 1996.
7 See Huntington, *The Clash of Civilizations: The Remaking of the World Order*, New York: Simon & Schuster, 1996, and David Rieff, *Los Angeles: Capital of the Third World*, New York: Simon & Schuster, 1991.
8 Kaplan's most recent book-length publication is *An Empire Wilderness: Travels into America's Future*, New York: Random House, 1998.
9 Kaplan, p. 83
10 Ibid.
11 Ibid., my emphasis.
12 Ibid.
13 Ibid.
14 In his earlier account of a sojourn in Togo, Kaplan describes it as a "country . . . less fact than fiction." (p. 70) Its capital, Lome, is a place that "seemed to lack foundation." (p. 71) Of Sierra Leone—a place in which "borders were crumbling, and they weren't all geographical"—Kaplan poses the question to a Catholic relief worker: "is [it] a country?" (p. 66)
15 Kaplan, p. 71.
16 Ibid., p. 4.
17 Ibid., p. 7.
18 Ibid.
19 Ibid., p. 4.
20 Ibid., p. 298.
21 Ibid., p. 348.
22 Ibid.
23 Ibid., p. 349.
24 Ibid., p. 35
25 Ibid., pp. 24–5.
26 Ibid., p. 36.
27 Ibid., p. 26.
28 Ibid., p. 27.
29 Ibid.
30 Mary Louise Pratt, *Imperial Eyes: Travel Writing and Transculturation*, London, New York: Routledge, 1992, p. 213.
31 Kaplan, p. 80.
32 Ibid., p. 57.
33 Ibid., p. 54.
34 My translations here and throughout. Original citations listed in corresponding end notes. "[D]ie globale Gesamtmasse der produktiv vernutzten abstrakten Arbeit sinkt aufgrund der permanent gesteigerten Produktivkraft erstmals in der kapitalistischen Geschichte auch absolut . . ." p. 263.
35 "[D]ie Menschen werden von den kapitalistischen Bedingungen ihrer Bedürfnisbefriedigung abgeschnitten." p. 263
36 " . . . die nur noch durch wenige dünne Adern mit dem globalen Blutkreislauf des Geldes verbunden sind." p. 191.
37 " . . . die Basis des gewaltigen westlichen Kapitalstocks, von der aus die weiteren Steigerungen erfolgen, kann innerhalb der Warenlogik in den anderen Weltteilen insgesamt nie mehr erreicht werden." p. 198–9.
38 "Diese stets zunehmende und über das Fassungsvermögen der Wareproduktion hinauswachsende Produktivität konnte nicht ohne katastrophale Rückwirkung

auf die nachholenden Prozesse der ursrpünglichen Akkumulation bleiben."
p. 221.

39 Ibid., p. 223.

40 See Kurz, p. 208.

41 Kaplan quotes from a letter from a friend, a US diplomat in Africa: "The greatest threat to our value system comes from Africa. Can we continue to believe in universal principles as Africa declines to levels better described by Dante than by development economists? Our domestic attitudes on race and ethnicity suffer as Africa becomes a continent-wide 'Wreck of the Medusa.'" (4) Note that this decline is not a subject for economics, only for myth and metaphysics. Kaplan himself sounds a similar warning: "It may be easy to say that a place like Sierra Leone does not matter, but if we don't care at all about such places, why should, for instance, suburbanites in Tucson care about the inner city in Philadelphia? To be completely heartless about Africa, I mean to suggest, is to start down a path which imperils our own nationness." (68) Here Kaplan comes uncannily close to a historical insight that, however, his "environmental" apology for global capitalism cannot develop further. One must not remain "heartless." But moral sympathy will have to be its own—and Africa's—only reward. Since even Western aid programs can do nothing but stimulate further population growth, Africa, with all the moral "care" that can be mustered for the occasion, must be set, "Wreck of the Medusa"-fashion, adrift.

Chapter 4

1 Jean Paul Sartre, *Search for a Method*, trans. Hazel Barnes, New York, Vintage Books, 1968, p. 7.

2 Michel Foucault, "What is an Author?," in *Language, Counter-Memory, Practice*, trans. Donald F. Bouchard and Sherry Simon, Ithaca: Cornell University Press, 1977, p. 133.

3 Edward Said, *Orientalism*, New York: Vintage Books, 1979, p. 2.

4 Ibid., p. 154.

5 Aijaz Ahmad, *In Theory*, London: Verso, 1992. See chapter 6, "Marx on India: a Clarification."

6 Karl Marx, *The Eighteenth Brumaire of Louis Bonaparte* in *Surveys from Exile: Political Writings, Vol. 2* ed. and trans. David Fernbach, London: Penguin, 1972, p. 239; references to the German original are to *Der achtzehnte Brumaire des Louis Bonaparte*, Berlin, Dietz Verlag, 1984.

7 Said, *Orientalism*, p. 21.

8 Ibid., p. 292.

9 Ibid., p. 293.

10 References here are to the version of the essay published in 1988 in *Marxism and The Interpretation of Culture*, eds. Lawrence Grossberg and Cary Nelson Champaign-Urbana: University of Illinois Press, pp. 271–313. A somewhat revised version—with nothing in it to alter my critical assessment of it here—appears embedded in Spivak, *A Critique of Postcolonial Reason: Towards a History of the Vanishing Present*, Cambridge, London: Harvard University Press, 1999. See pp. 247–70.

11 Spivak, "Can the Subaltern Speak?," pp. 280–1.

12 Ibid., p. 279.

13 Ibid., p. 277.

14 Ibid., p. 276.

15 Ibid., p. 278.

16 Ibid., p. 276.
17 Marx, *Surveys from Exile: Political Writings*,vol. 2, p. 240.
18 Ibid., p. 242.
19 Ibid., p. 150.
20 Ibid., p. 149.
21 Georg Lukács, *History and Class Consciousness*, Cambridge, Mass.: MIT Press 1997, trans. Rodney Livingstone, p. 61.
22 Ibid., pp. 70–81.
23 Neil Larsen, "Shades of Althusser, or, the Logic of Theoretical Retreat in Contemporary Radical Criticism," *Socialism and Democracy*, vol. 9, no. 2, Fall 1995, pp. 25–43.
24 Lukács, *History and Class Consciousness*, p. 178.
25 Spivak, "Can the Subaltern Speak?," p. 294.
26 "Bonaparte would like to be the most obliging man in France and turn all of the property and labour of the country into a personal obligation towards himself. He would like to steal the whole of France in order to be able to give it back to France . . ." *Surveys from Exile: Political Writings*, vol. 2, p. 247.
27 Robert Kurz, "*One World* e nacionalismo terciário," in *Os ultimos combates*, Petropolis, Brazil: Editora Vozes, 1997. p. 55; my translation from the Portuguese. Originally published as "*One World* und jüngster Nationalismus" in "Frankfurter Rundschau," January 4, 1992.
28 Ibid., p. 56.
29 See Robert Kurz, *Der kollaps der Modernisierung Vom Zusammenbruch des Kasernso-zialismus zur Krise der Weltökonomie*, Frankfurt am Main: Eichborn Verlag, 1991 pp. 223 and 228.
30 The last place to look for any such logic is in Spivak's "Scattered Speculations on the Notion of Value," twin to "Can the Subaltern Speak?" in its here even more grotesque, Derridean confabulation of Marx. Basing her "reading" of *Capital* and the labor theory of value, in true Althusserian fashion, on a single passage from chapter 1, volume I in which the verb "darstellen" is used—a passage she distorts and willfully misreads in the most absurd fashion—Spivak repudiates the "continuist [i.e. non-Althusserian/poststructuralist] urge" to treat that "common element"—value—that makes one commodity exchangeable with a certain quantity of others as the labor objectified in commodities. See "Scattered Speculations on the Question of Value," in *In Other Worlds*: *Essays in Cultural Politics*, New York, London: Methuen, 1987, p. 158.

Chapter 5

1 See, on this subject, Román de la Campa's *Latinamericanism*, Minneapolis: University of Minnesota Press, 1999.
2 See *Proceed with Caution, When Engaged by Minority Writing in the Americas*, Cambridge: Harvard University Press, 1999.
3 On questions of "hybridity" in relation to Latin American see chapter 6 in the present volume.
4 *Misplaced Ideas: Essays on Brazilian Culture*, trans. John Gledson, London: Verso, 1992.
5 Georg Lukacs, *History and Class Consciousness*, trans. Rodney Livingstone, Cambridge: MIT Press, 1993, p. 1.
6 New York: Routledge, 1994, p. 60.
7 *Hopscotch*, trans. R. Kelly Washbourne and Gregory Horvath vol. 1, no. 1, 1999, p. 117. The original Portuguese, more nuanced, is as follows: "A implicação mais

inovadora, contudo, refere-se à *aplicação* de categorias sociais européias (sem exlcusão das marxistas) ao Brasil e às demais ex-colônias, um procedimento que leva ao equívoco, ao mesmo tempo que é inevitável e indispensável. Fique de lado a crítica ao uso chapado de receitas, sempre justa, mas tão válida no Velho Mundo quanto entre nós. A dificuldade de que tratamos aqui é mais específica: nos países saídos da colonização, o conjunto de categorias históricas plasmadas pela experiência intra-européia passa a funcionar num espaço com travejamento sociológico diferente, *diverso mas não alheio*, em que aquelas categorias nem se aplicam com propriedade, nem podem deixar de se aplicar, ou melhor, giram em falso mas são a referência obrigatória, ou aínda, tendem a um certo formalismo. Um espaço *diverso*, porque a colonização não criava sociedades semelhantes à metrópole, nem a ulterior divisão internacional do trabalho igualava as nações. Mas um espaço *de mesma ordem*, porque também ele é comandado pela dinâmica abrangente do capital, cujos desdobramentos lhe dão a regra e definem a pauta. À distância, esta meia vigência das coordenadas européias—uma configuração desconcertante e *sui generis*, que requer malícia diferencial por parte do observador—é um efeito consistente da gravitação do mundo moderno, ou do desenvolvimento desigual e combinado do capitalismo . . . ." See *Seqüências brasileiras* São Paulo: Companhia de Letras, 1999, p. 95.

8 *Misplaced Ideas*, p. 27.
9 "The Politics of Literary Postcoloniality," *Race and Class*, vol. 36, no. 3, January–March 1995, p. 5.
10 See note 7.
11 "It suggests that imitation is avoidable, thereby locking the reader into a false problem." ibid., p. 15.
12 Ibid. p. 16. The original Portuguese is more suggestive here: "depois de vermos que origem não é argumento, fica indicado quanto é decisivo o seu peso real."
13 "Why should not the imitative character of our life stem from forms of inequality so brutal that they lack the minimal reciprocity . . . without which modern society can only appear artificial and imported?" Ibid.
14 Ibid, p. 28.
15 Ibid. On the problem of the inadequation of concepts see especially the essay "Adequação nacional e originalidade crítica," in *Seqüências brasileiras*, pp. 24–45.
16 See chapter 2 in this volume.

Chapter 6

1 Carlos Monsiváis, "Mexico 1890–1976: High Contrast, Still Life," *Mexican Postcards*, trans. John Kraniauskas, London, New York: Verso, 1997, p. 20.
2 *Labyrinths: Selected Stories and Other Writings*, eds. Donald Yeats and James E. Irby, New York: New Directions, 1962, pp. 177–85.
3 For a more developed discussion of this question see chapter 12.
4 *Hybrid Cultures: Strategies for Entering and Leaving Modernity*, trans. Christopher Chiapara and Silvia López, Minneapolis: University of Minnesota Press, 1995. See pp. 135–44.
5 *History and Class Consciousness*, trans. Rodney Livingstone Cambridge: MIT Press, 1971, pp. 110–49.
6 In *Surveys from Exile*, *Political Writings: Volume 2,* ed. David Fernbach, London: Penguin Books, 1973, p. 146.
7 "All fixed, fast-frozen relations with their train of ancient and venerable prejudices and opinions are swept away; all new-formed ones become antiquated

before they can ossify. All that is solid melts in air, all that is holy is profaned, and man is at last compelled to face with sober senses his real conditions of life and his relations with his kind." Karl Marx and Frederick Engels, *The Communist Manifesto*, New York: International Publishers, 1948, p. 12.

8 Trans. Marjorie Urquidi, Austin: University of Texas Press, 1971.

9 Ibid., p. 274.

10 The expression belongs to Walter Benjamin's essay on Surrealism in *Reflections*, trans. Edmund Jephcott, New York: Harcourt Brace Jovanovich, 1978.

11 Mariátegui, p. 187.

12 See p. 203. My emphasis. The translator's rendering of the original Spanish "cimiento" as "cement" is admittedly subject to question, however. "Foundation" is probably the better translation. My thanks to Sebastian Faber for pointing this out to me.

13 Mariátegui, p. 188.

14 See note 4.

15 Ibid., p. 3.

16 Ibid., p, 157.

17 Ibid., pp. 218–19.

18 Ibid., p. 221.

19 Ibid., p. 222.

20 Ibid.

21 Monsiváis, *Mexican Postcards*, pp. 25–6.

22 *Misplaced Ideas: Essays on Brazilian Culture*, trans. John Gledson, London: Verso, 1992, pp. 41–77.

23 Ibid., p. 15.

24 Ibid., p. 52.

25 Ibid., p. 69.

26 Ibid., p. 68.

27 Ibid.

28 Ibid.

29 Ibid., p. 7.

Chapter 7

1 Julio Cortázar, *Hopscotch*, trans. Gregory Rabassa, New York: Avon/Bard, 1971, p. 502.

2 Jaime Concha, for example, pointedly refers to Cortázar as "el gran cuentista argentino," the "great Argentine short-story writer." Concha, "Criticando *Rayuela*", *Hispamérica*, 4.1, August 1975, pp. 131–51.

3 Cortázar, *Hopscotch*, 1971, p. 468.

4 Roberto Schwarz, *Misplaced Ideas: Essays on Brazilian Culture* trans. John Gedson. London: Verso, 1992, p. 190.

5 Concha, "Criticando *Rayuela*," p. 137; my translation.

6 Cortázar, *Hopscotch*, pp. 45, 103.

7 See, for example, Stephen Boldy's comment that "Cortázar excels at the subtle depiction of bad faith in his characters and, indeed, it is on this aptitude that much of the density and ambiguity of his prose depends." Stephen Boldy, *The Novels of Julio Cortázar*, Cambridge: Cambridge University Press, 1980, p. 74.

8 See, especially, Oliveira's outpourings in chapters 21 and 48 of *Hopscotch*.

9 As Boldy writes—with a critical aim opposite to mine, of course—"historical and political action has been excluded from *Rayuela* and, indeed, there is little action of any sort in the novel." Boldy, *The Novels of Julio Cortázar*, p. 74.

10 Cortázar, *Hopscotch*, p. 112.
11 Ibid., p. 117.
12 Ibid.
13 Ibid., p. 406.
14 Ibid., p. 407.
15 Ibid., p. 406.
16 Concha, "Criticando *Rayuela*," p. 140; my translation.
17 Cortázar, *Hopscotch* p. 477.
18 Ibid., p. 478.
19 Ibid.
20 Ibid.
21 Ibid., p. 483.
22 Ibid., p. 484.
23 Ibid., p. 438.
24 Ibid., p. 302.
25 For a fuller account of this shift see the introduction to my own work, *Reading North by South: On Latin American Literature, Culture and Politics*, Minneapolis: University of Minnesota Press, 1995.
26 Oscar Collazos, Julio Cortázar, Mario Vargas Llosa, *Literatura en la revolución o revolución en la literatura*, (polémica) Mexico: Siglo Veintiuno Editores, 1970.
27 Julio Cortázar, "Acerca de la situacion del intelectual latinoamericano," in *Último Round*, tomo 2, Mexico: Siglo 21, 1974, p. 267; my translation.
28 José María Arguedas, *El zorro de arriba y el zorro de abajo*, Lima: Editorial Horizonte, 1988, p. 22; my translation.
29 Ibid., p. 23.
30 Ibid., p. 25.
31 Quoted in *Casa de las Américas*, #57, November–December, 1969, Año X, pp. 136–8; my translation.
32 Ibid.; my translation.
33 Cortázar in *Último Round*, 1974, p. 270; my translation.
34 Ibid., p. 272; my translation.
35 See Samir Amin, *Eurocentrism*, trans. Russell Moore, New York: Monthly Review Press, 1989. See also my earlier discussion of Borges and the "concrete universal" in chapter 6 of the present volume.
36 David Viñas, *De Sarmiento a Cortázar*, Buenos Aires: Ediciones Siglo Veinte, 1971, p. 125.
37 Ibid., pp. 124–5; my translation.
38 ". . . the graduate of the Mariano Acosta Normal School for Teachers goes in search of his 'spirit' in Paris, and, in fact, crosses paths with the graduate of the Ecole Normale Superieure, on his way to America in search of the concrete embodiment of the theories he has learned . . . ." Viñas, *De Sarmiento a Cortázar* p. 122; my translation.
39 Ibid., pp. 131–2; my translation.
40 Julio Cortázar, "Apocalypse at Solentiname," in *A Change of Light and Other Stories*, trans. Gregory Rabassa, New York: Knopf, 1980, pp. 119–28.
41 Ibid., p. 119.
42 Ibid., p. 123.
43 Karl Marx, *Grundrisse*, trans. Martin Nicolaus, New York: Vintage, 1973, p. 101.
44 For further discussion see "Indigenism, Cultural Nationalism and the Problem of Universality," in *Reading North by South*, op. cit. See also Silverio Muñoz, *José María Arguedas y el mito de la salvación por la cultura*, Minneapolis: Instituto para el Estudio de Ideologías y Literatura, 1980.

Chapter 8

1 Roberto Schwarz, *Misplaced Ideas: Essays on Brazilian Culture*, p. 2, London: Verso, 1992.
2 References are to John Sturrock's English translation of the novel, *Explosion in a Cathedral*, New York: Farrar, Strauss and Giroux, 1989.
3 Parts of this essay are drawn from an earlier, shorter article of mine, "A Note on Lukács's *The Historical Novel* and the Latin American Tradition" which appeared in *The Historical Novel in Latin America: a Symposium*, ed. Daniel Balderston Gaithersburg, MD; Ediciones Hispamérica, 1986, pp. 121–8.
4 *The Theory of the Novel*, trans. Anna Bostock, Cambridge: MIT Press, 1971, p. 46.
5 Carpentier, *Explosion in a Cathedral*, p. 331.
6 On the relation of Surrealism to "lo real maravilloso" see the following chapter.
7 See *El Reino de este mundo*, Buenos Aires: América Nueva, 1974. Also, *Tientos y diferencias*, Mexico: Universidad Nacional Autónoma, 1964.
8 *El reino de este mundo*, p. 14; my translation.
9 Ibid., p. 15.
10 For further discussion see my own work, *Modernism and Hegemony: a Materialist Critique of Aesthetic Agencies*, Minneapolis: Minnesota University Press, 1990, pp. 49–54.
11 Walter Benjamin, "Surrealism: The Last Snapshot of the European Intelligentsia", *Reflections*, trans. Edmund Jephcott, New York: HBJ, 1978, p. 179.
12 Georg Lukács, *The Historical Novel*, trans. Hannah and Stanley Mitchell, Lincoln and London: University of Nebraska Press, p. 296.
13 Ibid., p. 23.
14 Ibid., p. 176.
15 Ibid., p. 190.
16 Ibid., p. 192.
17 Schwarz, *Misplaced Ideas*, p. 23.
18 Ibid., p. 22.
19 Ibid., p. 20.
20 Carpentier, *Explosion in a Cathedral*, p. 274.
21 Fanon, *The Wretched of the Earth*, trans. Constance Farrington, New York: Grove Weidenfeld, 1963, p. 176.
22 "In its beginnings, the national bourgeoisie of the colonial countries identifies itself with the decadence of the bourgeoisie of the West. We need not think that it is jumping ahead; it is in fact beginning at the end. It is already senile before it has come to know the petulance, the fearlessness, or the will to succeed of youth." Ibid., p. 153.
23 For more on Schwarz see chapter 5.
24 Roberto González Echevarría, *Alejo Carpentier: The Pilgrim at Home*, Ithaca: Cornell University Press, 1977, p. 233.
25 Ibid., p. 226.
26 Ibid., p. 235.

Chapter 9

1 Including Breton's collaboration with Trotsky we might extend this somewhat. But by the outbreak of World War II at the latest the break is effectively complete. For an excellent study of relations between Surrealism and Communism see Helena Lewis, *The Politics of Surrealism*, New York: Paragon, 1988.
2 In *Reflections*, trans. Edmund Jephcott, New York: Harcourt Brace Jovanovich, 1978, p. 191.

3 In Theodor W. Adorno, *Notes to Literature,* vol. I, trans. Sherry Weber Nicholsen, New York: Columbia University Press, 1991, pp. 87 and 90.

4 More remarkably still, it seems virtually certain that, as late his completion (1931) of the first volume of *Residencia en la tierra,* containing some of his most "Surrealist" poetry, Neruda had no knowledge of Breton's manifestos.

5 The "miraculous" or "le merveilleux" was evidently a favorite Surrealist catchword.

6 *Les Vases Communicants,* cited in *Marxism and Art,* ed. Maynard Solomon, Detroit: Waynes State University Press, 1979, p. 510; my emphasis.

7 An analogous vulnerability is detectable in the Brechtian theory of the "alienation effect." This is not the context in which to engage in a lengthy discussion of Brechtian aesthetics in light of Surrealism, if only because the former did not actively influence radical literary and artistic practice in Latin America until the world-wide resurgence of interest in Brecht in the 1950s and 1960s. The Freudian theory of the unconscious is, of course, not in any way a direct influence on the theory of the alienation effect, which, with its emphasis on the production of a detached attitude of political, class awareness on the part of the theater-going public, owes its greatest debt to the pre-Freudian principle of de-familiarization or "estrangement" (the "ostranenje" of the Russian Formalists) as mediated by German Expressionism. And one might argue that Brecht effectively bypasses the formal principle of montage itself, by bringing into juxtaposition, not disparate images or objects, but rather the disparate attitudes towards *actions* on the part of the dramatic characters themselves, on the one hand, and on the part of the audience, on the other. But whether or not one accepts Lukács' notorious (and often misunderstood) strictures against the left-wing Expressionism of the "alienation effect," it is apparent that for this theory to make good on its pledge to stimulate class consciousness by means of a species of political shock effect it would have to be able to discount its own susceptibility to, as it were, a re-familiarization. Taking up, for the sake of argument here, the Lukacsian, realist perspective, one might observe that the mere act of pre-empting an "Aristotelian" moment of identification or catharsis need not necessarily produce results favorable to a politics of the left. As with Surrealism so with the alienation effect: there would seem in principle to be no restrictions placed on the appropriation of a shock-based aesthetic by fascism or the radical right. Shock, or "alienation" (*Verfremdung*), offers no intrinsic guarantee against artistic falsehood or untruth in the classically realist sense. For a full elaboration of this problem, and a fascinating account of Brecht in Brazil, see Roberto Schwarz's "Altos e baixos da atualidade de Brecht" in *Seqüências brasileiras,* São Paulo: Companhia das Letras, 1999, pp. 113–50.

8 *One Hundred Years of Solitude,* trans. Gregory Rabassa, New York: HarperCollins, 1991, p. 2.

9 Adorno, "Looking Back on Surrealism," p. 88.

10 Excepting, perhaps, the writings of the Haitian novelist Jacques Stephen Alexis, from whom the Cuban Carpentier adopts the term—"lo real maravilloso"—that conveys in Spanish the new conception of montage.

11 See chapter 5, "De Profundis": "One afternoon, while lunching on a puff pastry, the owner of the Coq-Chante plantation had fallen, suddenly and without previous signs of distress, dragging down with him the wall clock he had been in the process of winding." [my translation] *El reino de este mundo,* Buenos Aires: América Nueva, 1974, p. 34.

12 Benjamin, "Surrealism," p. 189.

13 Benjamin, "Paris, Capital of the 19th Century," *Reflections,* p. 148.

14 Domingo F. Sarmiento, *Facundo: civilizacion o barbarie: Vida de Juan Facundo Quiroga*, Mexico D.F.: Editorial Porrua, 1998, p. 12.
15 For more on Mariátegui see chapter 6 of the present volume.

Chapter 10

1 See, for example, William Rowe and Vivian Schelling, *Memory and Modernity: Popular Culture in Latin America*, London, New York: Verso, 1991, p. 208–09, 211–12, 214.
2 *Modernism and Hegemony*, Minneapolis: University of Minnesota Press, 1990, pp. 49–71.
3 Fernando Ortiz, *Contrapunteo cubano del tabaco y el azúcar*, Barcelona: Editorial Ariel, 1973.
4 Angel Rama, *Transculturación narrativa en América Latina*, Mexico City: Siglo Veintiuno, 1982.
5 Luis Harss, *Into the Mainstream Conversation with Latin American Writers*, New York: Harper and Row, 1967, p. 274.

Chapter 11

1 Mario Vargas Llosa, *A Fish in the Water: a Memoir*, trans. Helen Lane, 1st ed., New York: Farrar, Straus, Giroux, 1994. The allusion, of course, is to Mao Zedong's famous metaphor for the communist guerrilla fighter who blends into the people like a "fish in the water." As at least one of his Peruvian readers was heard to remark, a "fish out of water" would have been the more fitting title.
2 Ibid., p. 371.
3 Ibid., p. 371-2.
4 Ibid., p. 372.
5 Hernando De Soto (with Enrique Ghersi and Mario Ghibellini), *The Other Path: The Invisible Revolution in the Third World*, trans. June Abbott, New York: Harper and Row, 1989. (Prologue by Vargas Llosa.).
6 Mario Vargas Llosa, *A Fish in the Water*, p. 172.
7 Ibid.
8 Ibid., p. 174.
9 Ibid.
10 Mario Vargas Llosa, *Captain Pantoja and the Special Service*, trans. Gregory Kolovakos and Ronald Christ, New York: Harper and Row, 1978.
11 Vargas Llosa, *A Fish in the Water*, p. 78.
12 Mario Vargas Llosa, *Aunt Julia and the Scriptwriter*, trans. Helen R. Lane New York: Farrar, Straus, Giroux, 1982.
13 See "The Dirty War," a grotesquely entitled chapter referring to García's campaign of dirty tricks against *Movimiento Libertad*, but in allusion to the bloody repression unleashed in the 1970s by US-backed military regimes in Chile, Argentina and Uruguay—and directed against people whose left-wing political beliefs are precisely those attacked, in words, by Vargas Llosa.
14 Mario Vargas Llosa, *In Praise of the Stepmother*, trans. Helen Lane, New York: Farrar, Straus, Giroux, 1990.
15 Vargas Llosa, *A Fish in the Water*, pp. 411–12.
16 The author reminds us that in 1963 the Peruvian military had publically burned copies of *The Time of the Hero* (*La ciudad y los perros*), an early work that had exposed corruption and violence in a Lima military academy.

17 Readers of the *Eighteenth Brumaire*—with which *A Fish in the Water* often resonates in strange, inadvertent ways—will note the reappearance in Vargas Llosa's political adventure of the *Parzellenbauern*—here the "parceleros" who were seeking, according to *A Fish in the Water*, to convert into small private plots the large, state-owned farms created in the late 1960s by the Velasco government's land reform. Vargas Llosa (pp. 358–9) proclaims the "parceleros"—along with the "informales" in the cities—to be the "heroes of his discourse." He readily concedes, though, that they too voted against him. Vargas Llosa does not say as much explicitly, but it seems they, like their nineteenth-century French counterparts, "must be represented" by a Napoleon III, here in the guise of the neo-liberal in populist clothing, Alberto Fujimori.

18 Vargas Llosa, *A Fish in the Water*, pp. 477–80.

19 Ibid., p. 477.

20 Vargas Llosa, *The Green House*, trans. Gregory Rabassa, New York, Harper and Row, 1968.

21 Vargas Llosa, *A Fish in the Water*, pp. 514–15.

22 Ibid., p. 515.

23 Vargas Llosa, *The War of the End of the World*, trans. Helen R. Lane, New York: Farrar, Straus, Giroux, 1984.

24 *A Fish in the Water*, p. 530.

25 James Petras and Henry Veltmeyer, for example, have recently written as follows: "As the end of the millennium approaches, the conditions of long term stagnation and crisis are becoming more and more visible. Foreign reserves are being depleted, bailouts multiply as currencies threaten to collapse, negative growth rate and double digit unemployment (18 percent in Brazil, and 14 percent in Argentina) are matched by permanent reserve armies of under-employed (the informal sector) reaching 50, 60, and 70 percent of the population. Export earnings are crashing; imports being reduced; and debts, both domestic and overseas, are reducing any state resources that might be used to stimulate the economy. The neoliberal cycle is crashing even as the regimes continue to apply the empty formulas to enrich a narrowing circle of class cronies—the upper 10 percent of the population." See James Petras and Henry Veltmeyer, "Latin America at the End of the Millennium" *Monthly Review*, vol. 51, no. 3, July–August, 1999, pp. 31–52.

26 Vargas Llosa, *A Fish in the Water*, pp. 44, 45.

27 Ibid.

28 Ibid., pp. 506–7.

29 Roberto Schwarz, *Misplaced Ideas: Essays on Brazilian Culture*, trans. John Gledson *et al.*, ed. John Gledson, London: Verso, 1992, p. 23.

30 Vargas Llosa, *Cartas a un novelista*, Barcelona: Editorial Ariel, 1997, p. 37.

31 Mario Vargas Llosa, "The Chiefs" in *The Cubs and Other Stories*, trans. Gregory Kolavakos and Ronald Christ, New York: Harper and Row, 1979.

32 Vargas Llosa *A Fish in the Water*, p.248.

33 *Conversation in the Cathedral*, trans. Gregory Rabassa, New York: Harper and Row, 1975.

34 Ibid., p. 139.

35 Vargas Llosa, *Fiction: the Power of Lies*, La Trobe University, 1993, See also *La verdad de las mentiras: Ensayos sobre literatura*, Barcelona: Seix Barral, 1990.

36 See, for example, William Rowe, who accuses Vargas Llosa, in his middle and later work, of making "structures of conflict constitute the basis of sociality." "Nevertheless," writes Rowe, "the earlier novels, and especially *The Green House*, explore the making of connections across lines of power and cultural

divisions, with the multiple interweaving of conversations across time and space being a main technical device for such exploration. The result was the making of a liberated space through the (temporary) subversion of hierarchy. With *The Real Life Of Alejandro Mayta*, however, the technique of communicating vessels becomes subsumed into a political program. The connections do not traverse the political ordering of reality, they simply confirm it. [. . .] Irrationality invades politics, where it becomes destructive, and rationality (as authoritarian liberalism) controls writing." (pp. 58–9) William Rowe, "Liberalism and Authority: The Case of Mario Vargas Llosa", *On Edge: The Crisis of Contemporary Latinamerican Culture*, Minneapolis: University of Minnesota Press, 1992, pp. 45–64.

37 In his criticism of Arguedas, Vargas Llosa himself draws attention to the quickness to mythologize the "engaged" writer in Latin America—but erects in the process the opposing myth of the apolitical modernist as pure creative demiurge. See chapter 1 of *La utopía arcáica: José María Arguedas y las ficciones del Indigenismo*, México D.F.: Fondo de Cultura Económica, 1996.

38 See, for example, Antonio Cornejo Polar, "*La historia de Mayta* como apocalipsis," in *La novela peruana*, Lima: Editorial Horizonte, 1988: pp. 244, 256. Cornejo is unfailingly precise in his exposé of Vargas Llosa's neo-liberal, doctrinal *intent* in *Mayta*, but is, in my view, forced to misread the *novel itself* as a consequence.

39 Angel Rama, *La critica de la cultura en América Latina*, Caracas: Biblioteca Ayacucho, 1985, p. 335; my translation

40 Jorge Luis Borges, "Borges and I," in *Labyrinths,* New York: New Directions Publishing, 1964, pp. 246–7.

41 Rama, *La crítica de la cultura en América Latina*, p. 362, my translation.

42 Mario Vargas Llosa, *Death in the Andes*, trans. Edith Grossman, New York: Farrar, Straus and Giroux, 1996.

43 Mario Vargas Llosa, *The Notebooks of Don Rigoberto*, trans. Edith Grossman, New York: Farrar, Straus and Giroux, 1998.

44 See S.S. Prawer, *Karl Marx and World Literature*, Oxford: Oxford University Press, 1978.

45 Karl Marx and Frederick Engels, *Selected Correspondence*, trans. I. Lasker, Moscow: Progress Publishers, 1975, pp. 379–81.

46 Ibid., pp. 380–1.

47 Ibid., p. 379.

48 Ibid.

49 Georg Lukács, *Studies in European Realism*, New York: Grosset and Dunlap, 1964.

50 Ibid., p. 77

51 Ibid., pp. 77–8; my emphasis.

52 See Georg Lukács, *History and Class Consciousness*, trans. Rodney Livingstone, Cambridge, Mass.: MIT Press, 1994, p. 9.

53 Lukács, *Studies in European Realism*, p. 144.

54 Jean-Paul Sartre, *The Family Idiot: Gustave Flaubert, 1821–1857*, trans. Carol Cosman, Chicago: University of Chicago Press, 1981.

55 Vargas Llosa, *The Perpetual Orgy*, trans. Helen Lane, New York: Farrar, Straus, Giroux, 1986.

56 Ibid., p. 233.

57 Ibid., p. 148.

58 Gustave Flaubert, *Madame Bovary*, trans. Alan Russell, New York: Penguin Classics, pp. 161–3.

59 Vargas Llosa, *The Cubs and Other Stories*, trans. Gregory Kolovakos and Ronald Christ, New York: Harper and Row, 1979.

60 *La novela*, Montevideo: Fundación de Cultura Universitaria,1967.
61 "The narrative material is organized, according to the process of 'vasos comunicantes' by forging in a narrative unity, situations or facts that occur on different spatial or temporal planes, or those that are different in nature, so that those realities can enrich and modify each other, forging a different reality than the mere sum of its parts)[. . .]," Vargas Llosa, *Historia de un deicidio*, Barcelona: Barral Editores, 1971, p. 322; my translation.
62 I use the term here in a general narratological sense as the "breaking of boundaries that separate distinct 'levels' of narrative . . . "(See Chris Baldick, *The Concise Oxford Dictionary of Literary Terms*, Oxford: Oxford University Press, 1990, p. 134.) These can be spatial as well as temporal. The term is not meant here in Genette's narrower, more technical sense as a "leap" between diegetic and extra-diegetic levels. (See Gérard Genette, *Narrative Discourse: an Essay in Method* trans. Jane E. Lewin, Ithaca: Cornell University Press, 1980, pp. 234–6.
63 Vargas Llosa, *Conversation in the Cathedral*, pp. 288–9.
64 Vargas Llosa, *Cartas a un novelista*, p. 174; my translation.
65 Georg Lukács, "Narrate or Describe" in *Writer and Critic and Other Essays*, New York: Grosset and Dunlap, 1970, p. 115.
66 Vargas Llosa, *Conversation in the Cathedral*, p. 288.
67 Northrop Frye, *Anatomy of Criticism*, New Jersey: Princeton University Press, 1957.
68 See chapter 5, and Roberto Schwarz's discussion of the "different but not alien."
69 Vargas Llosa, *Time of the Hero*, see chapter 5.
70 Vargas Llosa, *A Fish in the Water*, pp. 292–3.

Chapter 12

1 Georg Lukács, *The Theory of the Novel,* trans. Anna Bostock, Cambridge, Mass.: MIT Press, 1971, p. 93
2 See Eric Hobsbawm, *Nations and Nationalism Since 1780,* Cambridge: Cambridge University Press, 1990; and Ernest Gellner, *Nations and Nationalism*, Ithaca: Cornell University Press, 1983.
3 Fredric Jameson, "Third World Literature in the Age of Multinational Capitalism", *Social Texts*, no. 15, 1986 pp. 65–88.
4 Fredric Jameson, *The Political Unconscious*, Ithaca: Cornell University Press, 1981. See chapter 1.
5 Benedict Anderson, *Imagined Communities*, London, New York: Verso, 1997, p. 6.
6 Ibid., p. 36.
7 Ibid., p. 6; my emphasis.
8 See here, for example, Franco Moretti, who, in his splendid work, *Atlas of the European Novel*, writes that " . . . the nation-state . . . found the novel. And vice versa: the novel found the nation-state. And being the only symbolic form that could represent it, it became an essential part of our modern culture." But Moretti, like Anderson, nowhere accounts for the historical *necessity* of this symbolic relation. Franco Moretti, *Atlas of the European Novel: 1800–1900*, London, New York: Verso, 1998. p. 17.
9 See Alfred Sohn-Rethel, *Geistige und Körperliche Arbeit*, Frankfurt: Suhrkamp Verlag, 1973. (I have referred to this more extensive German edition rather than to the English translation.)
10 Ibid., p. 19.
11 Ibid., pp. 186–7.
12 Walter Benjamin, "The Storyteller," in *Illuminations,* trans. by Harry Zahn, New York: Schocken Books 1976, p. 87.

13 Anderson, *Imagined Communities*, pp. 30, 35.
14 Karl Marx, *Grundrisse*, trans. Martin Nicolaus, London: Penguin Books, 1973, pp. 83, 84.
15 Lukács, *The Theory of the Novel*, p. 78; my emphasis.
16 Ibid., p. 81.
17 Henry James, *Washington Square*, New York: Penguin Books, 1979, p. 20.
18 Joaquim Maria Machado de Assis, *Dom Casmurro*, trans. John Gledson, Oxford: Oxford University Press, 1997.

Index